The Ten Secrets of Abundant Happiness

A timeless parable that will inspire & guide you to a happier life

By

Adam J Jackson

PRAISE FOR THE TEN SECRETS OF ABUNDANT SERIES

The Ten Secrets of Abundance books were first published in 1996. Since then, these remarkable books have been translated and published in over 30 languages.

~

'Adam Jackson created four incredible and inspiring books that are given by a Chinese man (fictional yet plucked from the universal consciousness) who steps into people's lives to give profound teachings for us all to adhere to in life.'

Helium.com

The Ten Secrets of Abundant Wealth...

'This is a tiny power-packed book. It's about getting your life in order...If you are feeling a bit jaded and read this sort of thing before then you might want a refresher and be inspired with this hand-sized book. If you are a sceptic, then this would be a low-cost way to find out more about looking at life differently. You have nothing to lose and everything to gain!'

Homeworking.com

'This is a book that should be read by anyone who suffers financial problems and feels that there is no

way of pulling himself out of them. It will give courage, hope, inspiration, and a more optimistic angle. This inspiring story reveals the 10 Universal Laws that rule everything in nature and life.'

simania.co.il

'This book is truly a wonderful book. Such an easy read and anyone who has read it will tell you that they wish they would have read it sooner...Pick it up, read it and you will never be sorry you did. '

blog.taivo.net

Blue Dolphin Press
An imprint of Bilberry Media Group
1 Coldbath Square, London EC1R 5HL
www.bluedolphinpress.com

First published as The Secrets of Abundant Happiness: *A modern parable of wisdom and happiness that will change your life.*
Thorsons an imprint of HarperCollins 1996

A catalogue record for this book is available from the British Library

ISBN 978-1-912424-04-7

Printed and bound in the UK by
CreateSpace

Disclaimer

All the material contained in this book is provided for educational and informational purposes only. No responsibility can be taken for any results or outcomes resulting from the use of this material.

While every attempt has been made to provide information that is both accurate and effective, the author does not assume any responsibility for the accuracy or use/misuse of this information.

Table of Contents

FOREWORD

Thank you for purchasing this book. It is now over twenty years since the first edition of this book was published in the United Kingdom. In that time, it has been translated and published in over thirty languages.

Happiness is as elusive today as it has been at any time in history. Due, in part, from the technological advances, we are becoming increasingly detached from the people closest to us and from what is happening around us. Just walk out onto the streets of any city in the developed world and notice how many people are shutting out the world around them, hard-wired into their smartphones and MP3 players. A train full of people, most of whom are totally unaware of those around them, focussed on their mobile devices. Headphones block out the sounds of life. It is not uncommon even to see groups of friends in the same room - sometimes around the dinner table or at parties - all totally focussed on their mobile handsets. We can have hundreds of 'friends' on Facebook and yet we still feel lonely.

Happiness cannot be found in detachment. We're becoming disconnected from what is going on around us and focussed instead on a virtual reality, and the virtual world can't fulfil our need for friendship and community in the same way that the real world does. Similarly, shutting off the world by putting on headphones stifles awareness both in terms of what is happening in the moment and in terms of the 'inner' voice, our intuition.

Indian philosophy speaks of two types of people - those who are asleep and those who are awake. Many of us in the Western world have lost connection to our intuitive nature, we are living in a trance and as each day passes, we are losing our capacity for inner peace and happiness.

I'd like to think that you choosing this book was not an accident. There is meaning and purpose in every event, if we choose to see it. Happiness is something to which we all aspire, yet few find. Deep down, we all know what we need to do, how we need to live and the type of people we need to become if we are to experience real joy and happiness in our lives.

My hope is that this small book will serve as a reminder of those things that are important, and perhaps inspire you to discover a new awareness, and to re-connect with the world.

The Ten Secrets of Abundant Happiness contains the essential tools needed to experience lasting happiness. The stories contained in the book are all based on true stories. I hope that they inspire you as much as they inspired me and that, whatever your current situation, these timeless principles will help you find joy and happiness in every day.

With best wishes,

Adam Jackson
December 2017

INTRODUCTION

You traverse the world in search of happiness,
which is in the reach of every man

Horace

Ask people what they most want from life, and the answer you most commonly hear is: 'I just want to be happy'. Why is it then that so few people are happy? Why is it that one of the biggest growth areas in the drug industry is anti-depressants? Why is it that the number of people who consider themselves to be happy is so small? Could it be that we have been looking for happiness in the wrong places?

I believe that we all have the power to be happy. It does not matter how much money you do or don't have, what job you do, or where you live. Whatever your circumstances are at this moment, you have the power not just to be happy, but to experience happiness in abundance.

Abundant Happiness is not just a matter of being free from depression and misery it is rather a feeling of joy, contentment and wonderment for life. This does not mean that it is possible or even desirable to be in a continual state of ecstasy; after all, there are times when personal tragedies and loss touch our lives and lead quite naturally to sadness, grief and disappointment. But there are ways through which we can cope and deal with those experiences, and often we can turn the challenges and adversities of life into triumph.

Unlike most parables, all the characters in this book are based upon real people (except for the old Chinese man who is based upon a composite of several wise old men and women I have met). I have, of course, changed their names and modified their circumstances to hopefully benefit the story but nevertheless they all triumphed over their personal crises and found personal happiness as recorded in each chapter. It is my hope that their stories will uplift and inspire you to follow their example and experience the blessings of Abundant Happiness in your own life.

Adam Jackson

THE DRIVER

It all began one cold and wet October evening on his way home from work. It was 8 pm, the third time that week he'd had to stay late at the office. The sky had been overcast all day and the heavens had decided to let loose a torrential downpour just as the young man had set off on his journey home. A question on the radio interrupted his thoughts. It was a simple question, one which the young man had never consciously asked himself, and the answers to which it led disturbed him.

The question had been prompted by a national survey which found that only one person in fifty considered themselves to be happy or contented, and less than one person in ten could remember a time even a moment when they had been truly happy. It was a simple, straightforward question. The radio presenter asked his listeners: 'Are you happy?'

The question caused the young man to suddenly reflect upon his own life. He lacked nothing to speak of: he was in reasonable health, he had a good job, he always somehow managed to pay the bills and occasionally put a little aside for minor luxuries. He had a close circle of friends and a loving family. But despite all this, he felt empty inside, disillusioned with life. Something was missing; he didn't know what it was, all he knew was that something was missing from his life. There were many words he could have used to describe his life, but happy was definitely not one of them.

It was Thoreau who said that most people live their lives 'in quiet desperation', and the young man thought that this was a fair description of his own existence. Each day seemed, from beginning to end, to be a struggle; one day converging into the next, with the same or similar frustrations and the same stresses. He couldn't help feeling that his life had turned into an endless, monotonous cycle. What had happened to all his boyhood hopes and dreams? Where was the passion and joy he knew as a child? When had it all begun to be such a struggle?

He had read somewhere that some religious philosophies taught that life was a continuous struggle, but the young man couldn't accept it 'Surely,' he told himself, 'there has to be more to life than this?' He felt confused, lost, as if trapped inside a giant labyrinth, not knowing how he had got there and unsure of the way out.

At that moment, the young man's thoughts were interrupted; but this time by smoke rising from under the bonnet of the car.

'Damn! If it's not one thing, it's another.' he muttered to himself as he pulled the car to the edge of the highway. He got out of the car, lifted the bonnet to take a look at the engine and was hit full in the face by a gush of piercing steam that almost knocked him backwards.

He raised his jacket over his head, hunched over to protect himself from the wind and rain, and walked one and a half kilometres along the highway to the nearest telephone and called the breakdown service for help. The operator advised him that a service mechanic would be with him within an hour or so. There was nothing he could do but return to his car and wait

A question echoed in his head: 'What is the point of it all? What is the point?'

There was no answer, of course. He didn't expect one. All he could hear was the sound of the traffic passing him by,

And so, cold, tired and miserable, the young man wearily walked back to his car. He was not aware that this event was to mark the beginning of one of the most profound changes in his life. Had he known what was to follow, there is no doubt and he would freely confess this in later years, he would have smiled and known the feeling of Abundant Happiness.

THE MEETING

As the young man approached his car, he noticed a man leaning against it. A curious looking character; an old Chinese man in white overalls, wearing a bright yellow baseball cap. He was a small man with a kindly, lined face and long, flowing white hair, but what the young man noticed most about the old man was his eyes. They were very deep, dark brown, smiling eyes.

The old man was smiling as the young man approached. 'A wonderful storm, no?' he said.

'Cold, wet and miserable, if you ask me,' muttered the young man.

But the old Chinese man continued undeterred by the young man's mutterings. 'Do you feel the energy? Can you smell the freshness in the air? Doesn't it make you feel wonderful?'

'Not really,' the young man thought to himself, but stayed silent. He took a closer look at this peculiar old man. The storm had passed only a minute or so before he arrived back at the car and it was still drizzling but the old man was not wet at all. There was not one drop of rain on him, But, before the young man had time to comment, the old man spoke.

'So, what took you?' he said,

'What do you mean? I was told that I would have to wait an hour for someone to arrive,' replied the young man.

'Well, life's full of surprises,' said the old man with a broad grin. 'So, what's the problem?'

'I'm not sure what's wrong,' explained the young man. 'I was driving along when smoke started rising out of the bonnet and the engine just cut out.'

'Okay, let's take a good look,' said the old man and he rolled up his sleeves, stepped forward and began to examine the engine.

After a few minutes the old man looked up and turned to the young man and smiled. 'You don't need to look so worried. It's nothing that can't be fixed,' he said.

Thank goodness for that,' said the young man with a sigh of relief.

'It might cost you a few thousand pounds...but it definitely can be fixed!' said the old man.

'Oh, no. You've got to be joking!' exclaimed the young man.

The old man patted the young man on the arm and laughed, 'Of course I am.'

The old man turned around to pick up a spanner but stopped briefly as he met the young man's gaze, and then turned back to the engine. It might never happen, you know.'

'What?'

'Whatever it is that's troubling you,'

'Nothing is troubling me,' said the young man.

'Ah... I see. That's good then,' said the old man, and he picked up a screwdriver and began whistling a tune as he continued working on the car.

'It sounds like you've had a good day,' said the young man.

'Of course. When you reach my age,' said the old man, 'every day that you are above the ground is a good day!' He turned around to face the young man. 'If you ask me, life is simply too short and too precious to waste feeling miserable. Did you know that the average life is 76 years? That is just 3,952 weeks! And 1,317 of those weeks you will spend asleep. That leaves just 2,635 weeks or 63,240 hours of living!

'How old are you?' asked the old man.

'Thirty-three.'

'So, that means that, if you are fortunate enough to live an average life, you have only about 1,114 weeks left to live!'

'Well, that is a cheerful thought!' said the young man in a blatantly sarcastic tone.

'It simply shows you that your time is precious, too precious to waste feeling unhappy. Life is meant to be lived; each day should be a joy not a struggle. It should be like strolling through a field on a sunny day, not battling through a never-ending storm.'

The young man fell a shiver run down his spine and the hairs on the back of his neck rise. How did the old man know how he was feeling? He tried to reassure himself that it was just a coincidence, after all, the old man could not possibly know what he was thinking.

'It always surprises me that so many people choose to be unhappy,' said the old man as he turned back to his work on the car engine. The young man leaned against the side of the car.

'What do you mean?' he said. 'People don't choose to be unhappy. It all depends upon their circumstances, it's what happens to someone that makes them happy or unhappy.'

'Of course, you may be right. But, if your happiness is determined solely by your circumstances, why is it that another person can experience the same tragedies or joys as you, but react and feel completely differently about it? I once knew two men who were both badly injured in the same car accident. One became depressed, but the other was remarkably cheerful,'

'Why were their reactions so different?' asked the young man.

'The depressed man was bitter and repeatedly asked, "Why did it have to happen to me?" whereas the cheerful man said. Thank God I am still alive!" It's like the poem: Two men looked out between closed bars, one saw mud, the other stars.

'I don't believe that your circumstances, whatever they may be, have any power to make you feel happy or unhappy,' said the old man. 'It is only your opinion about your circumstances that determines how you feel.

'After all, who is happier, the man who sees his cup as half full, or the man who sees his cup as half empty? Ah ha...found it. Could you pass me that wrench?' he said, holding his hand out behind his back to the young man.

'Here you are,' said the young man, 'but surely something either makes you feel happy or it doesn't?'

The old man put down his wrench and turned, resting against the car and faced the young man. 'So, what would make you happy?' he asked.

The young man thought for a moment 'I'm not sure. I suppose more money would help for a start,' he said.

The old man turned back to the young man whilst getting another tool from his toolbox. 'Do you really believe that money brings happiness?' he asked.

'I'm not sure, but at least it allows you to be miserable in comfort,' said the young man, breaking into a smile.

'Good point,' admitted the old man with a grin. 'But, comfortable misery is still misery! You may be in more comfortable surroundings, but you will feel just as uncomfortable as if you had nothing. If money brought happiness, millionaires would be the happiest people in the world, but we all know that the rich know misery and depression just as well as the poor. All money can buy is material possessions like your car here, but these are temporary distractions, they cannot bring you lasting happiness.'

The young man looked away, thinking about what the old man had said, and the old man picked up a spanner and went back to repairing the car.

'What about a different job?' said the young man. 'I think I would be happier if I had a different career.'

'Now you're beginning to sound like the stone cutter!' said the old man with a laugh.

'What do you mean stone cutter?'

'In my country, there is a story of a stone cutter who was unhappy and wished to be someone else with a different position in life.

'One day, he passed a wealthy merchant's house and saw all of the great possessions the merchant possessed, and he noticed how well respected the merchant was about the town. The stone cutter was envious of this great merchant and wished he could be exactly like him. Then he would no longer have to be a mere stone cutter.

'To his astonishment, his wish was granted, and he suddenly became the merchant and had more power and more luxuries than he had ever dreamed of. He was also envied and despised by the poorer people and had more enemies than he had dreamed of as well.

'Then he noticed a high official being transported by servants and surrounded by soldiers. Everyone bowed to the great and mighty official. He was more powerful and respected than any other throughout the kingdom. And the stone cutter, who was now a merchant, wished he could be like the high official, with servants and soldiers to guard him and more power than any other.

'His wish was again granted, and he became the high official, the most powerful man in all the kingdom, before whom everyone bowed. But the official was the most feared and hated in all the kingdom as well, which is why he needed so many soldiers to guard him, and the heat of the sun made the official very uncomfortable and weary. He looked up at the fierce sun shining brightly in the sky and said, "How powerful it is, I wish I could be the sun."

'And no sooner had he wished it than he became the sun, shining down on the earth. But a big black cloud came along and blocked the sun's rays. "How mighty the cloud is," he thought "I wish I was as powerful as the cloud."

'Then he became the cloud covering the sun's rays and raining down on the villages. But a mighty wind came and blew the cloud away "I wish I could be as powerful as the wind," he thought, and as he said it, so he became the wind,

'But whilst the wind could uproot trees and destroy whole villages, it was powerless against a great boulder. The huge stone was immovable, resisting all force of the wind. "How powerful the stone is," he said. "How I wish I could be as powerful as stone."

'Then he became the great stone which resisted the most powerful wind. He was now happy at last the most powerful force of everything on the earth. But then he heard a noise. Chink. Chink. Chink. Chink. A hammer was banging a chisel into the stone, breaking it away, piece by piece. "What could be more powerful than I?" he thought, and there at the foot of the great stone was...a stone cutter

'Many people spend their whole lives in search of happiness, and never find it simply because they look in the wrong place. You won't see a sunset if you're facing east and you won't find happiness searching amongst the things around you. The story of the stone cutter teaches that you cannot find happiness by changing anything in your life... except yourself.

'But I still don't understand,' said the young man. 'What about personal tragedies and disappointments? How can someone still be happy in those circumstances?'

'Each of us is like a ship,' continued the old man, 'travelling across the sea of life. Winds and storms, natural disasters, personal tragedies will come and go, but so long as you control your rudder and sails, you can travel wherever you please, regardless of those storms and winds. In fact, storms and rain can enrich life; it depends on how you look at them.'

'I'm not with you,' said the young man,

'Storms clear the air and bring rain, and what would life be without rain? There would be no growth, no richness in life, and there would be no rainbows. Storms bring winds, and if you know how to sail your ship, you can always use the power of the wind to your advantage.'

'I can see how it fits into your analogy, but I don't agree. How can adversity be turned into an advantage?' interrupted the young man.

'You have heard that every cloud has a silver lining?'

'Yes, of course. But that's just a saying, I've never found a tragedy to be an advantage.'

'Perhaps that is because you have never looked for it. There is no problem that does not bring with it a gift. Everything that happens has a purpose, a reason and a lesson that can enrich your life. Many people drift through life, slaves to circumstances and ruled by the storms and winds because they do not realize that they have a rudder and sails, let alone how to use them. They have forgotten how to sail their ship and, so they blame the weather. They do not realize that, whatever their circumstances, they can still choose to be happy.'

'But you can't choose all your feelings,' persisted the young man.

'Whatever you sincerely believe is, for you, true,' said the old man. You must therefore think carefully about what you choose to believe!'

'Come on, now,' argued the young man. 'Surely, you're not saying that you believe anyone, whatever their circumstances, can be happy? What about a person who is crippled or blind or deaf and dumb? How can such a person be happy?'

'Obviously, you have never met anyone who is handicapped,' said the old man. I know it seems strange, to think that someone who has fewer advantages in life than you can be happy when you are not, but it's nevertheless true. Do you know what Helen Keller who was blind, deaf and dumb throughout her life said when asked what her life had been like with such severe handicaps?'

The young man shook his head.

'She said,' continued the old man, '"My life has been so beautiful" and the great writer Milton who was himself blind explained, "It is not miserable to be blind. It is only miserable not to be able to endure blindness." Similarly, wealth, health, fame and power are no guarantee of happiness, When Napoleon, the emperor of the French empire and one of the most powerful men in the world of his time, was asked if his life had been happy, he answered, "I have not known more than six days of happiness."'

The young man was amazed. 'What is the explanation? How can someone with such terrible handicaps be so happy and someone who has so much power and wealth be so unhappy?'

The old man finished his work on the car and turned to face the young man.

'Happiness is one of the greatest gifts of life, and it is available to everybody. You see, you don't find happiness, you create it, And, whatever your circumstances, you have the power to create your own happiness.'

'How can you create happiness?' asked the young man.

'The Universe is governed by laws, precise laws which control the natural order of things.' said the old man. 'From the motion of the waves to the rising and setting of the sun, to the timing of the seasons, everything in Nature is governed by laws. Scientists have discovered many of these laws - laws of gravity, laws of motion, laws of magnetism. But there are also laws which are not as well known, and among them are the laws of happiness.'

'Laws of happiness?' asked the perplexed young man, 'What are they?'

'They are 10 timeless principles which, if followed, cannot fail to create happiness. Throughout the ages, civilizations discarded these laws in their search for great wealth and, in time, the laws were forgotten, known only to those few people who remained faithful to them. And so, they came to be known as "secrets".'

'How can I find out about them?' asked the young man.

'One moment . . . nearly done. There you are . . . finished. Good as new,' said the old man, wiping his hands on a cloth. You will find out soon enough. Here, take this,' he said, handing a piece of paper to the young man. The young man looked at the piece of paper; it contained no secrets, no laws, no aphorisms just a list of 10 names and 10 telephone numbers. He turned the paper over expecting to find something on the other side, but it was blank.

'What is this? Where are the secrets?' but when he looked up, the old man was no longer there. 'Hey!' he shouted, walking around the car. 'Where are you? This is just a list of names!' He looked up and down the highway, but the old man was nowhere to be seen.

Just then a pickup truck began flashing the young man and slowly pulled up behind his car. The young man walked briskly up to the driver's door.

'How in the name of heaven did you...?' He stopped mid-sentence. It was not the old man.

'What's the problem?' said the mechanic as he climbed down.

'Hold on a minute,' said the young man. 'Where's the old man?'

'What old man? What are you talking about?' said the bemused mechanic. 'You reported a breakdown, didn't you?'

Yes, but a man has already been and fixed it... the old Chinese man.'

'What old Chinese man? Let me call back to the breakdown operator and see what has happened. Perhaps there's been a mix-up It wouldn't surprise me. It happens now and then; the operators get so busy that they send the same report to two mechanics.'

The mechanic climbed back into his van and radioed the service operator. A few minutes later he got back out. 'Well, they definitely only gave your report to me. It's all on the computer. Apparently, I'm the only mechanic on duty in this area this evening. Anyway, I'd better check the car for you whilst I'm here. Turn on the engine will you.'

The engine turned over immediately and was running smoothly. The mechanic held up his hand signalling for the young man to turn the engine off.

'All seems fine,' he said. I can't see any problem.'

Ten minutes after the mechanic had left, the young man was still sitting in his car wondering about the old Chinese man. Who was he? Where had he come from? What were the secrets of happiness of which he had spoken?

A few more minutes passed before the young man started the engine and resumed his journey home again. There were no answers to his questions; all he had was a piece of paper containing a list of ten names and phone numbers.

THE FIRST SECRET – THE POWER OF ATTITUDE

The young man began making telephone calls to the people on the old man's list as soon as he arrived home. He managed to speak to six of them. The other four were out but he left messages for them to return his call. One strange thing he noticed as he talked to the people on the list was that they all seemed to become very animated and excited when he mentioned the old Chinese man. He arranged to meet each of them in turn over the following weeks.

The first person on the young man's list was a man by the name of Barry Kesterman. Mr. Kesterman was a teacher and worked at the local school. He was teaching classes until 5 pm the following day but he gladly agreed to meet with the young man afterward.

Mr. Kesterman was still relatively young in appearance; the young man thought he was probably in his late thirties or early forties, certainly no older. Mr. Kesterman was marking his students' papers when the young man knocked on his classroom door.

'Ah! Come in, come in,' Mr. Kesterman said warmly, shaking the young man's hand. 'It's a pleasure to meet you. Please take a seat.

'So, you met the old man yesterday,' said Mr. Kesterman.

'Yes. He fixed my car.'

'My goodness, He certainly pops up in the most unexpected places. And he told you about the secrets of Abundant Happiness?' Mr. Kesterman said.

Yes. You know of them?' asked the young man.

Yes. Of course.'

'And do they really work?' asked the young man.

'Most definitely. Fifteen years ago, I reached one of the lowest points in my life; I had just lost my job, I was living in small bedsit 500 kilometres from my home town, I hadn't made many friends, and I felt utterly depressed, almost despondent. It was like being engulfed in a black cloud and I just couldn't see a way forward. I went to the park and just sat down on a bench overlooking the lake and mulled over all my problems in my head. After a few minutes I turned around to find I was no longer alone; there was an old Chinese man sitting next to me.'

The young man could hardly believe what he was hearing. A small tingling sensation ran up his spine,

'Do you mind if I make notes?' he asked,

'No. Not at all,' said Mr. Kesterman, and he continued his story 'It was probably obvious that something was troubling me, but I got the impression that the old man knew exactly what my problems were, as if he could see inside me.

'We talked for a while; he told me that he was on his way to visit a friend who was feeling depressed. "My friend has simply forgotten the golden rule of Abundant Happiness," he said. I had never heard of any golden rule of happiness abundant or otherwise, but then he explained: "It is very simple," he said. "You are as happy as you have made up your mind to be."

'I didn't really understand it at the time, but I later found that it is absolutely true, and I can honestly say that that simple statement is one of the most important lessons I learned in life. It encapsulates the first secret of Abundant Happiness... the power of your attitude.'

The young man listened intently as Mr. Kesterman continued.

'Let me explain. Like most people, I had always thought things made me happy, but the truth is we can choose to be happy. I remember once seeing a hypnotist in a stage show. People were hypnotized on stage and were given a raw onion. They were all told that the onion was the most delicious fruit they had ever tasted. All of them bit into their onion and licked their lips with relish, savouring every mouthful. They were then given a ripe peach and told that it was a raw turnip. This time, as they bit into the peach, they immediately spat it out in disgust. It was the attitude which they acquired under hypnosis that determined their reaction to the onion and the peach.

'You see the problem is, as we go through life, we often acquire negative attitudes, and these are the real culprits that make us unhappy.'

'What sort of negative attitudes?' interjected the young man.

'Well, a good example is what we expect from life. For instance, I was always taught that we should expect the worst, because then we won't be disappointed,'

'Yes, I was taught that as well. It seems logical,' said the young man.

'It's a common belief,' said Mr. Kesterman, 'but it's a false one, and one that most often destroys our dreams and prevents us from experiencing happiness,'

'How can that be?' said the young man. 'If you expect the worst and it happens, you won't be disappointed; but if it doesn't happen, you'll be pleasantly surprised. If you hope for the best, you are only setting yourself up for disappointment.'

'I know it seems that way, doesn't it? But, I can demonstrate to you right now, prove to you that if you expect the worst, you will invariably experience the worst, and vice versa.

'Take a good look around this room right now and try to notice everything that's brown.'

The young man looked around the room. There were numerous things that were brown: the wooden picture frames; the light brown settee; the curtain frame; the desks, books and numerous other small items in the room.

'Okay,' said Mr. Kesterman, 'Now close your eyes ...' The young man closed his eyes.

'... and tell me everything you saw... that was ... blue!'

The young man smiled. 'I didn't notice anything blue,' 'Open your eyes,' said Mr. Kesterman. 'See, there's blue all around you,'

And there was too: a blue vase; a blue photo frame; a blue paisley pattern in the carpet; a blue letter holder on the desk; blue books on the bookshelves, and Mr. Kesterman was even wearing a blue shirt. The more he looked for blue, the more and more things he noticed which were blue.

'Look at all the things you missed'

'But you tricked me,' said the young man. 'I was looking for brown objects, not blue.'

'That is my point, entirely!' said Mr. Kesterman. 'You were looking for brown and, then you saw brown and missed all the blue. This is what you do in life; you look for the worst and, so you see the worst and miss out on the best. This is precisely what your belief of expecting or anticipating the worst leads to... it makes us lose sight of all the good things in our life. This is one of the reasons why many rich and famous people who have everything you could possibly imagine still manage to get depressed and become drug addicts and alcoholics. They focus on what they haven't got instead of everything they have got, and therefore they only "see" what is lacking in their life. In this way, they create their own misery.

'Similarly, many people who live a very modest existence are very happy because they focus on what they have got. This is why a person who regards his glass as half full will be happier than a person who regards his glass as half empty.

'You see, contrary to popular belief, everything external to us; money, cars, possessions, fame and fortune is irrelevant. It is our attitude to life that determines our happiness in life. Therefore, to experience happiness, we don't need to have more money or a bigger house or a better job, all we need to do is change our attitude. This is what led Samuel Johnson to write:

The fountain of content must spring up from the mind; and he who has so little knowledge of human nature as to seek happiness by changing anything but his own disposition, will waste his life in fruitless efforts and multiply the grief which he proposes to remove.

'I had never thought of it that way,' said the young man, 'But I suppose that makes sense.'

'It's interesting, isn't it? Also, consider what generally tends to happen if you are about to do something when anticipating the worst,' said Mr. Kesterman.

'What do you mean?' asked the young man.

'Well, let's say for instance, that you are about to give a speech in front of hundreds of people. You might be nervous and start thinking of all the worst things that could happen; for instance, you might forget what you were going to say, you might stutter and stammer, and you could end up making a complete fool of yourself in front of all those people. If you think these thoughts, how is that going to prepare or motivate you to do the speech? Is it going to make you feel confident or will it make you feel even more nervous?'

'I'd feel more nervous,' admitted the young man.

'Of course, you would, who wouldn't? And the same principle applies to everything we do in life. Who is more likely to jump out of bed in the morning eager to face the day; the person who expects that the worst things might happen in the day ahead or the person who anticipates a fantastic day? And which of them is more likely to enjoy the day?'

'I see your point, but what happens when things don't meet your expectations? What happens when bad things occur?'

'Remember the golden rule: you choose how you feel! You can look for the blue or the brown in any situation. You can focus on what's good about a situation rather than on what might appear bad.'

'What if there is nothing good?'

'Sometimes, of course, when tragedies touch our lives, what seeds of goodness there are may be difficult to see. But one way to cope with tragedy is to find something positive, something meaningful in our grief. Perhaps the greatest of tragedies is when a parent suffers the heartbreak of losing a child, and in many such instances, the only way we are able to overcome our grief is to create something positive.

'For instance, one young Californian mother was devastated by the loss of her 13-year-old daughter who had been killed by a drunk driver in a road traffic accident, When the mother discovered that the driver had a history of drink-driving offences and that the law was not protecting the public from him and others like him, she initiated a nationwide campaign to do something about it. Mothers Against Drunk Drivers successfully lobbied Congress and was responsible for over 950 anti-drink driving laws. The campaign soon spread to Canada, the United Kingdom and New Zealand and has since saved hundreds and thousands of lives. And it all began because one woman decided to turn her grief and her loss into something positive.

'There is no experience in life that doesn't bring with it a gift something that can benefit our lives and those around us, we just have to choose to look for it. For instance, when I met the old Chinese man all those years ago, I had lost my job, and all I could think about was that I was a failure and might never get another job. But after a long discussion with the old man that day, I began to see that losing my job might be something very positive,'

'How can losing your job be positive?" asked the young man.

'For a start, it was an opportunity for me to start a new career, something that I would really believe in,' said Mr. Kesterman. 'So, instead of feeling depressed about losing my job, I began to feel excited, enthused and optimistic. If you remember one thing today, remember this:

It is the meaning that we attach to the events in our lives not the events themselves that determine our feelings about them.

*With this attitude, losing my job represented a new beginning, a turning point in my life. When I was honest with myself, I knew that I had never really been enthused about my job. It was just a means of earning a living. But then I had a chance to think about what I really wanted to do with my life. I wanted to be able to make a difference, to have an impact a positive impact and make a real contribution to the community, I decided that I really wanted to be a teacher and it didn't take long for me to decide that I would go back to college.

'Let me give you another good example,' said Mr. Kesterman. 'Imagine that you split up from your girlfriend; you could decide it means that you are unattractive, unlovable and will never find another girlfriend. You might think that even if you did meet someone, you would never be able to make another relationship last. Alternatively, you could re-frame the situation and decide that splitting up from your girlfriend is an opportunity for you to find someone better, someone who is more suited to you. You see, it all depends upon your attitude,

You can re-frame most experiences in life to have a positive meaning. In some parts of the world even death is considered to be a time for celebration because they believe that, when we die, the soul returns to its real home and that we will all meet up with our loved ones in another time and place.'

'But it's not always easy to see a positive side to a situation,' insisted the young man.

'Only if you don't look for it. If you can't see a positive side, it generally means you're not searching for it. We can also help create a positive attitude by asking ourselves positive questions. Instead of asking "Why did this have to happen to me?" you can ask, "What can I learn or how can I benefit from this experience?"'

'I'm not sure what you mean,' said the young man.

'All day long you are asking yourself questions.' explained Mr. Kesterman, 'about the things you see, things you hear, things you smell, things you have to do, things you did and things you are doing.

From when yon get up in the morning to when you go to bed at night, your subconscious is constantly asking questions. In fact, the process of thought is nothing but a series of questions. Questions lead to answers and answers produce feelings. Therefore, if you feel unhappy or depressed, it usually means you are asking the wrong questions. You are asking yourself what is wrong with your life instead of what is right with it.

'Most people, when faced with a difficult situation, will ask themselves questions like: "Why did this happen to me?" or "What am I going to do?" These are negative, dis-empowering questions that produce negative, dis-empowering answers and create feelings of self-pity, hopelessness and depression. If instead we asked positive, empowering questions we would produce completely different feelings.'

'What questions are empowering?' asked the young man.

'Those that create feelings of power and hope. For instance, whenever I find myself in a difficult situation I consciously ask myself three powerful questions that instantly change the way I look at the situation.

'The first question is "What is great about this situation?" '

'But what if nothing is great?' interrupted the young man.

Then I ask: "What could be great about it?" You see that question makes you look for something great in the situation and, invariably, you'll find something just as you only noticed the blue things in this room when you consciously looked for them.

'This is what is meant by the saying that every cloud has a silver lining and that every problem is merely a gift in disguise. Everything can be re-framed and, in doing so, you have the power to enrich your life through every experience. This is the first secret of Abundant Happiness.'

'The old man gave me a list of people, all of whom taught me about the secrets of Abundant Happiness and many of whom had suffered crises in their lives, but they all rose above their troubles because they had learned how to re-frame every situation with a positive meaning.'

The second question is: "What is not perfect yet?"

'This presupposes that things will be perfect and creates a different feeling than asking, "What's wrong?"

'The third question is: "What can I do to make things the way I want them to be, and have fun in the process?" This question helps you find all the things which are within your power to remedy the situation and also how to make the process enjoyable.

let me give you a few examples of how these questions work. When your car broke down yesterday evening, if you had asked, "What's great about this situation?", you may have come up with 'It's great that I'm not hurt" or "It's great that there's a breakdown service who will help me" or "It's great that I didn't break down on a country lane, miles from anywhere."

Then by asking, "What's not perfect yet?" the answer in this case is obviously, "My car." And then, "What can I do to remedy the situation and have fun in the process?" Once you've called the breakdown service and are waiting for the mechanic, you could use the time to leisurely read the newspaper or a book, or listen to a programme on the radio that you never usually get a chance to hear. You could use the time to creatively plan your next holiday, write a letter or start writing that book you've always been promising yourself that you'd write (assuming you've got pen and paper), or you could simply lie back and take a well-earned nap until the mechanic arrived.

'Another example: imagine you're depressed because you're overweight What's great? It's great that you have finally reached the point that you are unhappy about your weight and really want to change; It's great that you're aware of the need to change because being overweight increases your risk of heart disease. What's not perfect yet? Your weight and shape. What are you willing to do to remedy the situation? Learn about what causes obesity, change your eating habits and start exercising. And how can you enjoy the process of slimming? Join a slimming club so you can meet other people with the same problem, or find an exercise class that you enjoy, perhaps even take up dancing which is a great form of exercise. Find healthy foods that you enjoy and learn to cook healthy, low fat meals.'

'This is fascinating,' said the young man. 'So, people can consciously change their attitudes by expecting the best, focusing on what is good in their lives and asking empowering questions?"

'Absolutely,' answered Mr. Kesterman. 'But the essence of creating a healthy, happy attitude to life can be summarized in one word... gratitude! One of the surest secrets of Abundant Happiness is simply to cultivate an attitude of gratitude.'

'And how do you do that?'

'Look for things to be grateful for,' replied Mr. Kesterman, 'Ask yourself every day "What do I have to be grateful for?"'

'But what if there is nothing to be grateful for?' persisted the young man.

Mr. Kesterman looked at the young man with raised eyebrows. 'A few years ago, I visited an old friend who was dying, The doctors had given him less than a year to live. I expected him to be depressed but instead found him to be not just cheerful, but positively joyous.'

'How can a man with less than a year to live feel joyous?' asked the bemused young man.

'I asked him myself. "Why are you so happy, Jim?" I said. And he said, "Because I woke up this morning and today I'm alive!" I found his answer humbling. If a dying man can find things to be grateful for, how much more should the rest of us find?

'No matter how bad our circumstances,' continued Mr. Kesterman, 'there is always something and usually many things that we can all find to be grateful for.

The difference between a person who lives a magical life and a person who lives a mundane life lies not in their circumstances it lies in their attitudes. Attitude is the paintbrush of the mind with which we colour our lives. We can choose whatever colours we wish.'

On his way home, the young man reflected upon what he had learned. He could see now that he had a lot to learn about himself and his life, but more importantly, he was beginning to understand why he had felt so unhappy for so long.

That evening the young man read the brief notes he had made at the meeting with Mr. Kesterman.

The First Secret of Abundant Happiness: The Power of Attitude

The foundation of my happiness begins with my attitude to life. I am as happy as I have made up my mind to be. From now on I will make up my mind to be happy.

If I expect the best, very often I'll get it!

Happiness is a choice that I can make any time, any place and anywhere.

Every experience can be framed to have a positive meaning. From now on, will look for something positive in everything and everyone.

In any difficult or stressful situation ask the three empowering questions:

What is great? Or, what could be great?

What's not perfect yet?

What can I do to remedy the situation and have fun in the process?

Gratitude is the seed of Abundant Happiness. From now on I will find things to be grateful for. It is only my thoughts that make me feel happy or unhappy, not my circumstances. I control my thoughts; therefore, I control my happiness.

THE SECOND SECRET – THE POWER OF THE BODY

The second person on the young man's list was a man by the name of Rodney Greenway. Mr Greenway was a well-known fitness instructor; not only did he own one of the leading health clubs in the city, but he had also written several books on health and fitness which had become international bestsellers. The young man arrived at Mr Greenway's health club promptly at the arranged time of 8 am and was met by a tall, muscular, clean cut man casually dressed in blue denim jeans and a white T-shirt. Mr. Greenway certainly looked the part with a slightly tanned complexion, short, dark brown hair and bright green eyes that seemed to glow when he smiled.

Mr. Greenway led the young man into his office and they both sat down on the easy chairs. 'Would you like something to eat or drink?' Mr. Greenway asked the young man. 'We've got fruit juice, mineral water, herb teas...'

'A fruit juice would be great Thank you,' said the young man. Mr. Greenway poured out two glasses of fresh apple juice and handed one to the young man.

'So how can I help you?' he asked.

'I'm not sure,' said the young man, and he proceeded to tell his story.

'The secrets of Abundant Happiness!' said Mr. Greenway. 'I came across them over 10 years ago. In those days I was still working as a lawyer.'

'A lawyer?' repeated the young man. 'You gave up a career in law to become a fitness instructor?'

'Yes, absolutely.'

'But why? How could you give up something that you must have studied for many years, and which would have provided a lucrative career for the rest of your life?'

'Very simple,' said Mr. Greenway 'I was unhappy. When I was a student, I really had no idea what I wanted to do with my life and the law seemed like a sensible option. I reasoned that even if, once qualified, I didn't like it, it would be an excellent stepping stone to other careers.'

'But not to becoming a physical fitness instructor?'

'No. That's true. I became a fitness instructor because that's what I wanted to do. I did fairly well as a lawyer for a few years, but my heart just wasn't in it. I became more and more tired and depressed as time went by. I even reached the stage when I found it difficult to get out of bed in the morning.'

'I know the feeling well,' said the young man. '

Then one day I had to stay late at the office and the caretaker came in. He could see something was wrong. I had my head in my hands, rubbing my eyeballs. I told him I was okay, just feeling a bit down. Then he asked me if I wanted to feel "high". I said, "No thank you." I didn't take drugs. "What makes you think I was talking about drugs?" he said. I was intrigued; I couldn't imagine what else, other than drugs, could make you feel high.'

The young man took out his pen and notebook from his pocket and began to scribble notes.

'And do you know what the caretaker said? "Exercise!"'

'Exercise?' exclaimed the young man looking up from his notebook.'

'Yes. Simple physical exercise.' '

How on earth can exercise make you feel high?' asked the young man.

'Physical exercise isn't just necessary for physical health, it is also necessary to maintain long term mental and emotional health, and there are sound reasons for this; you may have noticed that the advice people most often give to someone who is feeling a little depressed is to do something. It's good advice too, I use the acronym, GOYA.'

'What does that stand for?' asked the young man.

'Get Off Your... Backside!'

The young man smiled as he wrote it down.

'The reason why it's good advice is because it works. As George Bernard Shaw once wrote: The secret of being miserable is to have the leisure to think about whether you are happy or not" But, getting up and doing something doesn't just help take our mind off our problems; it changes our perceptions of those problems and relieves the stress that the problems create.'

'How can exercise change the way we feel?' asked the young man in disbelief.

'I will have trouble telling you anything which is more important than this today: Motion affects emotion!'

The young man wrote it down. 'When we move our bodies, we change our emotional states. It is well known that people who don't exercise regularly develop muscle atrophy, physical weakness, calcium loss from their bones, and are more than twice as likely to die prematurely than people who do exercise regularly. But, what is not as well known is that people who do not exercise regularly also tend to become introverted, tense and oversensitive as well as suffer more from depression, anxiety and mental fatigue.'

'Why is that?' asked the young man.

'Scientists discovered that there is a very good explanation for this phenomenon. They found that exercise causes the brain to release certain chemicals and hormones, endorphins and enkephalins, these are natural stimulants which make you feel enervated or "high".'

'Are you saying that we will feel happier if we exercise regularly?' asked the young man.

'Absolutely,' replied Mr. Greenway. 'What sort of exercise?'

'"Aerobic" exercise. Now before you ask, that does not necessarily mean you should do a Jane Fonda workout,' said Mr. Greenway smiling. '"Aerobic" literally means "exercising with oxygen" and therefore includes any activity or sport in which you breathe as you do the exercise such as swimming, cycling, brisk walking, even dancing. Non-aerobic exercise, on the other hand, involves exercising without using oxygen and includes those activities in which you hold your breath such as sprinting and weightlifting, and is not as good for your emotions or your health.'

'Why is that? 'The young man was curious, 'Because when you do non-aerobic exercise, instead of burning oxygen, your body will burn glycogen which is food for the brain.'

'How much exercise do you need to do to start to notice the benefits?' asked the young man.

'Only about 30 minutes or so every day that's all.

' That doesn't sound too difficult,' said the young man.

'It's not,' replied Mr. Greenway, 'although, like any change to your lifestyle, it does require determination to do it regularly and make it become a habit'

'So you're saying exercise can help you feel happier?'

'Yes, I had my doubts too,' said Mr. Greenway, seeing that the young man was not convinced. I had a long talk with the caretaker in my office that evening. He mentioned the 10 secrets of Abundant Happiness, and I must say that they all radically changed my life. But the one secret which I think I most needed to learn and the one which I am now most qualified to help you with is... the power of your body.'

'By 'body' I assume you mean exercise,' said the young man.

'No. There are a number of other equally important aspects about the way in which we use our bodies which also have a profound and immediate effect on our emotions of which exercise is only one.'

The young man was fascinated and wrote notes as Mr. Greenway continued. 'The first thing is our posture; the way we stand, sit and walk, If our posture is poor (i.e. bent over or leaning to one side instead of being straight and erect) our health and emotions suffer.'

'I find that hard to believe. How can the way we stand or sit possibly affect our emotions?' asked the young man. 'Let me explain,' said Mr. Greenway. 'Imagine that outside this room, there is a man who is feeling lethargic, tired and depressed. How do you think he will be sitting or standing?''

'I'm not sure.'

'Well, would he be holding his head erect or would his head be slumped and facing the floor?'

'Facing the floor.'

'Would his chest be pushed out or slouched?'

'Slouched, I suppose'

'Would his facial muscles he pulled up, tight and smiling, or would the muscles be flaccid and frowning?'

'Well, it's hardly likely they would be smiling,' said the young man.

'And would he be breathing deeply or shallowly?'

'Shallowly, Okay, I get the picture,' said the young man. 'We adopt different postures according to the emotions we are feeling.'

'Exactly. But it's a two-way street. Our emotions affect our posture, but our posture also affect our emotions. If we slouch and hunch over all the time, we will begin to feel depressed, whereas if we stand erect we immediately feel better. It sounds incredible, doesn't it, but by changing our posture we can instantly change our emotional state. Did you know, for instance, that if you stand erect, breathe deeply and smile, it is virtually impossible to feel depressed? Researchers have even taken people who are manic depressives some of whom have been on medication for over 20 years and monitored how they felt in different postures. The scientists were amazed to find that while they were standing like this, none of the patients felt depressed or needed medication. Can you imagine that?'

'But, surely you're not suggesting that the answer to everyone's problems is to spend more time standing erect, breathing deeply and smiling?'

'No, of course not. But its a great start. It does help us to feel better and it works instantly. Its simply a way in which we can take control of our emotional states using our bodies.

'One of the secrets of being happy is being aware of your posture, We often develop bad posture through continued misuse sitting hunched over a desk at work or slouched in front of the TV, but this will make you feel depressed.'

'But it is so uncomfortable standing erect,' said the young man. 'Its like being a soldier on parade.'

'Good posture is not standing to attention. In fact, that's very poor posture because it creates so much additional tension in your back. A healthy posture is simply keeping your back straight and relaxed. You shouldn't feel any tightness or pain at all. One of the best techniques which helps improve your posture is what I call the 'rope technique'.'

'Rope technique? Sounds interesting,' said the young man.

It's quite straightforward and very easy to do. All you do is imagine that there is a rope attached to the top of your head and that there is a man standing above you who is gently pulling the rope upwards.'

The young man tried doing it and immediately felt he was not only straighter but taller as well.

'When you do this, you feel like you are being gently lifted and straightened, don't you?' said Mr. Greenway, 'And, as a result, you feel better.

'Another very powerful technique using your body to help change your feelings is called 'anchoring'.'

'Anchoring?'

'Yes. It's very simple and extremely effective. It's a bit like Pavlov's dog. You might recall that every time Pavlov's dog was given food, a bell was rung. The dog subconsciously associated the sound of the bell with food, and eventually just the sound of the bell alone made the dog salivate. Pavlov's dog had subconsciously associated or anchored the sound of the bell with food. The same thing happens with humans. How do you feel when you hear a dentist's drill? Tense? Uncomfortable? It's the same thing, we associate the sound of the drill with pain, discomfort and tension.

'Often we subconsciously create anchors that are not conducive to happiness. I'll give you an example; if two people continually argue, there will come a time when all they have to do is see each other or hear each other's voice and they become angry.'

'I'm still not sure how this applies to being happy,' said the young man.

'We have positive anchors as well. You must have seen sports men and women clenching their fists and shouting "Yes!' to pump themselves up. It's because this makes us feel confident and energetic Try it for yourself now and see.'

It's okay.' said the young man, his face reddening. 'I'll take your word for it.'

'Don't take my word for it, try it,' said Mr. Greenway. 'Stand up, clench your fists and shout 'YES!'

The young man stood up, clenched his fists and said, 'Yes!'

"No. Don't just say it,' said Mr. Greenway, 'Shout it.' So, the young man did it again, but this time shouting it aloud. And to his amazement, he instantly felt energized. That's amazing!' he said. 'It really works,' 'Of course it does. There's more as well,' said Mr. Greenway. 'You can create your own anchors to produce specific emotions. Let me show you. Think back to a time when you felt really happy,' said Mr. Greenway. The young man had to go back 10 years to the time when he celebrated getting his first job offer.

Think of it as clearly as you can. Close your eyes and try to re-experience it. What you were saying? What you were doing? How were you breathing? Try to notice everything,' said Mr. Greenway. The young man pictured the scene and then he suddenly felt Mr. Greenway touch on his right shoulder. 'Now remember it again,' Mr. Greenway said and once again, as the young man was visualizing the experience, Mr. Greenway touched his right shoulder, 'What are you doing?' said the young man, 'Don't worry. We need to do it a few more times and then I'll explain.'

The same process was repeated seven more times before the young man said, 'What's this all about?'.

'I have just created a 'happy' anchor for you,' smiled Mr. Greenway.

'I don't understand . . .' the young man said, but just then Mr. Greenway touched him on his right shoulder and, to the young man's amazement, and for no apparent reason, he suddenly felt happy

I helped your subconscious associate happiness with being touched on the right shoulder,' explained Mr. Greenway. 'You see, it's that simple to create a feeling of happiness using an 'anchor'! All you need to do is: remember a time when you felt happy, really very happy and then, in the peak of the emotion as you are remembering it, do something unusual pinch your ear, tweak your nose, squeeze your wrist It doesn't matter what you do so long as it's specific and not something you do every day.' 'Why's that?' interrupted the young man. 'Well, it's like Pavlov's dog again, if it heard the bell all day long, it wouldn't have associated it with the food. The wonderful thing is that you can use anchors to trigger any kind of emotional state; confidence, affection, compassion, literally any emotion.'

That sounds incredible,' said the young man. 'So, for instance, if I want to feel confident all I have to do is remember a time when I felt confident, do a specific action like pulling my earlobe whilst I'm remembering it, and if I do it over and over again, eventually all I will have to do to feel confident is pull my earlobe?'

'Precisely. It can take time to practice visualizing an experience and remembering a specific memory, and you must be in the peak of the emotion before you create the anchor, but if you persevere, you'll see how easily it works,'

'It sounds a bit simplistic,' said the young man.

'I know, but it really does work. In fact, it works so well that advertisers use 'anchors' all the time to get you to associate good feelings with their products.'

'How do they do that?' asked the young man. 'Advertisers can't touch you.'

'Anchors can be created through any of the senses touch, sound, taste, smell or sight. Pavlov's dog was anchored using the sound of a bell, and remember the example I gave you earlier of two people arguing who eventually would become angry just by seeing or hearing the other?'

'Yes. I see what you mean,' said the young man.

'What advertisers commonly do is take one of the top pop stars and play his or her music whilst advertising a product. People feel good when they hear the music or see the pop star and pretty soon that feeling becomes anchored to the product. Why do you think a major soft drinks manufacturer paid Michael Jackson over $15 million to use him and his music in their adverts?

'Advertisers use anchors all the time, and we can use them in just the same way, but for our own needs instead of theirs. This is the power of your body, But, that's not all. There are other very important ways in which our bodies affect our emotions. Food for instance.'

'How does food come into all this?' said the young man.

'The food we put into our bodies influences the way we feel. For instance, processed sugary foods such as white bread, cakes and chocolates all affect your blood sugar level and can make you feel tired and irritable, and excess coffee and tea and alcohol are known to contain stimulants that can cause depressed feelings. Some common artificial food additives have also been shown to cause depression. Research studies have, for instance, revealed that aspartame, one of the most common artificial sweeteners used in many 'sugar free' drinks and foods throughout the world, may actually cause clinical depression in some people.'

'Are there any foods that help you feel good?' inquired the young man.

'Well medical studies have revealed that rutin, a bioflavonoid found in buckwheat, has a beneficial effect on our brain waves and can help 'lift' people out of depression. But, basically it is important to have a nutritious whole food diet with lots of fresh fruits and vegetables and whole grains (such as brown rice, oats, barley, millet and whole wheat bread and pasta) because this will help regulate blood sugar levels, reduce irritability and help counter the effects of stress.'

The young man thought about all the ready-made meals he was used to having. There was no way that there was much freshness in TV dinners. Perhaps this had also been a contributing factor to his general lethargy and unhappiness.

'But one of the most neglected areas in emotional well-being,' continued Mr. Greenway, 'in relation to our bodily needs, is natural daylight.'

'Natural daylight?' repeated the young man as he scribbled down his notes. 'Well, we all get that, don't we?'

'Unfortunately, we often don't. Many people work in factories or offices that have no windows, or windows that are tinted to block out the sunlight. It's a lot worse in the winter of course when the days are so much shorter. In fact, depression caused by lack of daylight is now an established medical disorder, Seasonal Affective Disorder or

SAD for short That is why there are so many more suicides recorded in winter months.'

'So, what we can do about it?'

'Either get out in the daylight for at least an hour a day or, if that is not possible, use natural daylight bulbs.'

'This has been absolutely fascinating,' said the young man. 'I never realized how important our bodies are to the way we feel. Why aren't people made aware of all of this?' That is why they are called 'secrets',' said Mr. Greenway. 'I think, deep down, we all 'know' how to use our bodies and how to be happy it's the most natural state in the world it's just that living in the modern world, we have forgotten and sometimes we need to be reminded.

'After I first learned all of this, I started to try and incorporate it into my daily routines. I went for a brisk walk every morning before work, I was conscious of my posture, I started eating sensibly with plenty of fresh fruits and vegetables, pulses, pasta, rice and potatoes, and I tried to spend an hour every day out in the daylight

'The results were incredible. After one week, I was so amazed by the difference in the way I felt that I decided to devote my life to sharing this with others. I trained in physiotherapy and personal fitness and to begin with I worked some evenings and at the weekend. Within a few months my business had taken off so well that I was able to do it full time. It's incredible how much better you feel when you really believe in and enjoy your work. In fact, I wouldn't call it work at all. It's fun.'

'And it was all thanks to your office caretaker,' said the young man,

'Yes, it was. I tried to contact him a few weeks later to thank him for his help, but nobody had ever heard of him.'

'Hold on,' said the young man. 'Was he ... an old Chinese man?'

Mr. Greenway smiled. 'Who else?'

When the young man arrived home he sat down and read his notes.

The Second Secret of Abundant Happiness: The Power of your Body

Motion affects emotion.

Exercise relieves stress and causes a chemical reaction making us feel good. Exercise regularly daily if possible for a minimum of 30 minutes.

My feelings are influenced by my posture. A strong posture creates a happy disposition.

The feeling of happiness can be consciously triggered at any time using an 'anchor',

The foods we eat influence the way we feel. Avoid depressants such as coffee, tea, alcohol, sugary foods and artificial additives. Have plenty of fresh fruits and vegetables, whole grains and pulses.

Lack of natural daylight can cause feelings of depression. Get out in the daylight for an hour a day, if possible.

THE THIRD SECRET – THE POWER OF LIVING IN THE MOMENT

'It happened almost 20 years ago. Things weren't going well at work and I was having problems at home as well. Then one day I was walking briskly up the main street in the centre of town at about four in the afternoon, on my way to give a presentation to one of our major clients. Suddenly, I heard a horn blowing and a woman scream. I looked up and saw a huge juggernaut heading straight at me.

'Everything seemed to happen in slow motion, I just stood there, paralyzed by fear as the juggernaut skidded towards me. I thought that was it, I was going to die, but at the last second, I felt someone grab me and pull me backwards. It was a close thing, I can tell you. I felt the side of the Juggernaut skim past my overcoat. Another centimetre and I would have been hit and doubtless killed. I turned around to see who it was who had saved my life and there he was, a little old Chinese man!'

Tony Brown was in his mid-forties. He was a successful freelance photographer whose photographs regularly appeared in the national newspapers and magazines. The young man had met Mr. Brown at his studio in the centre of the town.

'I was a little shaken by the incident and sat down on a nearby bench,' continued Mr. Brown. The old Chinese man came and sat down next to me, and asked if I was all right and I told him that I'd be fine, 'That was close,' he said 'I know. Thank you,' I said. 'You saved my life.' I explained that my mind had been elsewhere when I had stepped out into the road, and then he said something that made me think. He said: 'There is a saying in my country: the only place to live is here, the only time to live is now!'

'We talked; only for a few minutes, but just before he left, he handed me a piece of paper.'

'And it contained a list of 10 names and phone numbers?' interrupted the young man.

Yes,' replied Mr. Brown with a smile. This is how I learned the secrets of Abundant Happiness.' 'What did they do for you?' asked the young man.

'They taught me how to create happiness. And one in particular left a very deep impression on me, probably because it was something I had never considered ... the power of living in the moment.'

'How can a moment contain any power or secret of happiness?' asked the young man.

'The secret is not in the moment, it is living in the moment,' said Mr. Brown. 'Happiness cannot be found in years, months, weeks or even days it is found only by living in the moment.'

'What do you mean?' asked the young man, still confused. 'You're not saying that you cannot be happy for more than a minute, are you?'

'Of course not. But I am saying that you can only experience happiness moment by moment. Look at these pictures over here,' said Mr. Brown. 'What do you see?'

The young man studied the photographs on the wall next to him. Each frame captured an expression. There was a young mother cradling her baby; a father and son laughing, playing ball; two elderly men hugging; two friends in an airport crying, and a crowd of children playing in a school playground.

Finally, he said, 'Well, there's a lot of intense emotions and feeling. They're very good,'

'Thank you,' said Mr. Brown, 'It's the emotions I try to capture. This is the beauty of photographs, they record one split second of time a split second that will never be repeated again in which we experience an emotion. Have you ever thought about how people place value on things such as television sets, computers, cars, money, clothes, jewellery... all things that can easily be replaced? But, time is the one thing in life that can never be replaced and, yet we think of it as having no value. It is the most valuable resource we have, and yet we tend to squander it Thinking about the past or worrying about the future deprives us of the present and the present, the here and now, is all we have, and all we can ever have.'

'I'm not sure that I understand,' asked the young man.

'When you look back on your life,' explained Mr. Brown, 'and remember happy times what comes to mind?'

'Let me think...' said the young man looking away. He thought of his fifth birthday when his father had still been alive, and then there were the family holidays by the sea, graduation from college...'

'How do you remember those times?' asked Mr. Brown. 'As years or months or weeks or days ... or moments?'

'I'm not sure,' said the young man.

'Well, think of one that really stands out'

'Okay, my fifth birthday party.'

'When exactly did you feel happy?'

'Just before the party began, I remember my mother hugged me and whispered: 'You are my special boy and I love you!' Sometimes, when I close my eyes, I can still hear her saying it in my ear.

'Excellent!' said Mr. Brown, pleased to be able to prove his point 'You see that was a moment! All children live in the moment. Imagine what would have happened if, at the time, you had been thinking about school work? You may not have heard what your mother said, and you would have missed that feeling of happiness. Your mother would have also missed out on the happiness that your reaction no doubt gave her.'

'I see what you mean,' said the young man.

'All of our memories are made up of moments when we saw, heard or felt something. We don't remember years or months or even days, only moments. We can therefore only get the most out of life by getting the most of each moment. If a moment is special, magical, then life becomes special and magical. The secret is to collect as many of those moments as you can. There will never be another now, so the best we can do is make the most of it. Always remember that whilst life at this moment may not be all you want, at this moment it's all you have.

'So,' as one wise man once said, 'why not stick a flower in your buttonhole and be happy?"

The young man remembered the story he had been told by Mr. Kesterman of the man who, despite being terminally ill, remained cheerful because he was grateful for each day he lived. The dying man must have learned the power of living in the moment. Living moment by moment; day by day, he had been able to be happy in spite of his illness.

'There is a saying,' continued Mr. Brown." living yard by yard, life is hard but inch by inch, life's a cinch!' Everything is easy when it's broken down into small pieces. If you live in the moment you have no time for regrets and no time for worries, you only have what lies before you,'

But the young man was still confused. 'How do you get the most out of a moment?' he asked.

' By being aware,' replied Mr. Brown. 'Dante said, 'Think that this day will never dawn again!'.

'If you're not aware that someone is offering you an apple, you won't take it. It's a bit like a highly ranked tennis player in a big championship tournament who, in an opening round against an unranked player, thinks about the opponent he will have to play in the final and, as a result, makes an unforced error which loses him a point. He plays the shot over in his mind, and is unable to concentrate on the next shot. Consequently, he makes another error. Again, he chastises himself for the needlessly lost points and becomes anxious: 'What if I lose the match?' Needless to say, worrying about something which has not yet happened also prevents him from concentrating on the present shot, and he loses yet another point Before he knows it, it is all over game, set and match.

'The same thing happens in our lives. We mull over the past and worry about the future and, consequently, we never give the present our full attention. This leads to feelings of regret for things done and anxiety over things which haven't happened. If you do not live in the moment you cannot win the game of life.'

The young man raised an eyebrow. It seemed so obvious and yet he had never really thought about the significance of time in this way.

'If we are to be happy,' continued Mr. Brown, we must learn to appreciate what we have, and all we have is here and now. Today's decisions are tomorrow's realities. We must learn to take things as they come and to let them go as they depart. As Thomas Carlyle wrote: 'Our main business is not to see what lies dimly at a distance, but to do what lies clearly at hand.' If we focus on the distant future, we can become overwhelmed and depressed. Many people spend their time worrying about things which have never and probably will never happen, Montaigne, the French philosopher wrote: 'My life has been full of terrible misfortunes...most of which never happened.'

'This is one of the reasons why so many people are burdened by worry and stress. For them, today is the tomorrow they worried about yesterday! Living in the moment leaves no room for regret over the past or anxiety about the future. Instead of seeing what is ahead of you or behind you, you focus only on what is in front of you.' This is why to live in the moment taking one moment at a time is one of the best ways to overcome worry and fear.

'Most religions adopt this philosophy. When Jesus was asked how a person should pray, he recited in the Lord's prayer: 'Give us this day our daily bread.' Not tomorrow's bread or next week's or next year's, only today's. One of the ways people manage to survive personal tragedies in their lives is by taking one day at a time, and if. that philosophy can get us through the worst times, imagine how much better it can make the good times! This is why it is written that, to a wise man, each day is a new beginning. I keep this,' he said, handing the young man a plaque from the wall, 'and read it every day to remind myself of that wisdom and to make sure I live in the moment. It helps me make the best of each day and therefore the best of my life.'

The plaque was inscribed with the prose of an Indian poet entitled: Salutation to the Dawn

Look to this day!

For it is life, the very life of life.

In its brief course

Lie all the verities and realities of your existence:

The bliss of growth

The glory of action

The splendor of beauty

For yesterday is but a dream

And tomorrow is only a vision

But today well lived makes every yesterday a dream of happiness

And every tomorrow a vision of hope.

Look well, therefore, to this day! Such is the salutation of the dawn.

Kalidasa

'Try it for yourself,' said Mr. Brown. 'For the rest of the day focus your mind only on what you are doing instead of what you have done or what you will be doing.'

'I think I understand,' said the young man. But what about concern for the future?'

'It is only by living in the moment that we can create the future that we desire. Every moment offers us choices which will shape our destiny, Thought is the seed of action, action creates a habit, habits mould character and our character creates our destiny.

'The thoughts that we choose in any one moment determine where we will be in the next. The decisions and actions we take in any moment create our future. When you talk to people, you will soon find that all too often they are living in the past or future, in other times and places, instead of making the best of what they have here and now. This is precisely what happened to me, and the fact that I was often thinking about things other than the matter at hand nearly got me killed, if you don’t live in the moment, you might not get run over by a truck, but you'll miss most of the experiences and opportunities that come your way.'

'So, you're not suggesting that people should not plan ahead, are you?' asked the young man.

'Not at all. Planning is vital before we take any action. But don't plan something when you're doing something else and don't do something else when you're planning something. Whatever you are thinking or doing, focus on that activity, one thing at a time. When you are talking to someone give them your full attention; when you're working, focus your mind on the job at hand, and don't make the same mistake I did.'

'What was that?' asked the young man.

'When you cross the road, be aware of the traffic! Once you live in the moment you reduce feelings of anxiety and depression, improve your performance at work, enhance your personal relationships and generally enrich your life. This is the power of living in the moment.'

For the rest of that day, the young man tried to keep his mind attentive to what he was doing. It wasn't easy to stop his thoughts straying at times but generally he managed to concentrate on what he was doing, and he was left in no doubt that he was better off for it. Instead of worrying about the backlog of paperwork on his desk, he tackled one letter at a time and for the first time since he joined the company three years ago, at the end of the day, the 'to do' tray was empty. When he spoke to work colleagues he gave them his full attention and was surprised when one man said, Thanks for listening. You were really helpful.' And that made him feel good about himself.

Later that evening, after dinner, the young man sat down and examined the notes he had made in his meeting that day.

The Third Secret of Abundant Happiness: The Power of Living in the Moment

Happiness is found not in years or months or weeks or even days, but it can be found in each moment.

We get the most out of life only by getting the most out of each moment.

Memories are made up of special moments so collect as many as you can.

Living in the moment dispels regret, overcomes anxiety and reduces stress.

Remember each new day is a new beginning a new life.

THE FOURTH SECRET – THE POWER OF SELF-IMAGE

It was not until the following week that the young man was able to meet the next person on his list. Ruth Moses explained that she would be away on a study trip for her degree course in Archaeology, but she would gladly meet with him on her return.

When the young man arrived at Ruth Moses' apartment he was met by a fresh-faced elderly lady dressed in denim dungarees and a print sweat shirt.

'Hello,' he said, 'I'm here to see Ruth Moses.'

'Yes. Hello,' said the lady smiling. 'Please do come in.'

The old lady led the young man into the lounge. 'Make yourself comfortable,' she said. The kettle has just boiled. Would you like some tea? I've got Earl Grey, decaffeinated coffee and a selection of herb teas; fruit, chamomile, peppermint, orange blossom.'

'Peppermint tea would be nice. Thank you,' answered the young man.

A few moments passed before the old lady returned carrying a tray with a pot of freshly boiled water, two cups, an assortment of herb teas, a jar of honey and a plate of homemade biscuits. She sat down opposite the young man and started pouring the tea.

'Now then,' she said, 'I was intrigued by your phone call. Tell me again what it's all about'

The young man looked perplexed. 'I'm sorry... you're Ruth Moses?'

'Of course!' grinned the old lady. 'Who did you think I was?'

'Erm... I... don't know... but I thought you said on the phone that you were a student?'

'I am. I'm currently doing a degree in Archaeology. God willing, next year I'll be doing a masters. Would you like some honey with your tea?'

'No thank you.'

She passed him a cup of tea and offered him some biscuits.

'Are you kidding me?' asked the young man.

'About what?'

'You really are an undergraduate?' persisted the young man.

Mrs Moses smiled, 'Yes, of course.'

'Well... er... forgive me,' said the young man, trying not to cause offense at his surprise. 'It's just that, after we spoke on the phone, I expected you to be a young student.'

'I am a young student,' insisted Mrs Moses with a mischievous grin. 'Eighty-two years young to be precise!'

The young man smiled. 'I can't argue with that,' he said.

'So, how can I help you?' asked Mrs Moses,

The young man proceeded to tell her about his meeting with the old Chinese man.

'Look at this,' Mrs Moses said handing the young man a photograph,

'Who is it?' asked the young man as he looked at the black and while photograph of an old, almost haggard lady with a walking stick. Your mother?'

'No. It's me, or rather, it was me... twenty years ago.'

The young man took a closer look at the photograph and whilst he could see a certain resemblance in the bone structure, the hairline and the shape of the mouth, there was very little else to suggest that the lady in the picture was the same lady who sat in front of him.

'It looks like you got younger rather than older since this picture was taken. What on earth happened? How did you do it?'

'I met someone who changed my life ... an old Chinese man! Shortly after I retired 20 or so years ago, I started to feel old for the first time. I had difficulty getting to sleep at night, but I was tired during the day, I began to lose my powers of concentration and memory, and my limbs were beginning to feet stiff and heavy. As you can imagine, I became pretty miserable, but then one day everything changed. I was waiting for a bus and standing beside me was an elderly Chinese man carrying a rucksack on his back.

'The old man smiled at me, so I smiled back, and we began talking. He told me that he was travelling around the world. I couldn't believe it. How could someone of his age have the strength and energy to travel around the world with a rucksack on his back? I asked him, of course, and he laughed. "We are only as old as we think we are," he said. We began talking about life after 60, and whilst I could only see problems and difficulties, he saw advantages and opportunities. "With age comes experience and wisdom," he said. And then he asked me something I had never considered before: Why should life be any less fulfilling just because you have lived longer? "If anything," he said, "life should be better because you have had more practice at it!"

'Talking with the Chinese man that day made me realize for the first time the truth in the proverb 'A man is as he thinks in his heart,' What makes a person old is not their age but their mind. I enjoyed talking to the Chinese man so much that I let at least four buses pass by. I was captivated by the secrets of Abundant Happiness through which anyone of any age; creed or colour can create happiness in their lives. The secrets gave me a new lease of life. It was like being reborn. It was as if everything changed from being black and white into the most wonderful, bright colours. But, of course, nothing changed except me. And that turned out to be the value of the secrets for me... the power of our self-image.'

'Self-image?' repeated the young man quizzically.

'Yes. How you see yourself, the beliefs you have about yourself. One of the reasons many people are so unhappy with their lives Is simply that they are unhappy with themselves. Can you believe that deep down many people do not really like themselves? A lot of people grow up with complexes; sometimes physical', such as, 'My nose is too big' or 'I'm ugly' or 'too young' or 'too old'; sometimes the complexes are intellectual, such as, 'I'm not as clever as other people', and they believe they have a defective personality such as, 'I have no sense of humour' or 'I'm boring'. But whatever the reason, if you are not happy with yourself, how can you be happy with life?'

The young man immediately thought about his own complexes, and there were plenty of them. 'Where do all these complexes come from?' he asked.

'Our life experiences. Usually from our childhood. I remember one man told me, "I grew up to have my father's speech patterns, my father's posture, my father's opinions . . . and my mother's contempt for my father!"

'Our impressions of ourselves are, of course, first formed in infancy. We don't know who or what we are or what we should be, but we learn from those around us, those who are older and wiser and supposedly love us.

'Let me give you an example: little Jimmy comes home from school with a bad report card. He wonders to himself: Why have I done so badly? Maybe it's because I watch too much TV. Maybe I haven't worked hard enough. Maybe I'm stupid, or maybe I'm just lazy." He hands his report card to his father. The father looks at the card, there are no As and Bs, only Ds and Es. He says to Jimmy, "Well, one thing's obvious you haven't been cheating!" But as he studies the report in more detail and reads the teachers' comments about his son, Jimmy's father becomes angry. He says: "The problem with you, Jimmy, is you don't work hard enough, you're lazy and stupid!"

'Now Jimmy has no more doubts about himself, he knows that he is lazy and stupid, and he carries this knowledge throughout his entire life. Every time he sees a challenge he says to himself, "I can't do that because I'm stupid and lazy." So, he avoids challenges, he sees himself as inferior to others and he resents being himself,'

'So, how can we get rid of these complexes or negative beliefs?' asked the young man,

That's a good question. The first thing we need to do is ask ourselves one of the most important questions we can ever ask: "Who or what am I?"'

'Why?'

'Because the answer will help us appreciate how special we all are. For instance, did you know that; even after your mother and father met and mated, the chances of you being born were less than one in 300,000 billion! There could have been 300,000 billion other completely different people born in your place, but you made it Not only that, but there has never been a person exactly like you in the history of the world, and neither will there ever be anyone exactly like you again.'

'The next question we need to ask is, "What are my beliefs about myself?"'

'What, such as, "I'm ugly or stupid"?' interrupted the young man.

'Yes. Then consider, "How do I know for certain that it's true?" Was it because of what someone else said or did, or do you know it for a fact to be true? You see most of the time we develop our beliefs about ourselves from other people. People are sort of like psychological mirrors of us. But let me show you something'. Mrs Moses pulled out some mirrors from her desk drawer. She held each mirror up for the young man to look at himself They were all curved and distorted mirrors, miniatures of those which are often seen at a funfair, and the young man hardly recognized himself. One made his head look a metre long, another made his ears look like wings and another made him look like the fattest man on earth. The young man laughed at his reflections.

'Which one looks like you?' asked Mrs Moses,

'None of them,' replied the young man.

'How do you know?'

'Because they're "play" mirrors. They can't give a true reflection.'

'Of course. But what would have happened if you had never seen a true reflection of yourself? You might have been horrified when you looked in these play mirrors. Fortunately, you know what you look like physically because you have seen yourself before in a proper, unbiased mirror. But when have you ever seen a true, unbiased image of what you look like psychologically? You see, whilst we have mirrors which reveal what we look like physically, we don't have mirrors which show us what we look like psychologically Instead, we rely on the reactions of other people to find out who we are on the inside. If people say you are selfish, you may believe that you are selfish. Similarly, if someone tells you that you're stupid, you might believe that too. People are mirrors of us, yes, but they are distorted mirrors that carry their own prejudices which distort their image of you.

'The biggest mistake you can make in your life is to rely on other people to find out who you really are. When a parent or teacher says to a child, "You are naughty," or "You are selfish" or "lazy" or "stupid", they are creating a negative and false self-image for the child. True, the child may have done or said something which was naughty, selfish, lazy or stupid, but that was the child's behaviour, not the child. It's a subtle difference, but an important one. It's the difference between saying, "You are a naughty girl" and 'It's naughty to throw juice over the carpet." '

'Isn't it the same thing, really?' asked the young man,

'Have you ever done something that you later regretted? Made a silly mistake or done something stupid?'

The young man nodded, 'Hasn't everybody?'

'Now, just because you made a stupid mistake, does it mean that you are a stupid person?'

‘I see what you mean,' said the young man.

'Many people confuse the behaviour with the person, and as a result we develop negative beliefs about ourselves which are not necessarily true, but which we carry with us throughout our lives.'

The young man scribbled some notes on his pad. 'I understand how we can develop negative beliefs or complexes about ourselves,' he said. 'But, once we have developed them, how can we get rid of them?'

'Well, being able to identify where the belief came from is the first step,' said Mrs Moses. 'Sometimes an awareness is all it takes to eliminate the problem. However, there are some beliefs which are so deeply rooted in our psyche that their eradication requires more than an awareness of their origins. In these cases, one solution lies in "positive affirmations".'

'What are "affirmations"?' asked the young man.

'An affirmation is a statement we say to ourselves, either aloud or in our head. A positive affirmation might therefore be something like: 'I am a loving, intelligent, unique human being."'

'Why should that help?' asked the young man.

'If we hear something often enough,' explained Mrs Moses, 'we start to believe It. That is, after all, where most of our beliefs come from hearing something over and over as a child. Advertisers use this technique all the time. They create a phrase, and have it repeated over and over again in the media and eventually we all believe it. To take control of your life, you must take control of your beliefs, and using affirmations is one way of doing that.'

'How often do you need to say a particular affirmation before your subconscious starts to believe it?' asked the young man.

'That of course depends upon how long you have had the opposite negative belief and how frequently you repeat the affirmation. It also helps if you say the affirmation with feeling, as if you really believe it rather than in an uncommitted, monotone voice. I would say try and repeat an affirmation at least three times a day morning, noon and evening. Write it on a card, if you like, and read it whenever you get a chance.

'Another technique which can help you change your self-image is to act as if you were the opposite of your complex. For instance, if you believe that you're unattractive, act as if you are attractive, or if you think you lack confidence, act as if you were confident.'

'Isn't that just pretending to be something that you're not?' said the young man.

'Yes. But an incredible thing happens when you act as if you're attractive, confident and happy... you start to feel attractive, confident and happy Perhaps I can explain it better by example. Imagine a young girl who thinks she is unattractive going to a dance with her friends. All night long she stands in the corner where no one can see her and hardly surprisingly no one asks her to dance. Now if that same girl acted as if she was attractive, she might wear a more flattering dress, she might mingle more with people. She would relax and enjoy herself and in doing so would actually become more attractive to others.

'Or imagine a man about to give a speech. He is so nervous; his knees are shaking. If he acted the way he feels, he would turn around and run straight for the exit. But, he knows he must go through with it and, so he tries to act as if he was confident After a confident sounding opening sentence, the audience applaud, and now he ' starts to feel confident. Likewise, sometimes we may not feel happy, but if we act as if we are happy and smile at people, more often than not, they will smile back, and you perk up inside.

'Another way to improve our self-image is to search for things we like about ourselves.'

‘That sounds good in theory, but how easy is it to do in practice?' said the young man as he jotted down notes.

'Very easy,' said Mrs Moses. 'All you need do is consciously ask yourself: "What do I like about myself?" or "What are the things I am good at?"'

'Yes, but the answer might be "very little" or, even worse, "nothing at all",' said the young man.

'One of the most wonderful things about the human mind is that it will always search for an answer to a question, and even if there is no answer it will often make one up. Most of the time, we ask negative questions "Why am I unattractive?", "Why am I so stupid?", "Why can't I get a job?" Your brain will always find an answer to any question you ask of it about yourself "Because you've got a big nose", "Because you were born with a small brain", "Because you're not as good as other people." All nonsense, of course, but your brain found answers!

'When we ask positive questions, we will likewise get positive answers. And, even if you have trouble thinking of something you like about yourself, rephrase the question: "If there was something I liked about myself, what would it be?" This question forces a positive answer. Other excellent questions that will change the way we feel about ourselves are: "What are my strengths?", "What am I good at?", "Where can I make an effective contribution?"'

'Affirmations, acting as if, and asking positive questions are simple, effective ways through which we can start to change the way we feel about ourselves. We then need to stop taking on board false beliefs from the reactions of other people. We need to remember always that whilst people are our mirrors, they are prejudiced, inaccurate mirrors.

'If you remember one thing today, remember this: it takes no talent, no brains, and no character to criticize. Only God can create a flower, but any foolish child can pull it to pieces! When people are hostile or rude, when they say cruel and unkind things, it is invariably a reflection of their own troubled spirit rather than a reflection of you. Therefore, don't listen to anybody who tries to tell you who or what you are (unless, of course, it is positive). If I listened to other people, do you think I would be studying at university at my age? If I accepted what other people used to say to me, do you think I would have learned to ski when I was 65? Or learned to paint when I was 68? If I listened to other people I'd probably be dead or living off memories by now.

'People said I was a fool to start all these things at my age. Many still think I'm a little mad. Perhaps I am, but I'll tell you one thing I'm happy with my life.

'I once read that the highest thing you can attain in life is to know yourself because only then are you truly free of the limitations and restrictions that others may wish to impose upon you, and free to live as we were meant to live... being happy,'

The young man felt inspired. This sounds so simple and it makes so much sense, but... does it really work?"

Mrs Moses smiled, 'There is only one way to find out. Try it!'

That night, before going to bed, the young man read over the notes he had made that day.

The Fourth Secret of Abundant Happiness: The Power of Self Image.

It is written, 'A man is as he thinks in his heart' We are what we think we are.

If I am unhappy with myself, I will be unhappy with life. Therefore, to be happy in life, I must first be happy with myself.

Every person is special. Every person is a winner because every person overcame odds of one in 300,000 billion when they were born.

People are mirrors of us, but they are distorted mirrors.

To overcome complexes and negative beliefs about myself, and create a positive self-image, I must first find out where they came from and whether they are true. (If they are true, resolve to change.)

Make positive affirmations every day affirming the type of person I wish to be

Act as if I am the way I would like to be.

Ask myself what I do like or respect about myself

THE FIFTH SECRET – THE POWER OF GOALS

Two days later the young man met the fifth person on his list, Dr Julius Franks. Dr Franks was a professor in Psychology at the city university and although 70 years of age, he had a certain youthful vigour about him that transcended his years and reminded the young man of the old Chinese man.

'I met the old Chinese man many, many years ago, explained Dr Franks. 'I was in a prisoner of war camp in the Far East during the Second World War. The conditions were terrible, almost unbearable; meagre rations of food, no clean water and everywhere you looked there was dysentery, malaria or sunstroke. Some of the prisoners couldn't cope with the physical and mental strain of the continuous heavy workloads in the hot sun and, for them, death became a welcome escape. I even thought about it myself, but one day someone restored my will to live . An old Chinese man.'

The young man listened intently to Dr Franks' account of what happened that day.

'I was sitting alone in the exercise yard feeling very weak and tired, and I was actually thinking about how easy it would be to run into the electrified boundary fence. The next thing I knew, an old Chinese man was sitting next to me. Even in my weakened state I was startled and thought I must be hallucinating. After all, how on earth could a Chinese man appear so suddenly and easily in a Japanese camp?

'He turned and asked me a question; a simple question that, quite literally, saved my life.'

He paused for a moment.

The young man was perplexed. How could a question save someone's life?' he thought.

'And that question was,' continued Dr Franks, ' "What is the first thing you are going to do when you get out of here?"

'It was something I had never even thought about, never dared to. But I knew the answer. I wanted to see my wife and children again and, all of a sudden, I was reminded that I had something to live for, a reason why I would do everything I could to survive. That one question saved my life because it gave me something I had lost - a reason to live!

'Right then and there, the struggle to survive became an easier burden because I knew that each day I survived brought me closer to the end of the war and therefore closer to my dreams. The Chinese man's question not only saved my life, it taught me one of the most important lessons I have ever learned.'

'What was that?' asked the young man.

'The power of goals.'

'Goals?' repeated the young man.

'Yes. Goals, Ambitions. Things to strive for. Goals give our lives purpose and meaning. True, we can exist without them, but to really live, and live happily, we need our lives to have purpose. "Without purpose," wrote the great Admiral Byrd, "the days would have ended, as such days always end, in disintegration." '

'Disintegration of what?' asked the young man,

'The soul. Have you ever wondered why so many people lose their health and die so quickly after they retire? Have you ever wondered why so many rich and famous people end up as drug addicts or alcoholics?'

The young man nodded. He had often wondered why people became 'old' once they retired and he had always been curious about why a celebrity, someone who seemed to have it all - a magnificent home or homes, more money than they could ever possibly spend in their lifetime, a family, a fabulous career, so often took to drugs or alcohol, or even committed suicide.

'One of the reasons,' explained Dr Franks, is simply that they feel their lives have no purpose. Their lives have no meaning to them. Have you ever heard of Helen Keller?'

'Yes. Just last week as a matter of fact. I was told that, despite being blind, deaf and dumb, she loved her life.'

'Yes., And do you know why she loved it?' asked Dr Franks. 'Because she gave her life meaning. When she was asked how she managed to be so happy despite her handicaps, she answered: "Many people have the wrong idea of what constitutes happiness. It is not attained through self-gratification, but through fidelity to a worthy purpose." The most basic requirement the human soul craves is the need for meaning in life, and that is what goals give us,

'Goals create purpose and meaning. With goals, we know where we are going, we are driven toward something. Without goals, life has little meaning, and we tend to drift aimlessly. It is because people are motivated by only one of two things, pain or pleasure. Goals focus the mind on pleasure, whereas lack of goals allows the mind to focus on avoiding pain. Goals can even make pain more bearable.'

'I'm not sure I understand,' said the young man. 'How can goals make pain more bearable?'

'Let me see ... yes, imagine a terrible abdominal pain. An intermittent sharp pain every few minutes. It's so excruciating that it's causing you to scream. How would you feel?'

'Pretty awful, I would imagine.'

'How would you feel if the pain was getting worse and becoming more frequent? Would you be anxious or excited?'

'What sort of question is that? How can you be excited about pain? You'd have to be a masochist.'

'No. You have to be a pregnant woman! She bears the pain, but she knows that; at the end of it, she will have a baby. She may even look forward to the pains becoming more frequent because she knows that each contraction brings her closer to the birth of her child as well as to the end of the pain. The purpose or meaning behind the pain makes it more bearable.

'It is the same reason why living through hard times is made more bearable when we have something to look forward to at the end of it. There is no doubt that having goals to live for gave me the strength to survive when otherwise I would almost certainly have ended my life. Whenever I saw a fellow prisoner looking despondent I would ask him the same question; "What is the first thing you are going to do when you get out of here?" and gradually his face would change, a small light would shine in his eyes as the realization dawned upon him that he had things to live for. He had a future to strive for and he would do his very best to survive each day knowing that he was a little closer to his goal And I'll tell you something else: seeing a man change so dramatically, and knowing that you played a small part in helping him is a wonderful feeling, So I made it my goal every day to help as many people as I could.

'One of the secrets of surviving the worst periods in our lives is the same as the secret of living life to the full in the best times. And that secret is goals. If goals can give people in a prisoner of war camp the will to survive, what do you imagine they could do for people in peacetime?

'After the war, I became involved in a very interesting study at Harvard University. We asked the whole of the graduating year in 1953 if they had any ambitions or goals for their lives. How many of them do you think had specific goals?'

'Fifty per cent?' guessed the young man.

'Less than three per cent!' said Dr Franks. 'Can you imagine, less than three people in every hundred had any idea what they wanted to do with their lives!

'We followed their careers over the next 25 years and discovered that those three per cent of undergraduates who had had goals had more stable marriages and better health, and were worth more financially than the other 97 per cent put together. It was therefore no surprise to discover that they also had led far, far happier lives,'

'Why do you think having goals makes people feel happier?' asked the young man,

'Because we get energy not just from food but from enthusiasm, and enthusiasm is produced by having goals, things to aim for, things to look forward to. One of the biggest reasons why so many people are unhappy is simply that they feel their lives have no meaning, no purpose. They have nothing to get out of bed in the morning for, they have no goals to inspire them, no dreams. They drift aimlessly through life with no direction.

'If we have something to aim for,' continued Dr Franks, 'the stresses and strains of life seem to disappear. They are seen only as hurdles which must be overcome to reach that goal. This is why I advise all of my patients to learn the rocking chair technique.'

'What's that?' asked the young man.

'It's a simple technique in which you imagine you have lived your life and are now sitting in a rocking chair thinking back over how you lived and what you achieved. What would you want to be remembering? What things would you like to have done? What places would you like to have visited? What relationships would you like to have built? And, most, importantly, as you sit there in the rocking chair, what type of person would you like to have become?'

The young man made a few notes. These were powerful questions that he had never thought of asking himself before.

'This technique helps you create long term goals. We then do the same thing with shorter term goals ten year and five year goals, one year goals, six month goals, one month goals and even daily goals. I then advise my patients to write down all of these goals and read them through first thing in the morning. That way, you always have something positive to get out of bed for in the morning and start the day enthused and excited.'

'I'll try that,' said the young man. 'I always have difficulty getting out of bed in the morning.'

'It's also a good idea to read through your goals some time during the day and last thing at night to keep them impressed on your mind,'

'What happens if my views change and I decide that I no longer want one of my goals?' asked the young man,

'That's a good question. Our priorities and values in life do change as we grow, and we simply change our goals accordingly. This is why the rocking chair technique should be done regularly at least every year. That way we always have goals that we are committed to, which create purpose and meaning in our lives, things that excite and motivate us.

'Goals lay the foundation of our happiness. People often think that comfort and luxury are the chief requirements of happiness, but all we really need to feel happy is something to be enthusiastic about. One of the greatest secrets of Abundant Happiness is that there is no lasting happiness in a life which is devoid of meaning and purpose. This is the power of goals.'

'Did you ever meet the old Chinese man again?' asked the young man.

'No. In fact, for some time I was convinced that he was an hallucination or figment of my imagination.'

'Why?'

'Because I had never seen him before and I never saw him again. Sometimes the hot sun can play tricks with your mind. But not long after the war, I found out that he really did exist,'

'How?' asked the young man.

'I received a letter from a young man. A young man who had been given my name by an old Chinese man!'

Later in the day the young man summarized the notes he had made during his meeting.

The Fifth Secret of Abundant Happiness:
The Power of Goals

Goals give our lives purpose and meaning.

With goals, we focus on gaining pleasure rather than avoiding pain.

Goals give reasons to get out of bed in the morning.

Goals make difficult periods easier, and good times even better.

The rocking chair technique helps you to decide on your lifetime goals as well as more immediate, short term goals.

Write down all your goals and read them through:

first thing in the morning

sometime during the day

last thing at night.

Remember to repeat the rocking chair technique at least twice a year to make sure that your goals are still what you really want.

THE SIXTH SECRET – THE POWER OF HUMOUR

'It may seem absurd, at first, to think that it helps to make light of or laugh about your troubles, but you will and that it is in fact one of the best ways of overcoming most stressful situations and creating happiness.'

The young man was totally taken aback by this statement. The man before him was Joseph Hart, a small but large framed man in his late fifties. Mr. Hart was a licensed taxi driver in the city and his was the sixth name on the young man's list.

'Ten years ago,' continued Mr. Hart, 'my business folded. It didn't take much; I lost my biggest customer, a few large creditors went into liquidation without paying their accounts, and there was just no way out. I saw virtually everything I had worked so hard for being taken from me. Everything was gone.

'As you can imagine, I was angry, frustrated, and very depressed about the situation. It all seemed so hopeless. I rented a room on the thirtieth floor of the Hilton hotel in the centre of town and, believe it or not, I was going to end my life.'

The young man was speechless as he listened to Mr. Hart's story.

'I sat down on the edge of the bed for over half an hour with my head in my hands trying to summon up the courage to do what I had planned. Eventually, I got up and walked out onto the balcony. Just as I reached the edge, I heard a voice behind me. I turned around; a porter had come into the room and asked if everything was all right. I nodded, and he came out onto the balcony and asked if he could get me anything. I said no. He looked out at the view of the city. There was a strong breeze and he took a deep breath.

'"What a wonderful day"' he said.

"What's so wonderful about it?" I said, and then he said something that hit me like a bucket of iced water.

'He said, “You try missing a few, then you'll find out!"

'I was in such a state of tension that I broke down in tears in front of him. He asked me what was wrong, and I told him that I had lost everything.

'He looked puzzled and said, "What do you mean? Can you still see?"

'"Of course,' " I said.

'"Good, so you still have your eyes. Obviously," he said, "you can still talk and hear, and it looks like you can walk, so what exactly have you lost?" I told him it was my money; everything I ever earned had been taken from me, "Ah!" he exclaimed, "so all you have lost is your money!" Then he threw another bucket of iced water over me; he said,

"Who has more, a millionaire who has terminal cancer or a healthy man who is penniless?"

'It dawned on me then that perhaps I had blown the problems out of all proportion. The porter explained that many people simply lose perspective of their circumstances and often this is the sole cause of their unhappiness.

'Talking to the porter didn't solve any of my problems, but it did help me to see them a little differently. It was enough to make me think about my life again and, although I never told him, his simple wisdom stopped me from taking my life that day,

'Just before he left, he gave me a list of people who he said would be able to help me with my situation. I thought that they were going to lend me money, but they gave me something much more valuable - the secrets of Abundant Happiness.

'It was through those secrets that I gradually learned to rebuild my life and create happiness for myself. There was a lot I needed to learn about myself and about life; the importance of faith, our attitude, our physical health, forgiveness, relationships but one of the things that I particularly needed to learn was... the power of humour.

'I was one of those people who take everything very seriously. It's not easy being happy if you never laugh!'

'But isn't that putting the cart before the horse?' said the young man.' I mean, we tend to laugh more and take things less seriously when we are happy, not as a means to make us feel happy.'

'You are right, laughter is a by-product of being happy; but it is also something which produces a feeling of happiness. You see, the process of laughing and smiling releases chemicals in your brain which creates a kind of euphoria. In fact, researchers have demonstrated that when we laugh, stress hormones in our blood adrenalin and cortisone are lowered and, as a result, we actually feel less anxious and less troubled.'

'Then why is it that some of the greatest comedians are or were themselves serious depressives?' asked the young man.

'People don't become depressed because they laugh too much,' said Mr. Hart 'But many people instinctively use the power of laughter and humour to help them cope with their sadness. Remember that humour is only one of 10 secrets of Abundant Happiness. We need to incorporate all of them into our lives if we are to create lasting happiness. Trying to be happy using only the power of humour is as futile as trying to be healthy by exercising but paying no attention to diet, rest, stress and all of the other factors that affect our health.

'It has also been shown that laughing improves our powers of concentration and dramatically increases our ability to solve mental problems.

Researchers at the University of Maryland conducted a very interesting experiment a few years ago; they took two groups of people and gave them all identical problem-solving lasts. The only difference between the two groups was that the people in one group were first shown a 30-minute educational video before having to do the problem solving, whereas the people in the other group were shown a 30-minute comedy show. Incredibly, those who watched the comedy solved the problems on average three times faster than the other group!'

The young man looked up from his notes. 'But when someone has a problem or is feeling stressed, anxious or worried,' he argued, they are hardly in the mood to laugh are they?'

'No. Of course not. But that's the point! If they did, they could help their situation because not only will they feel better and less stressed, but they will also be more able to resolve their problems. Have you ever experienced something that upset you or made you angry, but a few weeks later you were laughing about it with friends?'

'Yes, hasn't everyone?'

'Did the situation bother you when you were laughing about it?'

'No. How could it?' smiled the young man.

'That is precisely my point,' said Mr. Hart. 'How could it? It couldn't. So, wouldn't it be easier if we were able to laugh at things sooner rather than later?'

'Yes, I see your point. But how is it possible to laugh about something that is upsetting you?'

'The secret is finding something to laugh about. It all goes back to our mind. We choose our thoughts, we choose what we focus our minds on. Instead of focusing on "What's terrible about this situation?" we can just as easily ask ourselves, "What's funny about this situation?"'

'What if there is nothing funny?' asked the young man.

'Then ask yourself, '"What could be funny?" There is usually something funny in every situation that you can laugh about, it's just a question of looking for it. And, if there is nothing funny, find something else which is funny because being able to laugh is often half the battle.'

'It sounds reasonable in theory, but in practice it's not always easy to find a funny side to every situation,' persisted the young man.

'Not every situation can be laughed at,' agreed Mr. Hart, 'but most can. The thing is you'll only see the funny side of any situation if you look for it, I remember hearing a wonderful story about John Glenn, the first American Apollo astronaut. John was all kitted up ready to enter the rocket when a reporter stopped him. "John, what's going to happen if, once you're in space, the engines fail, and you can't get back down to Earth?" John turned to the reporter and, smiling, said, "Do you know what? That would really spoil my day!"

'Now I doubt that many people have gone through such a stressful situation as John Glenn faced that day. Probably most of us never will either. But, if we can learn to face life's challenges with the same sense of humour, we would experience more happiness in life.

'After the successful completion of the Apollo mission, a press meeting was held, and another reporter asked John what he was thinking about as he was re-entering the Earth's atmosphere. "What I was thinking about as I was re-entering the atmosphere was that the capsule I was in was manufactured... by the lowest bidder!"

'Now that can be a pretty terrifying thought, but John overcame his fears through his humour. It just goes to show that whatever challenges or obstacles confront you in life, one of the best things you can do is ask yourself: "What is funny about this situation?' or "What could be funny about it?"

'The problem with most people is that they take life far too seriously. If only we stopped and asked ourselves, 'Will it make any difference to anyone in 10 years' time?"

'If the answer is "no", then it doesn't warrant being too serious about, does it? It's a bit like the two step anti-stress formula.'

'What's that?' asked the young man.

'The first step is: don't worry about small things.'

There was a pause.

'And the second step?' asked the young man.

'Remember, most things in life are small!

'I have this wonderful piece of prose written by an 85-year-old woman who was terminally I'll,' said Mr. Hart, handing the young man a piece of paper. There is great wisdom in it.'

If I had my life to live over again, I'd try to make more mistakes next time. I wouldn't be so perfect I would relax more. I'd limber up. I'd be sillier than I've been on this trip. In fact, I know very few things that I would take so seriously. I'd be crazier. I'd be less hygienic.

I'd take more chances, I'd take more trips, I'd climb more mountains, I'd swim more rivers, I'd go more places I've never been to. I'd eat more ice cream and fewer beans.

I'd have more actual problems but fewer imaginary ones!

You see, I was one of those people who lived prophylactically and sensibly and sanely hour after hour and day after day, Oh, I've had my moments, and if I had it to do all over again, I'd have more of those moments, moment by moment.

I've been one of those people who never went anywhere without a thermometer, a hot water bottle, a gargle, a raincoat and a parachute. If I had to do it all over again, I'd travel lighter next time.

If I had to do it all over again, I'd start barefoot earlier in the spring and stay that way later in the fall, I'd ride more merry go rounds, I'd watch more sunrises, and I'd play with more children, if I had my life to live over again.

But you see, I don't

The young man smiled as he read It. 'You're right There's a wonderful message there. Can I have a copy?'

'Of course,' said Mr. Hart

'Thank you for sharing all this with me,' said the young man. 'You've given me a lot to think about'

'Good. I'm pleased I have been able to help,' said Mr. Hart 'Before you go, did I tell you what George Burns said was the secret of happiness:"

'No'

' "The secret of happiness?" he said. "Simple. A good cigar, a good meal and a good woman or a bad woman - It depends upon how much happiness you can handle!"'

As the young man reached the door, he turned back to Mr. Hart 'You didn't mention how you knew the old Chinese man who gave me your name?'

Mr. Hart smiled. 'Didn't I tell you? He was the porter at the hotel. I never told him what I had been planning to do that day. The following morning, I went to the hotel reception to thank him and let him know how much he had helped me, but nobody had heard of him.'

'So, you never got to thank him then?' asked the young man.

'No. No, I didn't,' said Mr. Hart with a smile. 'But I have a feeling that he knows. After all, he gave you my name, didn't he?'

That night, before going to bed, the young man read over his notes.

The Sixth Secret of Abundant Happiness:
The Power of Humour.

Humour alleviates stress and creates feelings of happiness.

Laughing improves our powers of concentration and

increases our ability to solve problems.

In any experience, if you look for a funny side, very often

you'll find one.

Instead of asking, 'What's terrible about this situation?'

ask, 'What's funny about it?' or 'What could be funny?'

Always refer to the two step anti-stress formula:

1. *Don't worry about small things.*

2. *Remember most things are small!*

THE SEVENTH SECRET – THE POWER OF FORGIVENESS

The next day the young man sat in the office of the seventh person on the young man's list, a man by the name of Dr Howard Jacobson. Dr Jacobson was a tall, large framed man with fair hair and bright blue eyes and, at 42 years old, he was the youngest Chief Surgeon ever to be appointed at the city hospital. His office was on the top floor of the building and the two exterior walls were entirely made of glass, giving a magnificent panoramic view to the west of the city.

'I first heard about the secrets of Abundant Happiness twenty years ago,' said Dr Jacobson.

'And did they help you?' asked the young man.

'Most definitely,' said Dr Jacobson. They completely changed my outlook on life. I was never very happy growing up,' confided Mr. Jacobson. 'I was always "going to be" happy. Originally, I was going to be happy when I got to college, but when I got there nothing changed. Then I thought that I'd be happy when I qualified as a doctor, but that didn't work either. Neither did anything change when I qualified as a surgeon, or when I got married and had children. But, the truth is, despite being successful and having a nice home with a loving wife and family, I was never really happy.

'Looking back, I think my problems all began when I was sent off at the age of 10 to boarding school by my father against my wishes. My mother had died in a car crash a year earlier. She died on impact, so I was told, but my father, who had been driving, survived with hardly a scratch. I think that subconsciously I blamed him for the accident and, although it's a terrible thing to admit, I grew to hate him.'

'Why?' asked the young man.

'I suppose I thought that he had sent me away to boarding school because he didn't love me or want me at home.'

Dr Jacobson paused for a moment and looked out of the window.

'I lived with this anger for over 15 years,' he said, and then, his voice lowered, 'It's difficult being happy when you're carrying so much anger and resentment inside.

'Then one day I was at the airport on my way to a conference when a message came over the loudspeakers "Would Dr Jacobson please report to the information desk?" I went along, and was handed an urgent message. My father had had a heart attack and was in the intensive care unit of the city hospital. I sat down and reread the message, confused, unsure what to do. I hadn't spoken to him for over five years.

'I screwed up the piece of paper in my hand and was about to throw it in the bin next to me when someone asked if the seat beside me was free. I looked up and there he was... a little old Chinese man. He sat down and immediately started talking. He was on his way to visit a friend who had lost a leg in an accident. A car hit him whilst he was crossing the road at traffic lights and completely smashed the man's right leg. He was lucky to be alive. It transpired that the driver of the car had been in a hurry and hadn't seen the man begin to cross the road. "I hate people like that," I said, but the man next to me looked horrified. "Why hate a man just because he made a mistake?" he asked. "Everyone makes mistakes at one time or another in their lives. If you hate every person who makes a mistake, you'll end up hating everybody... including yourself."

Then he turned towards me and, smiling, looked me squarely in the eye and said, "We have a saying in my country, "Those who will not forgive, will not be happy."'

' "It's not always easy to forgive," I argued, "It depends upon how bad the mistake is."

' "If that is so," he said, "heaven would be a very lonely place."

'He talked for a few more minutes and mentioned the laws of life and the secrets of Abundant Happiness. I had never heard such things before but hearing them stirred something inside me. A few minutes later, the old man had left me as he found me, staring at the screwed-up message in my hand, but now I knew what I wanted to do.

'I cancelled my trip and went instead to visit my father in hospital. He was lying in bed with tubes all around him and a heart monitor beside his bed. I went over to his side, sat down on the edge of the bed and did something I hadn't done since I was a child... I held his hand. He lay there motionless, not even able to speak, and the doctors weren't sure whether he could hear either. I bent over him and whispered in his ear, "Dad, it's me. It's Howard." Then the most beautiful thing I have ever experienced happened. A tear began to roll down his cheek and, for the first time in many, many years I wept. It was time to forgive and let go of the past.

'Over the next two weeks I visited him every day, and although his eyes remained closed, when I held his hand his eyelids flickered very slightly, and he gripped my hand tightly Then, at last, the miracle that I had been praying for happened, I arrived at the hospital and found him fully awake and drinking a cup of tea.

'We hugged which was something we hadn't done since I was a young child and we talked. We talked more in that one afternoon than we had done in the previous 15 years. And it was only then that I learned about the accident that killed my mother and why I had been sent to boarding school against my wishes.

'A lorry had skidded out of control on black ice and smashed into the passenger door killing my mother on impact. It was nobody's fault, it was an accident. And although he never showed it at the time, my father had been devastated. It still brought tears to his eyes to talk about it. My mother and he were childhood sweethearts.

'I had never stopped even once to think of the pain he had been going through, I had only thought of myself. He had a highly paid job, but it involved him traveling frequently to the Far East and America and, right or wrong, he thought I would be better off and receive a better education if I was at a boarding school.

'People say that time heals, but it doesn't. It's true that anger and bitterness usually fade over the years, but unless we are prepared to forgive, they never totally leave your soul. No, the key to forgiveness doesn't lie in the passing of time, it lies in understanding. The Sioux Indians have a wonderful prayer:

O Great Spirit, keep me from ever judging and criticizing a man until I have walked in his moccasins for two weeks.

'We often blame people for things, but we can never be sure that, given the same upbringing and circumstances, we would react any differently to another person.

'For instance, I had never thought of what my father might be going through after the death of my mother or why he had insisted I go to boarding school. I had only chosen to see it from my point of view. Subconsciously, I thought that by placing me in a boarding school, my father didn't want me or love me. But it turned out he did it because he loved me. He thought it was for the best. He had also lost my mother, his childhood sweetheart and he didn't know how to take care of me and wasn't able to take care of me because of his work commitments,'

The young man thought about his own life. There were plenty of people who angered him. His boss, who was always harassing him, and a close friend who borrowed money over a year ago and still hadn't repaid it, were two that immediately came to mind. It suddenly occurred to him that he hadn't even considered the matters from their point of view.

'I can see that when no malice is involved, things should be forgiven, but if someone intentionally harms you, why should you forgive them?' asked the young man.

'Why not?'

'Because some things are just unforgivable!' argued the young man.

'I'm not so sure,' said Dr Jacobson. Take child molesters as an example. You can't get a more heinous and repugnant crime, can you?'

The young man nodded.

'Yet, did you know that over 95 per cent of all child molesters were themselves molested when they were children? Can you be certain, if you had suffered in the same way, that you wouldn't have committed the same crimes?'

The young man shook his head, 'I suppose not, but its not so easy forgiving.'

'No one said it was easy. You know what they say? 'To err is human, but to forgive is divine!" But it helps if we try looking at things from the other person's view. And look what happens if you can't forgive? Who suffers? Who gets the stomach ulcers and the high blood pressure? You do!'

'Not if you get even first. Even the Bible says, "An eye for an eye and a tooth for a tooth." Isn't revenge good for the soul?'

The Bible also says, "Turn the other cheek" and "Leave revenge to God." If we sought revenge every time we were wronged, as Mahatma Gandhi once said, the whole world would end up being blind and toothless." Revenge cannot bring peace, it only breeds more revenge. It's a never-ending cycle.

'If your heart is full of hatred, how can there be room for love and happiness? Forgiveness frees your soul from hatred and allows room for love to enter.'

Dr Jacobson walked over to the far side of the room where there were two high backed chairs against the wall.

'It's like these chairs,' he said, 'One is love and happiness, the other resentment and anger. You can't carry both at the same time.'

'Well, you can forgive, but not forget,' insisted the young man.

'That is not forgiveness. Forgiveness is wiping the slate clean, completely erasing it. It's letting go of the anger and condemnation, just like letting go of a heavy rock. Carrying the rock will weigh you down; let it go and it has no power over you, you are free. This is why Confucius said, "To be wronged or robbed is nothing, unless you continue to remember it."

'Every religion in the world speaks of the power of forgiveness. How can we expect God to forgive us if we cannot forgive others? A man who cannot forgive burns the bridge over which he will have to pass himself, because we all at some time need to be forgiven.'

'But how many times can you forgive someone?'

'As many times as he wrongs you. Always remember, the only person who suffers if you don't forgive is you, because it will be you who carries the hatred and anger and resentment. Forgiveness frees you from that suffering. This is why it is so vital if you want to be happy. It is only by letting go of condemning judgments and grievances that we are free to experience joy and happiness.

'I believe that, in time, every man must pay the penalty for his own misdeeds, either in this life or the next. If there is one law in this universe it is the law of cause and effect or, as it is written: "We reap what we sow" our actions come back to us. If you believe this, you no longer need to hold on to anger or bitterness or hatred. Of course, I don't know for certain if the universe works this way I may be wrong, but I choose to believe it and I'm happier for it.

'But, do you know who is the hardest person to forgive, the one person who you will find it most difficult to be compassionate to?' continued Dr Jacobson.

'No.'

'Yourself!'

'What do you mean. Why should I need to forgive myself?'

'Whenever you make a mistake or do something you later regret. We need to remember that everyone is doing the best they can most of the time. We are humans and humans slip up and make mistakes. We all do things at times that we are ashamed of or embarrassed by and wish we could change.

'Every now and again it helps to step aside and see yourself the way you once were as a little child. Be gentle with that child. How can you be happy if you don't love and respect yourself? If God can forgive you, you can forgive yourself. There is an old proverb "The wise man falls down seven times each day, but he also stands up seven times."'

'I had never thought of it this way before,' said the young man. 'It sounds all well and good, but I don't think it is necessarily an easy path to follow. All I can do is try.'

Before he went to bed that night, the young man read over his notes.

The Seventh Secret of Abundant Happiness: The Power of Forgiveness

Forgiveness is the key which opens the door to Abundant Happiness.

You can't be happy if you carry feelings of hatred or resentment. Remember no-one suffers from your bitterness but you.

Mistakes and failures are life's lessons. Forgive yourself and forgive others.

Remember the Sioux Indian prayer:

'O Great Spirit, keep me from ever judging and criticizing a man until I have walked in his moccasins for two weeks.'

THE EIGHTH SECRET – THE POWER OF GIVING

Two days later the young man sat in the spectators' gallery overlooking the swimming pool at the community sports centre, waiting to meet the next person on his list, a man by the name of Peter Tansworth. The gallery was empty, but the young man could hear the screams and shouts of children splashing about in the pool,

'Hello. Are you the man I spoke to on the telephone last week?' shouted a man wearing a tracksuit by the poolside.

'Mr. Tansworth?'

'That's me,' said the man in the tracksuit smiling up at the young man,

'I'll be with you shortly. Ten minutes or so. We're just finishing off.'

'No problem!' shouted the young man. 'You carry on.'

The scene seemed very ordinary to the young man. Nothing unusual about 20 or so children enjoying a swimming lesson. But as the children began to get out of the pool, the young man noticed one little boy had only one arm, then another had no legs. As he looked around, he observed that all of the children were physically handicapped.

A few minutes later Mr. Tansworth joined the young man in the gallery.

'Hi. Pleased to meet you at last.' Mr. Tansworth said, shaking the young man's hand.

Mr. Tansworth had a slightly tanned complexion and large smiling eyes. The young man told him of his meeting with the old Chinese man and of the people he had subsequently met.

'When I met the old man almost five years ago now it also turned out to be a major turning point in my life,' said Mr. Tansworth. 'At that time, I owned a successful computer company. I was doing very well in the business. Making money had always been my main aim in life and when I reached my 35th birthday, I was a millionaire... but I was also very unhappy.'

'Why?' asked the young man.

'You know it is written: "What shall it profit a man if he shall gain the whole world, but lose his soul?" That just about sums up what my life was like. In my rise to the top I had left behind the things which really mattered to me: my wife divorced me, I had only a few friends and every day was simply a battle to acquire more money than I could ever spend.

'I remember one Christmas I was feeling so miserable that I bought myself a Rolex watch to cheer myself up. It cost over £5,000 and for a while I was very proud of my new acquisition. But within half an hour the feeling had worn off and I felt just as miserable as I had been without it. Looking back, I can't imagine why I thought a watch would make me happy, it was the same as most other watches all it did was tell me the time.

'I remember that day well. It was Christmas Eve ... the streets were bursting with people and I sat down on a bench in a shopping mall, watching the frantic bustle of people. Although I was sitting among thousands of people who were passing me by, I had never felt so totally alone. I became overwhelmed with a terrible feeling of loneliness.

'Christmas can be a wonderful time of year, but it can also be a very miserable and lonely lime. Every year hundreds of thousands of people sit in misery. Those with no family or friends; those with no money, no food, and those who are homeless. For them, Christmas is a time that only magnifies their lack. That day I got my first glimpse of how miserable and lonely life can be, but then something happened that changed the rest of my life.'

'What was that?' asked the young man.

'A little old Chinese man sat down beside me!' The young man smiled.

'He turned to me and said, "Did you know that the only time during the four years of fighting in the First World War when soldiers put down their guns and made peace was Christmas 1914?" I had no idea nor much interest, but he continued regardless.

"British and German soldiers climbed out of their trenches and greeted one another in No Man's Land and shared food and drink."

' Mr. Tansworth paused and then added, 'It's incredible when you think about it, isn't it?'

The young man nodded, 'Yes. I suppose it is.

' The old man then said, "People pursue happiness in having and acquiring, and getting served by others, but it takes a time like Christmas to remind us that real happiness is found in giving and in serving."

'The old man's words really made me think about my life, I had always thought that it was by acquiring things that we became happy - acquiring more money, a better job, a bigger house and a faster car. But the fact remained that even though I had acquired everything I had set out to possess, I was still unhappy.

'I had a long discussion with the old man and that was the first time I had ever heard of the 10 secrets of Abundant Happiness. Through him, I met some wonderful people who shared those secrets with me and all of them helped enrich my life. But there was one secret that was particularly important to me, and that was ... the power of giving.

'It is incredible to think that the one thing we crave most in life - happiness - we can get most easily... by giving it away. It is one of the most magical laws in Nature, the more you give, the more you receive. It's like sowing seeds, for every seed you sow, you'll get thousands back.'

'But how can you give away something you haven't got?' asked the young man.

Mr. Tansworth smiled. 'That's the beauty of it!' he exclaimed. 'You can get it by giving it away. When you give joy, you instantly receive it, it's like perfume.'

'Perfume?' repeated the young man.

'You can't pour It on others without getting a few drops on yourself. Take smiling: if you smile at someone, invariably they will smile back. You see happiness is like a boomerang, the more you give it away, the more it comes back to you.

'I am sure you can remember a time when you did something for someone else with no ulterior motive, even a small thing like giving someone who is lost directions or helping a blind person cross the street, or simply remembering a friend's birthday? Or giving someone a sincere compliment or showing your appreciation and thanking them?'

The young man nodded, 'Yes. Of course.'

'Didn't that make you feel good inside? Not just because the person might have been grateful for what you said or did, but simply because it feels good to do something for or to help a fellow human being.'

The young man thought about the time a few years back when he had been approached by a foreign woman who was lost in the city and needed directions. The address she was seeking was three kilometres away; it was the middle of winter and snowing, and the woman was shivering. There was no way she would have been able to find her way there, not in such terrible weather. So, he drove her to where she wanted to go. And now, looking back, he remembered how good he had felt about himself at the time.

'You see, deep down human beings are not by their nature selfish. We will do far more for other people than we will do for ourselves. Most parents, for instance, will willingly sacrifice their own comfort for the sake of their children.

'After talking to the old Chinese man in the shopping mall that day, I walked along the mall and came across a Salvation Army choir singing Christmas carols. There was a big sign saying, "Help the homeless this Christmas." Almost without thinking about it I took the Rolex watch back to the shop and instead gave a cheque for £5,000 to a Salvation Army collector. And do you know I will never forget the look of astonishment and gratitude on the woman's face. She showed it to her colleague and tears came to her eyes. "This will make such a difference," she said. "Thank you and may God bless you."

'It was only then that I first began to understand what the old man had said because I got more pleasure from giving away that cheque and knowing that I had made a difference, however small, in other people's lives than I would have got from wearing the watch for a lifetime.

'I remember reading some years back how a father wanted to teach his son the value of giving from an early age. It was his son's sixth birthday and he had been given lots of brightly coloured helium balloons by his grandmother. After the party, the father told his son that he had an idea how he could have even more fun with the balloons ... by giving some of them away! Needless to say, the boy wasn't too enthusiastic about this suggestion, but the father assured him that he would have fun and, reluctantly, the boy agreed.

'They went to an old folk's home and the little boy walked into the lounge carrying 20 helium balloons and gave one to every person in the room. Suddenly people were laughing and talking excitedly, and one old lady who hadn't had a visitor for over three years was so moved that she wept. It was as if the little boy had turned on a light switch and lit up the room.

'They all told him how wonderful he was to think of them, and soon everyone in the room was laughing and wanting a hug from him. And that little boy loved every minute of it, so much so that on the way home he asked his father when they could go back and do it again, it was a lesson the little boy never forgot. From that day on, he looked for opportunities to give rather than only to take.'

'That's a wonderful story,' said the young man.

'Let me tell you another one which particularly moved me,' said Mr. Tansworth. 'A few years ago, I met a man named Paul who told me how he had learned the power of giving when he was still a college student. Paul had been given a brand-new car for his eighteenth birthday by his older brother and naturally he drove it to college to show it off. One of the juniors walked around the shiny new car admiring it, "What do you think?" Paul said. "It's fantastic!" enthused the junior. "Fantastic". When Paul told him that it was a birthday present from his older brother, the junior was dumbfounded. Your brother gave it to you?" he said. "Wow. I wish ..." Paul knew what the junior was going to say: "I wish I had a brother like that!" But what the junior actually said was something quite different and his words stayed with Paul for the rest of his life. The boy said: "I wish I could be a brother like that!"

'Paul was so taken with what the little boy had said that he offered to give him a ride in the car during the lunch break. The junior couldn't hide his excitement and asked if they could stop by his house. Paul smiled to himself. He thought he knew what the boy wanted; he wanted to show his friends and neighbours that he had driven in a brand-new car.

'Ten minutes later the car stopped outside the junior's house and the little boy ran inside. The next moment he came back out pushing a little boy in a wheelchair. "Wow!" said the little boy with wide open eyes. And then something happened that brought tears to Paul's eyes. The junior said to his little brother: "Someday, Sam, I'm gonna buy you a car just like that one." Hearing this, Paul said, "Say, Sam, would you like to come for a ride as well?" And he lifted the tiny crippled boy into the car and the three of them went for a drive. That day, the proud owner of the new car was humbled and understood for the first time in his life why it is written: "It is more blessed to give than to receive."

'So, you see,' said Mr. Tansworth, 'by giving of ourselves to others, we don't merely take our minds off our own problems. To me it is the greatest secret of Abundant Happiness: all you have to do to bring happiness and joy into your life is to give it to others,

'This is why I always look for places and people to whom I could give help; not just money, but my time as well. That's how I ended up with this job, teaching handicapped children how to swim. It makes me happy to be able to make a difference in their lives. I don't believe there's any greater happiness than that which we get when we are able to help or bring joy to another human being.'

On his way home, the young man thought about what Mr. Tansworth had said in relation to his own life. The past few years he had been too wrapped up in his own problems to worry about other people's. The thought had never occurred to him that by considering other people and taking the time to do something for them, particularly those closest to him, he would in fact be helping himself.

When he arrived home that evening the young man summarized his notes.

The Eighth Secret of Abundant Happiness: The Power of Giving

Happiness is not found in having and acquiring for ourselves, but in giving to and helping others.

The more joy and happiness we give, the more we receive.

Every day I can create happiness in my own life by looking for ways to bring happiness to others.

THE NINTH SECRET – THE POWER OF RELATIONSHIPS

Two days later the young man met the next person on his list in a small coffee shop in the centre of town. Ed Hansen lived alone in a small apartment on the east side of the city He had not always lived alone; at one time he had lived in a four-bedroomed detached house with his wife and two children, but that was a long time ago, before the drinking started.

'I can't complain,' Mr. Hansen said to the young man. 'I messed up. I have nobody else to blame but myself. In fact, I'm grateful for having a second chance. I've been sober now for 10 years.'

'How did it all begin?' asked the young man.

'It started many, many years ago. The stress and pressure of work worries, anxiety you know what it's like. One evening I stopped in a local bar to have a drink with a few colleagues after work. All I had was a few glasses of wine, just to relax and unwind a little. It worked, and the following evening I stopped off again.

'Before I knew it, I was drinking a bottle of wine every evening after work and soon that increased to two or three. It didn't take very long, a few months maybe, before I was drinking during the day as well. As you can imagine, my life fell to pieces; my work deteriorated rapidly. I was given the sack, my wife took the children and left me, I couldn't pay the hills and a few months later I was evicted. The rest is a bit of a blur. I ended up homeless and living on the streets, begging.'

The young man was shocked by Mr. Hansen's story. He had never met someone who had been homeless before; he had always assumed that homeless people were outcasts and misfits, different from everyone else, but Mr. Hansen seemed so normal. It humbled him to realize that anyone who was desperately unhappy or couldn't cope with their worries or daily stresses could so easily find themselves in the same predicament.' There but for the grace of God go I,' he thought as he took a sip from his coffee.

'How did you manage to turn your life around?' he asked.

'It wasn't easy. I did it with help. At the time I would never have admitted that I needed help, but I did. I felt trapped, completely powerless. I remember one winter's night I was so cold, so freezing, that not even the booze could numb the pain. I really thought that I was going to die. I hadn't eaten for three days and I lay huddled and shivering in a cardboard box. All I could do was pray that my end would come quickly and painlessly.

'The next thing I remember, someone was standing over me. It was too dark to see who it was, but he had a soft, gentle voice. He said, "Come with me, Ed, it's time for you to leave here," and he held out his hand. I thought that perhaps I had died because as soon as he touched me, all the pain in my body vanished. He led me down the street and after a few minutes we stopped in front of a large building. I turned to face him; he was an old Chinese man. He handed me a piece of paper and said, "This is it, Ed. This is where your new life begins. Be well." I looked at the paper he had given me, but when I looked up again, he was gone.'

The young man had already guessed who Ed's mysterious rescuer had been, but still felt a lump rise in his throat and his eyes begin to glaze.

'There was a meeting going on in the building,' continued Mr. Hansen. 'An Alcoholics Anonymous meeting. But it was warm and there was a wonderful smell of hot coffee, so I stayed. I looked at the piece of paper the old man had given to me and...'

'There was a list of 10 names?' interjected the young man.

'Yes,' answered Mr. Stein smiling, 'but the amazing thing was... the last name on my list was the same name on the blackboard. It was the name of the speaker, Mr. John Mapland.

'After the meeting I went over to Mr. Mapland and showed him the piece of paper. He then put his arm around me and said, "Don't worry Ed, we're all friends here. If you need help, this is where you'll get it." That evening I began to live again just as the old man had promised. Despite my bedraggled appearance, everyone was very friendly. For the first time, people were willing to listen to me without being critical or judgmental.

'I regularly attended the AA meetings, and, with time and determination and the grace of God, I regained my sobriety. During that time, I met the other people on the list the old man had given me, and they inspired me and showed me how to live again with the secrets of Abundant Happiness. All of the secrets helped me in some way, and enriched my life. But the one that saved my life that night was... the power of relationships.'

'Relationships? What do you mean?' said the young man,

'Unconditional, loving relationships. Without relationships, life is empty. After all, life is meant to be a celebration and it's not much fun having a party by yourself, is it?

'Human beings are social creatures. We need to talk, we need to communicate, we need to feel wanted and needed. We all need each other. It is even written in the Bible: "It is not good for man to be alone."

'When I look back,' explained Mr. Hansen, 'I can see now how I neglected my friends and family in my struggle to succeed in business. Perhaps that was one of the reasons I began drinking in the first place. I don't know much, but I do know that I would never have been able to overcome my problems without the love and support of a room full of strangers, all of whom understood what I had been through and all of whom accepted me for what I was and offered me help without asking for anything in return. Sometimes in life you can find yourself in a hole so deep that you simply can't climb out alone. It's at times like those that you need someone to pull you up.'

Mr. Hansen paused momentarily.

'If you were to ask me what lessons I have learned in life, right up at the top of the list would be this: the quality of our lives is the quality of our relationships.'

'In what way?' asked the young man.

'Well, Happiness arises first from your relationship with yourself, but then from the friendship and love of your relationships with other people. After all, how much pleasure would there be if you could only do things alone?'

'It's very true,' said the young man. 'Last year I went on holiday by myself to the Seychelles and although everything was wonderful, there was definitely something missing. It wasn't the same as having someone there to share it with.'

'Exactly,' said Mr. Hansen. 'Having other people you care about makes good experiences even better, but they also make the difficult times easier.

Have you ever noticed how you automatically feel better after you have talked to somebody about your problems? They may not have given you any advice or tangible help, and you still may have the problem, but somehow, it doesn't feel quite so bad?'

The young man nodded. There were plenty of times when he had talked over problems with a friend and felt better for it

'But something that you may not have noticed,' continued Mr. Hansen, 'is that we tend to become most anxious or worried or depressed or unhappy when we keep our thoughts to ourselves. If we keep our problems to ourselves, we can easily blow them out of proportion and gradually they seem to get worse and we start to feel overwhelmed and powerless. The old saying; "Two heads are better than one" is absolutely true, not just because there is double the brain power to help find a solution to a problem, but also because the process of sharing problems, worries or anxieties often relieves them.

'Relationships enrich our lives. If you share joy, you multiply joy, but if you share a problem, you halve a problem, Lord Byron, the English poet, put it this way:

All who joy would win,

Must share it Happiness was born a twin.

It all made sense to the young man, He had always kept his problems to himself. Although he had close friends and family, he rarely discussed his problems with them. But the truth was, he had never found it easy developing close relationships.

'It's all very well,' he said, 'and I understand what you mean, but some people find relationships difficult.'

'If you find relationships difficult, you will invariably find life difficult,' said Mr. Stein.

'Yes,' agreed the young man, 'but for instance, in my case, I have always been a bit of a loner. I've never found it easy making friends or developing close relationships.'

"Have you ever heard the phrase: "The past is not the future'?'

'No.'

"What it means is that just because something happened yesterday, doesn't mean it has to happen again tomorrow. Just because you had problems with relationships in the past doesn't mean that you have to have the same problems in the future. It might mean that in the past you were simply going about it in the wrong way.' 'What do you mean?' asked the young man.

'Well, what makes you like someone?'

'I don't know, Sometimes I click with another person and sometimes I don't.'

'Okay. Let's look at it another way; do you feel at ease with someone who looks you in the eye when you meet them or someone who avoids eye contact?'

'Someone who looks me m the eye.!

'Good. And are you more comfortable with someone who has a firm handshake or someone whose grip feels like a wet squid?'

'Firm handshake.'

'Of course. And do you prefer a person to only talk about themselves or to be interested in you as well?'

'I'd prefer someone who was interested in me,' said the young man. 'But this is all obvious.'

"You're right,' said Mr. Hansen, 'it is obvious, but do you consciously do these things when you first meet people? You'd be surprised how many people don't, and then wonder why they have difficulty developing relationships with other people.'

The young man looked away briefly. "You're right. If I'm honest, I don't think I've ever really thought about it'

'And, if we want to keep our friends, we need to learn to accept them for who they are and overlook what we may see as their shortcomings, and instead focus on their positive or admirable qualities. We have to be willing to forgive them when they make mistakes, just as we would want them to forgive us ours.'

'Yes,' said the young man, 'I had a long chat with a man about the power of forgiveness last week.'

'Forgiveness is very important in being happy,' said Mr. Hansen, 'because without it we would end up alone and bitter. When we value our relationships, we automatically treat people differently. And, when we treat people well, they tend to treat us well,'

'But still, relationships are not always easy, are they?' said the young man. "There are bound to be problems and disagreements in any relationship.'

'Of course, there are. But I found one simple technique that helps all my relationships.'

'What's that?' asked the young man. 'I always try to treat everyone I meet as if I might never see them again. Can you imagine how your relationships with your friends, your work colleagues, your family and even strangers might change if you treated everyone you met as if it was the last time you would see them?'

The young man shook his head. 'I'm not with you.'

'How would you behave to your wife or girlfriend if you thought you might not see her again? Would you let her leave you without kissing or hugging her?'

'No.'

'Would you say "goodbye" with an unresolved argument?'

'No.'

'Would you let them go without telling them how much they meant to you?'

'No.'

'And what about work colleagues or friends or members of your family? If you thought you might never see someone again, wouldn't you try to make your time with them as memorable as possible? Wouldn't you do your utmost to avoid parting with bad feeling?'

The young man nodded. Mr. Hansen's words struck a chord deep within him. It brought back his memory of the last time he saw his mother. It was a hot summer's day and she was leaving for a holiday abroad. He was in a hurry to meet his friends for a game of tennis, and quickly gave his mother a peck on the cheek. He had no way of knowing that she would never return and that was to be their final farewell. He had thought about it often since; it was the moment in his life that he most regretted, and would do for the rest of his life. He understood now how to avoid making the same mistake with other people who he cared about and loved. It was simple as Mr. Stein had said, 'Treat people as if you may never see them again.'

'Many people,' said Mr. Hansen, 'simply don't value their relationships. I chose my career over my family and in doing so, lost both. Others choose money and possessions over their relationships. You'd be surprised how many brothers, sisters, parents and children are willing to fall out over money They sacrifice their closest relationships and unknowingly sacrifice their happiness as well.'

Later that evening, the young man summarized the notes he had made that day.

The Ninth Secret of Abundant Happiness: The Power of Relationships

The quality of my life is the quality of my relationships.

No man is an island. We all need relationships.

Close relationships make the good times better and the difficult times easier. A joy shared is a joy doubled, but a problem shared is a problem halved.

Treat everyone you meet as if you may never see them again.

THE TENTH SECRET – THE POWER OF FAITH

It was another week before the young man was able to meet with the last person on his list. During that time, he had the opportunity of reviewing and practising some of the things he had learned. He made happiness a priority and always tried to look for positive things in every difficult situation. He had also begun using the power of his body, particularly exercising regularly and taking care of his diet.

He had found the secret of living in the moment especially beneficial at work He had noticed that he was getting more done, more successfully, with less stress or worry. Even his boss noticed the change in the young man's performance and praised him for his efforts.

The young man repeated positive affirmations to himself every day to help improve his self-image and, by asking himself five empowering questions at the start of each day, he found he was more enthusiastic, more eager to face the challenges of each day.

He had used the rocking chair technique, setting lifetime goals as well as shorter term goals and he wrote each one of them down and read them all three times each day to keep them imprinted on his mind. He found that he had much more energy and enthusiasm when he had things to strive for and look forward to.

The young man had also begun to take himself less seriously and consciously looked for the funny side of events, especially in stressful situations. At the same time, he made sure that he treated everyone he met as if he might never see them again, and consequently he found himself treating people more considerately and he noticed that they in return treated him the same way He never let an opportunity pass without letting the people around him, his friends, his family, his work colleagues know that he appreciated them.

One major difference that the young man noticed immediately was that by looking for ways he could help and give to others, he spread happiness and received it at the same time. He found that bringing a smile to someone else always made him feel good. It was a wonderful feeling making a difference to someone else's life. And at the end of each day, the young man made it a rule to try and forgive anybody who had upset him that day. This way he found he never went to sleep with any feelings of bitterness or resentment.

Yes, there was no doubt that he was feeling more energetic, more enthusiastic and was a happier man he had ever been. There was no doubt in his mind that the secrets of Abundant Happiness were really working!

'What then,' he thought to himself, 'could the last person on my list possibly add to what I have already learned?'

Miss June Henderson lived in a small apartment in the suburbs a few kilometers north of the city She was a pretty woman, still in her early forties, very petite, with auburn shoulder length hair and large green eyes.

'So, you met the old man,' Miss Henderson said to the young man.

'Yes. He turned up a few weeks ago when my car broke down.'

'It is amazing, isn't it, that at times when you least expect it, something wonderful happens?' said Miss Henderson.

'I suppose so,' said the young man.

'It is called the eleventh-hour principle. Have you heard of it?'

'No,' said the young man, shaking his head,

'Well, it is simply that just as the night is often darkest and coldest just before the dawn, it is when things look really bleak that we often experience a dramatic turn for the better and something wonderful happens. The old Chinese man always turns up at the eleventh hour.'

'I suppose that's true,' replied the young man.

'When I met the old man I was very unhappy,' said Miss Henderson.

'Why?' asked the young man.

'My mother had died only a month before. I can still remember it as if it were yesterday.'

The young man was embarrassed for asking the question. 'I'm sorry,' he said.

'Thank you, it's okay. Really. I was only 21 at the time and I had just finished my final year's exams at university. It was a terrible shock. My mother, despite being a heavy smoker, had always enjoyed good health, but these things eventually take their toll. She died suddenly of a heart attack whilst on holiday.

'One day I was sitting alone on the veranda outside our apartment thinking about her. I don't know how long I had been there before I became aware that I was not alone. On the balcony of the neighbouring apartment was an elderly Chinese man. Our eyes met, he smiled and said, "Hello," and we began talking. It was very strange; I had never met him before, but it felt as if had known him for years.'

The young man recalled how he had also felt comfortable talking about intimate details of his life with the old man within five minutes of meeting him,

'The old man was so wise and gentle,' said Miss Henderson. 'He seemed to know that something was wrong and funnily enough it was him who brought the conversation around to the subject of death. He explained that in his country, death is a time of celebration, not one of sorrow,'

'How can losing someone you love and will never see again be a time to celebrate?' asked the bewildered young man.

'I asked exactly the same question,' said Miss Henderson. 'And the old man explained the golden rule of happiness.'

'Oh, yes. He told me as well,' said the young man. 'Our attitudes and beliefs determine our feelings, not our circumstances.'

'Exactly,' said Miss Henderson smiling. The old man explained that, in his country, they believe that our existence began a long time before we were born into this world. Our short life in this world is merely a school of learning from which we graduate when we are ready. So, when a person dies, their soul continues on its journey. All the major religions share the belief that while the body may die, the spirit lives on and in another time and another place, we will meet our loved ones again. Even the Bible describes death as "sleep" from which, one day, we will all awake.'

Miss Henderson pointed to a plaque on the wall next to the young man.

'I first read these words in a cemetery on a 300-year-old headstone,' she said. The plaque read:

There is an old belief

That on some solemn shore,

Beyond the sphere of grief,

Dear friends shall meet once more.

'If you believe death to be a final and complete separation, then it can be devastating. But if you believe that the separation is only temporary, and that the soul lives on, it is not quite so distressing.'

'But, even though death may not be permanent, any separation is sad, isn't it?' said the young man.

'Yes, even a temporary separation can be sad,' said Miss Henderson, 'although in some eastern faiths they are joyful because they believe the soul of the person has returned to its true home, on to a higher level of learning.

'But, talking to the old man that day did more than just help me come to terms with my grief, it made me review ail of my beliefs,'

'In what way?' asked the young man.

'Well, you might not believe it, but I used to be a terrible worrier,' she said. 'When I was only 12 years old I worried about the fact that one day I was going to die! Can you believe it? I worried about everything; things I had said or done, the things I had to do, things that had gone wrong and things that might go wrong. And if I had nothing to worry about I worried that there was something I should be worried about!'

The young man could empathize with this. He spent most of his days worrying about one thing or another; deadlines at work, bills, his health there was always something that might go wrong.

'Sitting there, talking to the old man,' continued Miss Henderson, 'made me realize the insignificance of most of the things I had always worried about. When you're faced with the death of someone close to you, all worries about bills, mortgages, exams, jobs ... absolutely everything fades into insignificance.

'The old man introduced me to the secrets of Abundant Happiness and I can honestly say that those secrets changed my life. It was a revelation for me, I had never considered that I was the architect of my own happiness or misery. I learned, for instance, the importance of my attitude and beliefs, the effect of my body on my emotions, the power of a strong self-image, the necessity of goals and a sense of humour, and I learned to value each day and try to live in the moment But, the one secret that I think I most needed to learn and which therefore had the most profound effect on my life was... the power of faith.'

'Faith?' repeated the young man. 'What does faith have to do with happiness?'

'We all need a certain amount of faith just to live, let alone be happy,' replied Miss Henderson. 'Let me give you an example, do you drive a car?'

'Yes.'

'How do you know that your car is safe to drive?'

'I had it serviced only a month ago.'

'How do you know the mechanic did his job properly?'

'Erm.., I don't know for sure, but..'

'So, you must have faith in the mechanic.

'And when you drive, how can you be sure that you won't have an accident?'

'I drive carefully,' said the young man.

'So, you have faith in your own ability to drive. That's good, but there might be other drivers on the road who are not careful, mightn't there?'

'Possibly,' admitted the young man, 'but I'd like to think most people are careful.'

'So, you also have faith in other road users. Can you see that, in order to drive your car, you have to have faith in the people who manufactured and serviced the car, other drivers on the road and yourself. You can imagine how much more faith you need to live, if you are not to live in fear and anxiety every day.'

'I can see your point,' said the young man.

'And there is one faith which we need most of all, 'said Miss Henderson. 'And that is a faith in God, a Higher Power, Universal Force. It doesn't matter what you call it'

'You're not saying we need faith in God to be happy, are you?' asked the young man.

'I'm not saying you can't be happy without faith in God. What I am saying is that, without it, it is difficult to find lasting happiness. Faith is the foundation for Abundant Happiness. It is like two people who build themselves houses. One builds his house on rock and the other builds his house on sand. Whilst the weather is favourable they'll both be happy, but as soon as a storm comes, the man who built his house on sand will be crushed. Faith is the rock on which lasting happiness is built, it overcomes all adversities, and provides hope and courage to those who have it.

'William James wrote: "Faith is one of the forces by which men live and the total absence of it means collapse." And Mahatma Gandhi said, "Without faith, I should have been a lunatic long ago." Without faith in a Higher Power, life becomes burdened with doubt, worry, anxiety and fear. Psychological studies have demonstrated that people with a strong religious faith suffer less depression and stress related disorders, and cope better with loss. In fact, let me show you this. 'She said reached for a book on the bookcase. It was entitled Modern Man in Search of a Soul by Dr Carl Jung, listen to what Dr Jung wrote,' she said.

Among all my patents in the second half of life that is to say, over 35 there has not been one whose problem in the last resort was not that of finding a religious outlook on life. It is safe to say that every one of them fell ill because he had lost that which the living religions of every age have given to their followers, and none of them has been really healed who did not regain his religious outlook.

'I understand what you're saying,' said the young man. 'But, I'm not sure I believe that a God exists.'

Miss Henderson thought for a moment 'If I was to tell you that the QE2 ship was formed over millions of years during which time bits of metal and wood and plastic and an assortment of chemicals linked together, you would say I was crazy, wouldn't you?'

'Yes, of course,'

'Because you can see that the QE2 has been designed, therefore there must be a designer?'

'Yes,' answered die young man.

'When you study the human body, you will see a design far more complex than the QE2,' explained Miss Henderson, 'For instance, the Columbia space shuttle was built with 5.2 million parts, yet the human eye alone has more than one billion parts. Scientists can only marvel at the workings of the human body and despite all our technological advances, we would need a computer the size of the Empire State building to compare with the human brain.

Throughout Nature we see incredible design and precision.'

'But if there is a God,' said the young man, still unconvinced, 'why is there so much misery in the world?'

' You said that a few weeks ago you were unhappy, 'said Miss Henderson. 'Why were you unhappy then, but not now?'

'Because I have learned the secrets of Abundant Happiness,' said the young man.

'So, if you have the power to create your own happiness, who has the power to create everyone else's?

'I see what you mean,' said the young man. 'We are all responsible for our own happiness.'

'Of course. So if we are unhappy, it is through our own thoughts and actions. It is not God's doing. To me, this is the most wonderful lesson of the secrets of Abundant Happiness; there Is only one person who can make you feel happy or unhappy, and that person is you.'

The young man nodded in agreement. 'Yes. I suppose it's true.'

'In the end,' explained Miss Henderson, 'faith is something we all need to find for ourselves. But I am a firm believer that if you search for truth, you will find it. And sometimes when we feel most confused and lost, something happens that touches our soul. A little miracle, If you like.'

'Such as ...?' inquired the young man.

'Such as a chance meeting with an old Chinese man!'

That night, before going to bed, the young man read over the notes he had made that day.

The Tenth Secret of Abundant Happiness: The Power of Faith.

Faith is the foundation of Abundant Happiness.

Without faith, there is no lasting happiness. Faith creates trust, leads to peace of mind, and frees the soul from doubt, worry, anxiety and fear.

EPILOGUE

He felt the first few drops of rain hit his forehead as he got into his car, and minutes later the storm broke. The thunder and lightning preceded a heavy downpour of rain which beat heavily against the windscreen. His thoughts drifted to the evening, a little over a year ago, when he had met the old Chinese man. He remembered how miserable he had been that evening and smiled as he pictured himself walking back to his car in the wind and rain on that stormy night, unaware that he was about to meet a mysterious man who would change his life forever.

Since that meeting the young man's life had changed immeasurably. He had more energy, more enthusiasm and was happier than he had ever been, Others noticed it too; there was a sparkle in his eyes, a spring in his step and, more often than not, a smile on his face. Yet he had the same job, he lived in the same apartment, drove the same car and had the same friends. There was only one thing that had changed in his life... and that was himself.

People would often ask him why he always seemed to be so cheerful. On those occasions he would gladly tell the story of his meeting with the old Chinese man and the secrets of Abundant Happiness. It always gave him great pleasure to share what he had learned because he knew it would make a difference in their lives just as it had in his. Many people would phone to thank him and tell him how the secrets had helped them in their lives. And on more than one occasion it had been suggested that he write the story in a book

Suddenly, there was a loud bang and smoke began rising from under the bonnet of the car. The young man pulled the car over to the side of the road, got out and walked the two and a half kilometres along the highway to the nearest telephone to call the breakdown service.

As he walked back to his car to wait for a mechanic, he could not help but smile to himself. He became excited, hoping that he might see the old Chinese man leaning against the car, waiting for him as he had done the year before, He wanted to thank the old man and let him know how much the secrets of Abundant Happiness had changed his life. But it was not to be, the old man was not there.

The young man walked round to the driver's door of the car and was about to put the key in the lock when he noticed a bright yellow object lying on the ground, He leaned forward and picked it up.

'Would you believe it?' he whispered to himself. In his hand was a yellow baseball cap!

As he sat in his car waiting for the service mechanic, a thought came to him. He picked up a pen, opened his notebook and began writing: *'It all began one cold and wet October evening...*

ABOUT ADAM J JACKSON

Adam Jackson is an internationally renowned therapist, motivational speaker, entrepreneur and author. His books include 'The Secrets of Abundant Health, Wealth, Love & Happiness' series and The Flipside. Adam's books have been published worldwide and translated into 34 languages.

Adam was born in 1962 in Sussex, England. He graduated with a degree in Law from the University of Southampton in 1983. He went on to qualify as a Solicitor and practise Law in the London. However, after three years, Adam decided to leave the Law and re-trained in Natural Health Sciences.

In 1995 Adam became a monthly columnist for the Nursing Times and Health Guardian, reporting on the latest developments and research relating to alternative therapies & complementary medicines. In 2001 he was invited to appear on behalf of the British Complementary Medical Association before the House of Lords Select Committee to give evidence on the role of Alternative & Complementary Therapies in primary healthcare in the UK.

Adam has appeared on national television in the UK (including Good Morning GMTV, The Big Breakfast Channel 4, and BBC1 Kilroy Silk) and North America (including CBC, 'The Health Show' & The Dini Petty Show). He has also been featured in the national press in the UK including Sunday Express, TODAY, as well as GQ and Here's Health magazines.

OTHER BOOKS BY ADAM J JACKSON

'*The Flipside* shows you that every cloud
can have a silver lining. Brilliant'
THE
FLIPSIDE
Finding the hidden
opportunities in life
Adam J Jackson

'This is an inspiring, really energising book. It is just the sort of thing you need when you have watched too many news broadcasts about how the world is going to the dogs...This is an empowering book. Read it first before you give it to that friend who really needs it.'

The Times - South Africa - 25th April 2009

'We are inspired by Adam J Jackson's writings in his book "The Flipside" which is based upon a simple and inspiring idea that "every problem or obstacle in our lives however big or small contains an equivalent or greater benefit or opportunity.'

Health budget speech tabled by Limpopo MEC for Health and Social Development, Mrs Miriam Segabutla. 18 June 2009. Department of Health and Social Development, **Limpopo Provincial Government**

'Life-affirming stories guaranteed to make us change the way we look at adversity'

Publishers Weekly

'An entertaining and relevant read when so many people are facing financial and emotional traumas.'

News of The World

CONNECT WITH ADAM J JACKSON

Connect with Adam and subscribe to his V.I.P. list to receive news, updates and exclusive promotions:

WEB

http://adamjjackson.com

TWITTER

https://twitter.com/adamjjackson

FACEBOOK

https://facebook.com/adamjohnjackson

If you enjoyed this book, please consider submitting a review on Amazon.com – thank you!

Join the V.I.P. Club

Join Adam J Jackson's VIP Club and receive exclusive access to news, updates and promotions as well as a chance to receive review copies of forthcoming books.

To join the club, click through to:
http://adamjjackson.com/vip-club/

ACKNOWLEDGEMENTS

The idea behind The Secrets of Abundance series was inspired by two very special relationships. Two elderly men who helped and guided me in my early twenties. Dr Emil Just and Fred Kurgan. Both men were remarkable in their own ways. Their relationships had profound effects on my life and much of the teachings within this book I received first from them.

I'd like to thank my literary agent, Sara Menguc, and her colleague, Amabel Gee. With their help, these titles have been published all over the world in over thirty languages.

Finally, to Karen my wife, my best friend and my most candid editor. Words cannot express my love for the one person who has always had faith in me and believed in my work.

Printed in Great Britain
by Amazon

62803141R00092

JENNY'S FIRST CLASS JOURNEY

By the same author:

THE TENT OF GOD

THE RIVER SLEA

OUR HUMAN CONSTITUTION

WALTER PATER

Jenny's First Class Journey

Anthony Ward

Norton Bailey, London

Norton Bailey & Co Ltd
103 Lonsdale Road
Barnes
London S.W.13

Clarke, Irwin & Company
Toronto

Printed in Great Britain

For Ed and Helene Dorn

ACKNOWLEDGMENT

Some of these chapters or earlier versions of them have appeared in Voices 2 (Michael Joseph) and in The English Intelligencer and The Park.

CONTENTS

Brick at first. The outside wall is made of smooth brick. It was added later. The building was a stable. The walls are thick, rubble for a core, faced with limestone. The limestone crumbled on the wall facing the street and it was replaced by the regular, smooth brick.

A boy is throwing a tennis ball against the wall, right-handed, arm horizontal to the ground; his left shoulder turns, poises. Then he catches the ball again as it rebounds, comes back lower, near his left foot. The ball smacks firmly into his cupped hands. He straightens, flicks the ball at the wall, hard, and catches it again.

It is in April. The wind has loosened the dust on the road. The gravel and the sand which had been thrown down to stop the cars slipping on the ice, rolls freely about. The ball bounces on the firm surface of the road now when the boy changes the rhythm of his game. It comes up from the road, into his hands, firm and clean. He can throw it again easily and with confidence. It does not slip. The boy can feel the slight wind on his arm and the blood throbbing with the sudden jerks he makes to throw the ball. Behind him a pub sign creaks, The Shoulder of Mutton.

The wind on his arms makes the boy think of the arms of his father which are white. The network of blue veins stands out in ridges across the white flesh. The flesh loops from one vein to another, like electric wires strung from pylons. There is a telegraph pole in the garden between the stable and the house. The wires sink and slope up again to the bracket on the wall of the house. The elbows of the father's arms are pointed, two thin arms in the rolled sockets of the sleeves of a striped shirt. The boy stops his game. He goes into the yard. He kicks an empty corned beef tin in an empty shed and stands for a moment to watch it lie still again in the shade at the back.

If you look at the boy from behind, say from the apple tree which is in front of the kitchen windows and which shades the lawn, you see his back. He has his head on one side and his hands in his pockets. The right hand is only hooked on to the pocket because he has already put the ball there. He is standing still for a moment, watching something inside the shed and he stands easily and with conscious pleasure as though he knows that there is a spectator to his action. Such gestures and movement as he makes give the impression of being directed at a public. At the moment he stands there, his own public. It is so that he refers to the past and memorizes and relives it. Such reference gives his existence physical continuity and a sense of weight. The boy feels heroic to have such power and moves suddenly, with vigour and high pleasure, up the yard to a cratch standing under a pear tree beyond the strip of concrete.

The cratch stands beside a railway sleeper, blackened with creosote, which acts as an upright pillar for a ruined shed. The beams the corrugated iron of the roof was nailed to, stretch across the space, about five feet apart, to the brick wall at the other side. There are two large oblong holes which take up the whole of the bottom half of the wall. They were pigsties once. Then the shed was built on to the end of the brick place. They are filled with lumber now. Two rusty chain blocks and tackle.

The boy picks up the two handles of the cratch and lifts. It moves forward slightly on its iron wheels. There are the cuts the saw has made and the marks from chopping meat. The wood has a softness which comes from its being scrubbed. There are traces of blood and fat on the board top. The boy thinks of the bones of the black-market sheep, buried in the garden, the constable bribed with the liver. He has held the front legs of a sheep open for his father to cut the throat. He has watched the blood mingle with the soap-suds and circulate in the warm water when he has washed the cratch. He has smelt the pungent smell, left the blood to dry on his arms and then rubbed it off, feeling pleasure and energy doing so, standing in large Wellingtons with his feet comfortable and sliding in the clotted black blood on the mosaic of a concrete and gravel floor.

It is an April evening and there is no smell of blood as he stands feeling the thick round handles. They grow warm as he holds them and make him enthusiastic. He squeezes, imagining strength to compress wood. The handles bed down into the flesh of his palms and he is satisfied. He puts the handles down again to stand the cratch on the back pair of its four legs and presses to lift the front two legs, which hook on to the iron axle. He lets go the handles and the hooks smack back again over the iron bar. He repeats the motion and weighs the cratch, rocking the front end up and down as he pushes down or releases the weight. He seeks the point of balance where the legs are at an angle which bisects the weight of the whole cratch, but it is impossible. He must press the handles down until they touch the ground and still the front is not reared enough not to slap down again on to the iron bar. The handles jerk up again. The cratch shuffles a little to one side. He becomes aware of the pear tree above his head. Twigs stretch down and impede his movement. He cannot swing the cratch round with the back legs for fulcrum because of the trunk of the tree. He drags the cratch off the earth and out into space on the broad concrete strip, in front of the gutted wooden building, with the beams stretching like the black iron rails of a fence near a river, with the sky showing through, and the clouds moving across, while the leaves of the tree stir slightly in the gentle wind.

The wheels of the cratch roll uneasily over the rough concrete. The boy pulls the handles up as far as he can, to the level of his chest, and then lunges forward and shoots the cratch into the ruined shed, letting it run free, watching the staunch back legs bouncing forward. It slews round and finishes up sideways. He fetches it back, pulling it after him, like a wheelbarrow, and repeats the motion. He presses down again on the back two handles and lifts the front legs, sways the cratch about, turns it from side to side. He begins to make the sound of a machine-gun but finds it implausible and stops. Soon he follows the sweeping motions of the front end of the cratch with the sound of his voice, 'Eeeeiooowww', and again. And becomes absorbed thus for a time but he is dissatisfied.

A year ago he went to a nautical college at Hull. This Easter he came home on the bus with a rolled-up twelve-foot rubber dinghy he had bought off a ship's steward. People grumbled when they tripped over it on the bus. It was too big to go on the luggage rack. He had to leave it in the aisle. Elderly ladies lifted their legs to step across it and straddled indecently for a moment the haphazard yellow packet. It had a sharp knife with a pink cork handle and the hooked blade perforated down the inside curve with large holes, slotted into a pocket. The boy had bought this and a celluloid chart of the heavens with the constellations figured on it in luminous paint. He had put this chart in the wooden shed and revolved the firmament so that the segment showing corresponded with the phase of the moon. He sat with it in the dark and navigated the shed with the aid of red Betelgeuse and Orion. The dinghy was on the lawn now, underneath the apple tree.

You're not to put it on the lawn, his mother had said, it will turn the grass yellow.

There isn't much grass to speak of - anyway what there is is covered with oil.

You can't answer that, his father said, laughing.

You shouldn't back the van on the lawn.

Jezebel. The father warmed the back of his hands, squatting, good-humouredly, at the fire; his thick, spatulate fingers turned in towards each other, moving up or down as he shifted his hands. The mother went out of the room carrying dishes.

You take after your father.

The boy watched his father go into the shop, take down a triangular piece of brisket from the silver rail above his head, put his cigarette down on the blackened piece of board the weights were stood on to stop them cracking the marble counter, cough, and reach up again for the cleaver. He went out, pleased, dragged the dinghy out of the back kitchen and deposited it on the lawn, underneath the apple tree.

Dissatisfied, he let go the handles of the cratch and went across the lawn to the dinghy. He took out the hooked knife and unwound it from the line, threw it. The point stuck in the gnarled bark of the tree. There was an armless statue of Diana at the foot of the tree, going green; with a spear they had had her in the house, now she stood derelict in the garden, beside the yellow dinghy, making ineffectual suggestions of attack at an object too shapelessly bundled to express anything but good humour. The dinghy, unconcerned by the statue, rested placid. The boy stirred it with his foot. But since there was no air in it and no water near and the dinghy was intended both for being inflated and floated, he left it, to return to the cratch.

There was no noise at the top of the yard except one or two birds singing on the pear tree. He went into the shed and could see them through the rafters. He kicked at a piece of wood embedded, by accident, in the concrete. And looked round. The two oblong holes, filled with lumber, attracted him. He rummaged and found the rusty block and tackle. He hung one from a beam. The chains fell to the floor. He pulled one and they ran out of the various wheels of the block down on to the floor where they fell in heaps. He pulled the other way and the bottom block was first dragged along the floor underneath the one which was hooked to the beam and then began to mount and draw near, climbing as he pulled down and down on the chain. Small clouds of red dust smoked from the pulley wheels. The links of the chain had made a twisting groove in the steel wheels. As more chain passed through, across, the wheels began to shine again, first only in the place at the centre of the worn groove, then the shine widening, the wheel running easier. The boy began to pull with long sweeps of his arm, at first gripping the chain near the top of the wheel where it entered under the bracket which held the hook, then hauling down with an uninterrupted pull, the length of his arm. The wheel began to move freely, turning with the momentum while his hand went up again to grip the chain, near the crown of the wheel.

The chains grew warm to his touch. The remnants of the corrugated iron rattled near the bottom end of the shed. The chain grew suppler as it freed itself from the rust. The solid clank as it hit the concrete and rested heavily, stolidly there, grew satisfying to the boy. He let out the pulley, bent to the heap of chain and lifted it, still surprised at the weight of such a pliable thing. He dropped it and watched how still it lay. There was no life in it. A rope twisted if you threw it down. Chain rested quiet with neither will nor desire, silent and unpretentious but still there and because there, attractive, but indigestible, unpalatable, resistant, cold, having none of the easy susceptibility of rope or yarn or cloth. Chain. Chain. Chain. Chain. Dug as rock at first with red ore streaking it. The ore melted out, the impurities burnt away, moulded into blocks of pig iron then and finally struck out into links by a smith or, as in this case, pressed by a machine, into a chain. Making it easier to lift by spreading the weight, geared.

The other pulley was still in the dark pigsty. It lay on a rotting sack of potatoes among green shoots. The sack fabric came apart as the boy dragged the heavy block off it and the sweet smell of the rotting potatoes, and the harsher smell of the earth they had moistened round them, came into him and stayed at the back of his throat.

He hooked on the second pulley to the next beam and worked it as he had done the first. To loosen it and to make shiny the twisting groove at the centre of the wheel. Dust puffed out of the powdering beam and the rust smoked off the iron as the chain warmed in his hand and he began to feel accustomed to its shape and behaviour.

The colours of the sky were changing now to darker blue. The sun burnished the four windows of the long back kitchen of the house. The white dust on the concrete gave the feeling of fluidity and relaxation. Through the beams in the roof the boy watched the light in the sky amongst the branches of the pear tree. He listened to the purling of a thrush. The telegraph pole rose up behind the creosoted railway sleeper. He sprang up and clutched on to a beam and hung, pulling himself up, panting, then down again, on to the dusty concrete, softly in his rubber shoes and with pleasure, dusting the dust and the black powder of the creosote off from his hands, feeling the warmth of the palms as they came together, putting them in the pockets of his loose trousers, and hunching up his shoulders so that his arms fell down the sides of his body, vertical, and standing thus for a moment, rocked back on his heels and tried to balance out the pleasure and the vigour of living in such a place.

The sea is in motion inside the feeling and movement of the boy. He is a boat as he rocks thus, to and fro, from the balls of his feet to his heels and back again, or water lapping. He has taken readings of the sun with a quadrant and sextant. He has worn a uniform, a golden anchor on a white peaked cap, learned to move on deck in rope-soled shoes, gutted fish in the Arctic Circle and chopped ice in a frozen hold, been seasick and slept amongst men with warm hands and ordinary pleasure in holding them both round a hot mug.

The ship's steward he bought the dinghy off was later arrested for the attempted rape and murder of one of the younger cooks on board. Ten shillings it had cost. He still watched the luminous dial of the chart in the shed and remembered watching the luminous dial of the wrist-watch on his pillow, waiting for the hands to move round to the time when he should go into the older man's bed to make love to him, in his father's house. He had dozed in spite of all and awakened bitterly disappointed in the morning.

Beaten with rope ends, knocked down in a ring by an instructor with tattoos on his arms and a lecherous face to teach him manliness, having had his balls blacked in ritual punishment by the prefects in the dormitory of the seamen's hostel, and then polished, to his everlasting shame, with a softer brush, buggered by a ship's steward and finally expelled for short-sightedness as pretext, he stood in the lean-to shed with the black fingers stretching over his head and the thrush singing on the pear tree, amongst the flowers of the small plot of garden before the four kitchen windows. He could smell the smell of baking and felt the air of festivity inside the house. He stood thus with his hands in his pockets, held up as a man, by means of the chain and the ship's steward and the sinking sun. His name was Jeremy, shortened to Jenny. This was a period of rest while he considered what to do.

The mother called from the kitchen window:
What are you doing, Jeremy?

He looked out of the shed at her:
Nothing.
Would you like a scone?

He went into the house and took a rough browned scone from the wire tray. There was tea made. He drank a cup and wolfed the scone then went out again cheerfully and back up the yard to the cratch and the two pulleys.

When he asked the ship's steward home at first it was as a boxer. They had met in a gym in Hull. The boy admired the boxer and loved him so he asked him home to meet his mother. The steward was much older than Jeremy but the parents were impressed by their son's ability to command the friendship of a man so mature and well suited. So they talked to him deferentially, feeling it odd and glad that their son had found such a respectable friend to look after him. They were a little overawed by his manners.

The steward was thick-set and had greased black hair, carefully combed and a little scented. He had a gold wrist-watch with a gold strap, the dial turned to the inside of the wrist. Jenny moved his watch round too. The steward had explained to him that it was to protect the dial if you were working. They swaggered thus together. The boy, in uniform, with his golden anchor glowing, the man, broad-shouldered, wasp-waisted, in a blue gaberdine suit, with his wrist-watch turned to the inside, walking down the High Street together for the benefit of the girls the boy had known at school.

They walked out one evening 'to see my father's field'. It was over the fen bridge, out of the village. They talked about boxing as they went. When they climbed over the gate to get into the field and were walking behind the thick hawthorn hedge the man twisted out his right arm, turning the white of the wrist upward to expose the dial of the watch and said, 'I'll give you five minutes.

Jenny took off his coat. The steward rolled up his sleeves and they sparred. He stood still while the boy danced round him, shooting out lefts and looking levelly over the right fist guarding his jaw. Suddenly the man fell heavily on the boy; dazed him with a right to the temple, encircled him in his brawny arms. The boy could feel something hard pressing into his thigh. They stood chest to chest, the man pressing his loins against the boy; he trying to twist away, crying, good-humouredly at first, Hey... this isn't boxing, smelling the scent of the man's hair, feeling his breath.

They fell to the ground, the man on top of the boy and pressing down on him, into him.
Hey! Jenny kept saying, Hey! And then, suddenly, in a spasm of loathing, brought up his knee into the man's balls to free himself.

They stood up, Jenny put his jacket on.
Did you feel anything Jenny? the steward asked.

When?
Just now.
No?
Didn't you feel anything hard?
No. Then. Come on, we'll be late for dinner, and over the gate to wait on the road while the steward rolled down the sleeves of his nylon shirt and slipped into his padded jacket.

The man put his hand on the boy's shoulder as they went back down the road and the boy felt comforted. They made the rendezvous that night but Jenny dozed off and remained intact until other violence was offered him in Hull.

He hooked the bottom pulley of one of the blocks suspended from the beams on to the handle of the cratch and pulled. The handle lifted, tilted and slid off. He tried putting the bottom hook of the other block on to the handle diagonal to the other and pulling them up together. But it was an inadequate support. The cratch lifted and its legs dangled like a dead animal's, but it was not stable. He lowered it again and went into the house to get some of the thick white string they used for sewing meat. He looped this round each pair of handles many times so that he made a rope and then hooked the pulleys on to the rope and started to pull. He sat on the cratch as it lifted, the chain of one set of pulleys in each hand; pulling down with one hand while he held the other still, then trapping the length of chain under his haunch so that it wouldn't run out as he let go and reached up to take it near the top hook again. There was no rattling sound now of the wheels running easily and no time to enjoy such perception. The muscles of arms and the weight of body trapping the chain held him aloft. The cratch was no more than three or four inches from the ground by this time but with his hand warming and his breath coming shorter the boy felt anxious not to let it sink down.

He pulled with his left hand, rolling over on to his right haunch, to take as much weight as possible from the other end, giving himself a straighter pull to hold the right hand pulley more easily. He felt the drama of the unlevel, changing attitudes of the cratch. It seemed to him that there was no alternative either to sailing or butchering. Such jobs as had been suggested to him, policeman, schoolmaster, bank clerk, were beyond his experience. He knew nothing of the lives of such people and was not equipped to choose. The policeman he had seen his father bribe with a liver, the schoolmaster had first encouraged him to draw pictures of the sea. Sitting on the cratch, suspended in mid-air, levelling the board top, to tilt it again, he was safer and more knit together. Two birds singing; above him the sky of Lincolnshire, streaked with red and magnificent, through the black rafters; below him the concrete floor he had made with his father, over broken asphalt. Sitting, he could feel the saw cuts and the grooves marked in the wood by the cleaver. The backs of his knees folded over the serrated edge. On the handles there were marks of grease. There was blood settled into some of the cracks which had been opened up in the wood by the boiling water when they scalded pigs, or by the weight of four quarters of beef, cracking down. His hands moulded to the chains. The muscles of his fingers ached and yearned. He worked himself higher, up to the roof, nearing the rafters and looked about. His tiring arms failed at first to respond to the efforts he made. He was in an awkward position for pulling, facing right with his feet dangling. He brought his legs up and swivelled round to face out of the front of the shed, seeking the lawn and the apple tree and the dinghy through the network of chains hooked on to the string rope which spanned the handles. He was sitting on the chain of the pulley behind him. He jerked up the front suddenly, hauling in the chain, hand over hand, collecting it in a tangled pool between his legs, feeling it there, holding it with his thighs. His back pressed against the taut chains behind him. The string rope holding the back handles slipped up near the join with the square top. He was cramped forward, his feet up, the cratch swaying and the dust powdering from the rafters as they creaked with a weight they had not born before. He sang, thinking of the waves round the trawler in the Arctic, swaying, the chains giving out, notch by notch, pulling them back and then releasing his grip to let them rush through the wheels of the pulleys, suddenly lowering one end or other as though he were plunging into the trough of a wave. 'Five points east', pulling the front chain, lurching his body to the left. The cratch rocked sideways and undulated forwards in a complex movement. The boy felt it and kept it going by following it with his body. Wind began to blow through the chains rigged in front and behind. Water spread over the concrete. Fish appeared. There were dolphins playing.

AMBY

At the top of the steps out of the Victoria Station, silhouetted, one glove off, ready to shake his hand, fat, wearing an overcoat heavy enough to smother him, Amby, and Jenny, the ticket in his hand and the leather grip, borrowed on a previous trip, one handle broken. The folding iron gate, narrowly opened, a return ticket, the round ticket office above him, to the left, like the bridge of a ship.

Hello Jenny. Did you have a good journey?

Shaking hands. The man's warm and thick, hard.

How are your father and mother?

Very well thank you. They sent their regards.

How's business? Still the same?

Dad says we're beginning to turn the corner.

Uncle Amby smiled, putting his tan glove on again. Three converging ridges, sewn up, on the back of it, imitation veins, buttoning the red button at the wrist.

They turned out into the light. A limousine parked in front of the Royal Station hotel.

Put your bag in the boot. I've got a surprise for you.

What?

You'll see.

High on an embankment here, overlooking the town, Attercliffe behind, the Norfolk market in front.

Traffic mingling from five or six roads at the bottom of the Victoria embankment.

Ha! Ha! There you are. What did I tell you? He won't hurt you.

Punch. Down! Get down. The dog yapped, its paws scrabbling on the back seat, leaping forward, nipping Jenny's ears, licking him, pushing at him with its cold nose. Amby was laughing. He had a kind face. He was square and soft. He was balding now. His hat off. He wore glasses. He smoked a pipe. He laughed shaking, breathing heavily when they got into the car, took off the glove again to heave himself to one side while he struggled with short thick fingers for the car keys, for his matches, lit the pipe, threw his trilby into the back, at the dog. The dog worried it, growling, leave it, leave it. And left it, put its paws on the back of Jenny's seat and licked his ears. He liked it. The dog's tongue was warm, his wet nose cold. The tongue pulled slightly at the flesh of the boy's ears, of his cheek. He laughed, tickled, Get down. Get down. Argh. Grrr. Get back you hound. That quietens him. He won't hurt you. Look at him. He knows who his boss is. The dog crouched on the back seat, watching Amby, who looked at it. Who made as if to hit him with the back of his hand, suddenly, quick, raised it. The dog shrank from him. But it was a game. When he turned to the wheel the dog put its front paws on the back of Jenny's seat again nibbled his ears.

Give up. He pushed it away. But it came back. Jenny sat forward on the seat, half twisted round, holding the dog from him.

Give up.

Ha! Ha! He won't hurt you. He wants to play. Saliva trembling from the jowl of the dog. Yapping. Ha! Ha! Ha! Ha! Are you frightened of him? He's only a pup. A bit excitable. He won't hurt you. Play with him. He wants to play. The dog's strong breath, wet on Jenny's cheek the sticky saliva. Shaking his head away, leaning forward so that the paws scratched

for him on the cream leather seat.
What do you call him? Laughing. Stop it! Ha! Ha!
Stop it. Stop it.
What? What's his name?
Punch.
Ha! Ha! Give up. Stop it. His hand in the slack flesh under the neck, under the dripping jowl, at the back of the neck, pulling it away from the flesh beneath. That shows he's healthy. Ha! Ha! Ha! Ha! stop it. The dog yapping. Its bark high. Excited. He's taken to you. You'll be company for him. I haven't the time to look after him. He'll get rid of some of his energy while you're here. It isn't often that he takes to people. He won't leave you alone now. You've made a friend of him. You've no need to be afraid of him, you know. If he annoys you, give it him. Good and hard. Teach him a lesson. It's the only way. Show him who's boss. He won't bite. He's still a pup. Like all thoroughbreds he's very highly strung. Don't worry about him. You'll get on all right. Down. Down now, Punch. Down. Get down. The dog crouched back again. Jenny smiling. Watching the town moving beyond the glass.
I thought we might have lunch out of town somewhere. What do you say? Jenny smiles softly. He wipes his neck and ears with a white handkerchief. He smelt the dog's smell on him. They moved smoothly away, down the long embankment, in front of the station, down, towards the tram lines, towards the wholesale warehouse of W. H. Smith, round, sharp to the left, a black road down into Attercliffe towards the steel works, past small engineering works, a wholesale frozen meat depot. Across, carefully, the tram lines

and up the hill towards the Norfolk market. Ay. We'll go out of town for lunch. There's a nice little place at Balborough. Shall we go there? You don't say much. Are you pleased to be here then?
Jenny sits in his expensive jacket. The sun is warm through the windscreen. The leather comfortable and the smell of Uncle Amby's pipe fragrant on the air. He watches the people beyond the glass. Smiling, thinking. The comfort cushions his reverie.

There was a boy in a school blazer opposite, sitting at another table, with a tall grey-haired gentleman with a white moustache. He was watching Jenny. Who caught his eye. They stared at each other until Jenny blushed, he turned away his eyes. His head dropped. The blush burnt in his face and neck. He looked down at the tablecloth, fiddling with the chipped silver knives and forks, blushing. I'll go and wash my face and hands, I think. Out in the hall, at the reception desk, Excuse me could you tell me where the toilet is please? Second on the left sir, at the end of the corridor. And there in the fluorescent light he regained his composure. Back again. Surer. Not of the distinguished boy. But of Mr Powell.
Is Punch all right? I can hear him yapping. The smell of clean soap on him. The dog's smell gone. His hands free of the stickiness. As his ears and cheeks. He's all right. Don't worry about him. He wants to get home.
Jenny ate his duckling. Margaret brought him coffee. Cream, sir?
Yes please. Warmer, fuller, his own belly out, further out and more used to Uncle Amby, they left, tipping Margaret handsomely, Jenny leaving sixpence

of his own under his plate, to travel back into Sheffield, down through Holmsfield, Fulwood to Nether Edge. It was during the time of a general election and in the evening and late into the night they watched the results, sitting on the sofa, on television. Amby put his arm round Jenny.

Fetch me a glass of rum. And another. And another. Lemon Hart. From a crate in the pantry. Jenny willingly fetched more. A coke fire burned. The television room was hot, the furniture leather-covered, the ceiling darkened by smoke. The smell of tobacco and rum. They sat together and the man's warm arm was soft round the boy who put his head on his fat chest. Allowed the languor and the peace to steal in upon him, his way of dealing with worries thus to melt them into the moods of his body so that no edge of judgment remained. Dreaming, in front of the grey light of the television, Maggie, of his home, the dog on the sofa with them, warm against him. Time. Here. Time. The General Election. Gain and loss reported. Amby told Jenny he had loved his father when they were young, together, they walked. Best man at the wedding. I don't know what went wrong with your father. Something did. He never used to carry on like that. I was going to marry your mother you know, until he took her from me. Still the best man won, I suppose. I might have been your father. But I've nothing to regret. Nothing to look back on. With shame. I've done quite well when all's said and done. My life's a bit lonelier now than it was then but I still enjoy it. Might as well enjoy yourself while you can. Here today and gone tomorrow. Tears were in his eyes.

Shall I bring you another drink?
Jenny took the glass from the arm of the chair. I never married, why should I? There was only one woman for me and I lost her. I said I wouldn't marry until I could afford it and when I could afford it it was too late. Still, you can't have everything. I've got a lot to be thankful for. All the same. I've kept in touch. They sat together. Jenny felt Uncle Amby's warmth. His voice. His strength. He smelled the rum on his breath and the pipe in his mouth. His teeth were stained with nicotine. The room was dark. They reminisced while results were pending. They talked quietly. Jenny turned in towards Amby and put his arm across round his comfortable belly. His father and mother were young again. At Scarborough. For Easter. A photograph. Amby in a striped blazer, arm in arm with his mother, while a white-faced father strode out with them, carrying tennis rackets. Smiling. Smiling. Towards the camera. Easter. The wind high. The spray whipped over the sea wall. Laughing up to the castle. To watch the white spray on the sea. His mother's dress blew on to her body so that it showed along her breasts and legs. She danced and held the skirt down, laughing, the balloon's going up, her hand down the material, thuddering. While, oh while she laughed and shouted, while she danced and sang, while the air went into his father's chest and the colour rose in his white face and the black lank hair rose and staggered. Down, right, into the town. Hotels rising over the beach. People running at the edges of the waves. Women walking with their heads ducking down, sideways, with their heads pointed into the wind, a hand holding the wide

hat, the other the thin skirt down, flapping behind them with silk showing. They ate tea at a little old-fashioned café and laughed. Where his mother with her cheeks tingling and her hair wild, while his father out of breath, coughing, saying, Like wine, Like wine! Jenny and Amby laughed together. Jenny felt the tyres of flesh under the Aertex shirt with the open neck. Punch in the kitchen tied in his wicker basket. Watching Jenny when he went to fill the glass of rum.

On the walls of the house in bright oilcolours, pictures, of Chinese wizards, green, at the head of the stairs, with a girl naked but for a thin gauze cloth, on his knee, his hands with long nails on her thigh, on her breast, outlined, underneath the gauze. On the wall beside the bathroom door she was off his knee, running from him, naked, he was laughing and the gauze was in his hand. On the large wall beside the dining-room a naked Indian rode bare-backed a grey stallion.

The artist, Geoff, who worked for Mr Powell, was highlighting and shading in the horse's belly. Jenny watched them through the banisters. Punch was yapping and springing at the foot of the stairs, jumping up the first three or four stairs, his paws scratching, scrabbling, then down again, skidding on the lino, slipping, spreadeagled, on his belly, scrabbled to push himself off again, yapping, to get a grip, to spring, up, at Jenny. Get down. You bleeding cur. Amby. His arm raised. The dog leapt behind coats hanging beside the entrance. Jenny then came down. Shall I put a sex on him, Mr Powell?

Yes. Ay. I think you should. After all he is a stallion. You'd better not make it too conspicuous but we must be honest, I think.
The brush flexed and the bristles spread and the grey paint flowed from it at the join of the horse's thighs, a thick stroke, and then another in the same direction, his wrist resting on his padded rest, the bristles out like a fan, smoothing the paint down, turning, twisting, with a fine torque up to the belly at the end of the stroke. Then a little white, highlighting it, a little black, carefully, there. Do horses have hair?
I don't know. What do you think?
Shall I give him some hair?
After all he is a stallion. Ay. I think you'd better.
P'raps we'd better go and look at an 'oss.
Shall I make it a bit bigger?
I think that's enough, don't you?
He put away his paints and brushes.
And they stood back to argue the horse's points.
The dog was worrying a pair of grey socks, tied together, given to it for that purpose.
There was a marble statue of Rebecca at the Well in the hall, my wife, said Amby, fondling her cold breast, do you like her? Faithful. Never answers back. Doesn't cost a penny. Never buy her a new dress. Just dust her. That's all. Give her a wash every spring. If I get tired of her all I need do is put her in the dustbin. She's beautiful. Aren't you, love? Patting her cold bottom, his warm fat arm round her neck, my little missus, never says a word, no trouble at all, doesn't want to be taken out, always satisfied, doesn't mind what I do, do you dear? hey? darling? do you?

What do you call her?
Rebecca.
Rebecca?
Rebecca at the pump. Ha! Ha! When he laughed his eyes ran so that he had to take off his glasses and wipe them on a large red silk handkerchief. Oh dear. His tits shook while he giggled, and then he sneezed, five times, as he also did, always whenever he looked at the sun, Jenny watching fearful lest the sneezing should become a final apoplexy.

The tears rolled down Amby's face so easily. Talking through the sobbing. He squeezed his eyes, finger and thumb, at the bridge of the nose and continued, When I did ask her she'd decided to marry your father. She was beautiful to look at then. I've often wished that it had been me. I'd like to have been your father and your brothers. I'd have made a good husband. I know I shouldn't boast but I think I would have been able to look after your mother. But there was my mother to think of. Your grandmother. She was a real lady. Always spick and span. Impeccable. Nobody could touch her. I never saw her with a hair out of place. I always said I'd look after her when my Dad was gone and I did. She married beneath her. She was brought up a lady. I used to say to her, Mother why did you marry my Dad? But she never told me why. I think it must have been on the rebound. Poor old lad he could neither read nor write. They did say that if he'd been able to write his name he would have come into a very large fortune. I can well believe it. He was a very aristocratic-looking man. There was something about him. They were both a cut above the ordinary. But my mother, my poor old mother, you'll understand when you lose yours, Jenny. You've only got one mother. There's nobody ever like your mother. It was cancer. You know that, don't you. She suffered. I've never seen suffering like that. When my turn comes I hope I shall go quickly. She was a wonderful woman. She had a lot to put up with what with one thing and another unemployment and thirteen children to feed. She wouldn't let me smoke in the house until I was past thirty and then I had to have a row about it. She had her principles. Poor old lass. She never sat at the table in her whole life without doing her hair first and taking her apron off. She went dressed like a queen. I said to her, Mother I'm going to ask you whether you'll mind if I smoke. I'll ask once and not again. I think I'm old enough now to make up my own mind, don't you, love? After all I am thirty.

The way I was brought up the men went into another room to smoke. You can either give it up or go out to the shed.

That was when I was thirty. I didn't mean any disrespect.

You know that, don't you, Mother. You know I think the world of you. You know I love you. I'll never touch another woman while you're alive, Mother. You know that. That I respect you too much to bring any other woman here. I do love you, Mother. But you won't mind will you if I don't ask you every time I want a smoke?

Well, Ambrose, I suppose you'll please yourself.

You're offended, aren't you?

I don't want to tie you down. I won't be a burden to you, you know that. If you stay with me after he's

gone it will be of your own free will.
Yes, Mother. I know. I know. I know you won't.
If you could find a nice girl, a really nice girl, one to make you a good wife after I'm gone.
There's years yet, let's not talk about that, let's be cheerful, shall I play you a hand of crib?
We were happy together then. I took her out a lot. We used to go to Richmond to the theatre, Harrogate, Matlock, Buxton. I took her to Barlborough occasionally. She was always beautifully dressed. I felt that proud to be with her. It was best that she should go though, as she did. The doctor said there was no hope, she begged me to put an end to her.
His tears fall into his Aertex shirt, sobs choke his voice:
She asked me to put an end to her. Please, she said. Please, Ambrose. She always called me Ambrose. Anything but this, Ambrose. Show me you love me. This is the last thing I shall ever ask you to do for me. You'll be free then. I can't hold on any longer. I'm tired. I want to rest now, son. I want to sleep. I'm old now. I want to rest. I shan't hinder you any more now.
You've never hindered me, Mother. Don't leave me. Don't leave me. You're the only person I've got to cling to. You know I love you. Don't say that, Mother. You've never hindered me.
Do you want another drink?
Mute, he proffered the glass, blowing his nose into the large red handkerchief. I loved her, Jenny. I thought the world of her. The doctor got it for me. She went on pleading. She was in terrible pain. It's a terrible thing to see. She just wasted away. Her

eyes were as big as saucers. His tears were wet in Jenny's hair. His face had collapsed. The veins were red in the slack flesh under his eyes. He took off his glasses and with finger and thumb pinched the eyes across the bridge of his nose, in which veins like wire-worms straggled about. Then dried his eyes with the inside of his wrist again as he put back the glasses. The pipe bubbling, wet, flecked with the whitish spittle, flicked the phlegm into the fire where it hissed. I asked the doctor. Get it for her, doctor. She can't last any longer. She's in terrible pain. It tears my heart out to see her suffer. She pleads with me. I can't stand it any longer. Every time I go up that's all she asks. That's all she thinks about. That's all she wants. Please, doctor. Put her out of her misery. It's cruel to keep her alive. He left me some medicine. Be careful not to give her too much, he said. If you only give her a bit too much she'd be too weak to resist it, I think. Call me at once when you need me. He shook hands with me. Thank you, doctor. Thank you. He'd left it on the kitchen table. I poured out about three times as much as the dose written on the label and went up and said Here you are, love. The doctor's left some new medicine. Go to sleep now. I put me arm round her to sit her up so that she could take it from the spoon. She was as grateful as a little baby. She was that light. And fresh. She was all white. Go to sleep now, love, I said and laid her down again. She died in her sleep. Well, there's no use crying over spilt milk. It was a release. Well. That's all water under the bridge now.

Aren't they beautiful pictures in the hall and on the

stairs? Amby was laughing. Jenny could feel his breasts shaking.
What are you laughing at?
I was thinking of Geoff wanting to know whether he should put the sex on the stallion. Jenny too laughed. They snuggled together through the long evening of television, in the soft metallic light and the red glow of the electric fire, the fan inside the painted logs revolving to create the flicker and shadow of flames.

As Jenny returned from the bathroom in his pyjamas Amby walked out of his bedroom. His long sex dangling beneath the loose hem of the vest and his fat white arse bobbed to the bathroom, the crack vertical, tight, the hams jammed together. He slept in rough blankets in a soft bed surrounded by damask curtains and Persian rugs. Beside his bed golden cupidons peeped out of an automatic teamaker. Beside the teamaker there was a photograph of his mother. A tall Japanese screen. His clean underclothes were arranged on a chair.

Alone, Amby out, Jenny felt the blankets and lay on the eiderdown, sank into the luxury, felt the pile of the rugs, looked in the drawers, behind the screen, found magazines of naked women, started to the window when he heard a car. The flesh of the girls on the walls cream in colour. He felt the brush strokes. Punch followed him, racing, scrabbling on the polished lino, barking, jumping, the saliva hanging elastic on each side of his soft black jowl. In the wardrobe in Amby's room there were long dresses and the smell of mothballs, there were ladies' silk underclothes in the drawers at the bottom of the wardrobe, broad felt hats with wavy brims and feathers in them, black straw hats, a row of pairs of buttoned shoes. He listened. The flimsy stuff of the dresses brushed his cheek, the back of his hand. He shut the door, startled, at a car door slamming in the street. And grew quiet, holding his breath. Amby. No. There was a blue coat frogged with braid like a hussar's jacket, tarnished, the cloth pulling away too weak for the braid. Quiet here in the room. And there were pots in a glass cupboard, blue, with Chinese dragons mouthing flames and delicate feathering of blue landscape, raised a little from the pot surface, feeling the paint with a fingernail. His grandmother. His mother detested her. All he knew. He put back the folds where he had disturbed them. The car stopped. Amby. He heard the car door slam. He was at the door, the knob in one hand, bending down, holding Punch who was straining forward, yapping, by the collar, he opened the door, to meet him: Hello.

Whoops. Down, Punch. Down. Lie down. Yes.

I've been reading, a book arranged open in the television room.

Hello. Jenny. Geoff was with Amby and a girl. This is Mary. A lovely girl with full breasts in a close-fitting dress with a flared skirt, scent, smelling it, bending down, holding Punch, his paws scrabbling towards him, bending towards him, her belly moving underneath the dress, there, under the dress and an edge of her petticoat. Stop it, Punch, Get down, hitting him with the flat of his hand. Like a flood of warm water, as though he had slipped naked into a warm bath came in the lovely woman, into his mind like a warm breath. Smiling at her, loving her, her hair shining, long, blonde, and she saying, Hello Jenny. Smiling. Get down. Laughing. Ow. Ouch. Laughing, watching, Jenny watching, she was pulling her skirt away from the dog, slapping it away, a lovely woman, open, supple like a long slack line, like a full line slack and easy. Amby put his green trilby on the cold marble head of Rebecca. At tea in the kitchen, holding the hot cup, listening, watching. Mary was to sleep in his bed, he was to sleep in the box room. Geoff with Amby. She had long long blonde hair which later she let down and brushed sitting chatting watching television. Jenny bringing the drinks. She drank Advocat. He listened to the brush crackle through her lovely hair, smooth. In bed then he waited with his door open watching the light under her door, naked in his bed. Geoff and Amby were already asleep. He had watched the procession to the bathroom. Mary in a long flowing housecoat. In his white pants now, having left his pyjamas under her pillow, he tapped softly at the door till she softly said, Jenny?

Yes.

Come in.

There lying flat out with the sheet round her waist, propped up by the pillow, the blankets falling to show the form of her legs and her lovely bosom heaving up into the delicate filigree of the lace, the dark point of her nipples, there, there, oh there, her soft shoulders and the flat and ridges of her ribs and belly. Jenny light, thin, smiling, soft, looking, her long soft arm, her warm smell, she was holding his green pyjamas. There you are. Her eyes soft and smiling, watching him, her shining blonde hair, spread over the white

pillow. Her eyes over his body, kindly, round his shoulders, and one by one, over his ribs, on his thighs and legs and on his naked feet.
Aren't you cold?
No. He felt his sides. His arms wrapped round, crossed. Her warm smell rose like a cloud from the bed, her warm soft smell, like a scent from the garden, like soft wind in an orchard where there is water, where light burns in pools of light, in luxury of light flecking, in rattle of leaves, clean, fresh, where sound is sharp. Where music makes peaceful peaceful people. Where flesh touches flesh and remains, where the warmth makes women blush with heat, rose. There. A lark, straight up. There. There. Singing, so still that he could hear the beating, flickering, of its wings. Quiet sounds, legs, white legs, heads thrown back, inclined, springing. Jenny standing holding himself yearning towards her.
Can I kiss you?
Yes. She opened her arms and he came into them, his head enveloped in the softness of her breast while she stroked his hair. Jenny's cold. He kissed her lips. Her big face. Scent. Enveloped.

She pulled the sheet over her body and snuggled warmly into the bed, her face soft with the pleasure, her chin down, mmmmmmm. Good night. He went back to his own bed in the box room where he slept dreaming she was touching him.

How many eggs? Amby, holding a poacher in which there were six shallow cups to insert in holes over a reservoir of water. Only one. Tired. Tired of the dog which never stopped worrying. There were six eggs on Uncle Amby's willow pattern plate, several slices of bacon, tomatoes, slices of black pudding. He could hear his teeth champing, the tea moistening the sound into a squelch as he drank with his mouth full, already more on his fork. Can you get it yourself? There was ginger hair on the top of his shoulders. His ringed hand patted his folding stomach as he finished. You're up early. For Jenny had now developed the habit of staying late in bed. I'll be back for lunch. Take Punch for a walk.

Can I come with you?

Hurry up.

He sat in the car throughout the morning, Punch licking his ears, while Uncle Amby attended to his business affairs. The smell of the pipe and of the leather of gloves and the deep upholstered seats, wearing the stained blue mackintosh, his face wan and his expression glazed. Poor Jenny. Watching. Finally to a variety of banks into which he entered to watch the money deposited. Towards noon a look of more open and active pleasure began to dawn. They went out of the town to a restaurant in a wood before which there were acres of lawn disposed in planes, rhododendron bushes and at the bottom of the long slope down which it had become his delight to run with Punch, a lake, kept in by blackened stone bordered by high beeches, the edge of the estate. Here too there was a deferential waitress. He had learned to sit confidently and to tell her what he wanted. Beneath his jacket he wore a Fair Isle pullover like his uncle's. Strolling in the grounds after lunch they took pictures. Jenny with a small box camera and the uncle with a varied apparatus of instruments for measuring light. Photographing the silver roots of a beech two university students passed them walking quickly and talking loudly but he failed to hear what they were saying. There were beech nuts on the ground. Here the dog ran. He threw a stick for it which it brought back and finally lay at his feet, panting, its pink tongue lolling over the clear white of its fangs. The fallen leaves smelt damp, strong. The air was fresh. Wind rushed in trees. Or rather brushed for this afternoon was quiet. Autumn but the sun shining. The sound of leaves dropping, of his feet through them, an oasis here in the middle of the city, formerly the private park of a steel magnate, now taken over by the Corporation for civic receptions, ordinary guests admitted when no official function was planned. The red water of the Rivelin coming down the narrow valley. The blood of the iron carried down there by the water into the heart of the town where it had served to turn grindstones to sharpen cutlery. And Jenny here listening and watching his uncle busied about his cameras with his pipe in his mouth and the long afternoon before them in which they might visit another house open to the public or just take a drive through the moors.

And in the house on their return with what pleasure poor Jenny smelt the odour of tobacco in the television room. How soft and open his face. He brought Amby's slippers to watch him push himself to the edge of the leather-covered chair, to fiddle with the laces of his veldtschoen. And he knelt to untie the lace, pull off the man's shoes from the fragrant sock tightly held up by the suspender, put on the leather slippers. Amby tired after their stroll.

Will you fetch me a bottle of rum?
Yes. Sitting deep in the chair he offered three pound notes to his nephew. He took them, put the choker lead on Punch, and went out into the quiet of the evening, walking with the dog to the off-licence, looking over privet hedges, over landscaped gardens in which dwarfs and pit animals conducted a bewildered dialogue with each other while their owners through leaded panes ate tea. All unknown. Except in the shop to which he had been many times before.
How's Mister Powell?
Very well thank you.
The usual is it?
Yes, please.
That's a lovely dog.
Yes it is, isn't it.
Yes.
Yes.
So into the comfortable light of the television and the service he might perform in bringing the beakers of Lemon Hart to soften Uncle Amby's sense of loss. Until he grew in this quiet and regular comfort to love the man. The image coming on the white paper, rubbing for it with a finger to ensure that no air bubble left a white spot. The roots of trees and the exteriors of churches. Jenny sank into this well-being. People thought that he looked like his uncle.
Is that your son, Mr Powell?
He does look like you.
Am I his son? Jenny shocked. Startled, unnerved. He was growing fat here. His belly in his Fair Isle pullover and his interest in photography. The dog tore at him now as always. He took pleasure when

fetching the rum to drag at the choker so that the breath rasped out of its throat. He beat it with the end of the lead to train it. Heel, Heel. But the dog fought him. Dragged. Coughed and dragged at the lead.

Have you adopted him then, Amby? Mrs Dunmore whom they went up to see one afternoon. How long's he been here now? Her eyebrows plucked and the thin black arch of the painted line gleaming on the puffed ridged flesh of the brow. Her face like wax. Her lips red shining with the spittle on them and her nails red like fangs.

He reminds me of Mother sometimes, said Amby and she put her own jewelled fingers over his to pat him and say,

You thought a lot about her didn't you, love.

There's a look he has sometimes.

The dog showed its fangs and snarled when he hit it with the hawthorn walking-stick. Alone then in the house. Punch at the top of the stairs, snarling. He fled when Jenny went up with the lash. His paws scrabbled on the lino, scratched, scraped, hollow on the skirting-board and then slithered as Jenny took his collar and dragged him with it across the lino, his four paws stuck out straight forward, braced. Down the stairs to the basket in the kitchen where he pulled him over the side, into it, Sit, Sit! Jenny with his leash high, willing the dog to obey him, glaring at him, poised, waiting, Stay there. Down. The dog watching him his head on one side, saliva drooling from his soft black muzzle. Down.

Away. Jenny lashed at him. The dog squealed,

yapped, skidded, slithered round the bottom of the stairs, up then, up, into Ambrose's bedroom. Jenny, blind, followed it, under the bed, its teeth were bared, it snarled at him, snapped at his hand when he reached for its collar, drew blood. Come out. Come out. Cur. You bloody cur. He grasped a long bamboo cane with a feather duster on the end of it, poked at the dog, who stayed put. He pushed him across the lino. There was dust under the bed. Get out. Get out. The dog watched him with bloodshot eyes, growling, quietly. Down the stairs again. In the kitchen. The boy's hand was in his collar. He was twisting it into the slack flesh of the neck. Twisting. The dog's tongue lapped out. It was trying to turn round its head to bite but the teeth only grazed the flesh, the angle too oblique, unable to get a purchase. The pointed white teeth there beside his hand. Its breath rasped. He beat it with the plaited leash. With the chain of the choke. The dog screaming and Jenny lost to himself. Cur! CUR! The slack skin moved over the flesh underneath, the collar slipping over an ear, the dog with its head on one side, dragging away twisting, the teeth were coming round, snapping, closer to his hand. He beat it. Beat it. Beat it. In black rage. The collar slipped off. Away up the stairs again. Jenny did not follow him, but put his bleeding hand under the tap and let the cold water chill it, drank then with his mouth under the tap, letting the water stun his face. Uncle Amby came back. Jenny moved quickly to take up a book in the chair. Punch's collar came off, he said. I couldn't catch him again.
Never mind. Did you have a good day?
Yes thank you.

What are you reading.
Nothing much.
I've had a long day.
I'll make you some tea.
Jenny handed him the cup. Amby, puffing, was bending down undoing his shoelaces, taking off his shoes, easing his feet into his slippers. He levered himself up from the chair, slipped to the edge of the seat then pushed himself up, the two veldtschoen dangling. He ambled out. To put his shoes beside the cooker in the kitchen. Jenny looked at him, fat and quiet with his slack double chin and the lower lip folded down underneath the pipe he sucked.
I like Mary, Jenny said.
Amby chuckled but looked surprised, watched the boy, frowning.
What do you mean?
When's she coming again?
When Geoff brings her.
Why didn't he bring her last time?
You'd better ask him.

Jenny sat in a separate chair. He watched Amby who was quiet, quietly smoked, quietly watched the flickering picture, listened to the politicians interviewed, comments made on the results of the election, on reasons for, on how, when, why, past, future. He was pale and did not look at the boy. Drank rum. Though at last he said, Yes. She's a nice girl. She'll make him a good wife. His square cut nails. His gold signet ring. Solid, comfortable flesh a bit hard, a bit brittle. Crackling. Holding his glass on the arm of the leather chair and his pipe burbling. Looking at the grey light of television, one elbow propped on the

chair arm, that hand with the finger crooked over the stem of the pipe. Holding the other arm with the other hand. And Jenny. Jenny lost, trying to watch the television. Both Amby and Jenny keeping their attention on the television. Watching the lines graining the picture in the screen. Amby sucking his pipe, drinking, lumbering to his feet to fill his own glass. Jenny going on watching the television. Why does he sleep with Geoff? But thinking of Mary, alone in the house with him once, washing her hair, a towel over her bare shoulders. Drying it. Pummelling her head with the towel in both hands. Rubbing. Mmmmmmm. She. The bitter scent of the shampoo, fresh and soft and warm and downy. Like a soft bird. Her feel like the breast of a goose, downy. Here Amby's squelching softness. Looking now at Jenny. Glancing at him. What's up? What's the matter?
Nothing. Why does Geoff sleep with him? Why doesn't he sleep in my room? In the other twin bed. What do they do? Where's Mary? Why doesn't she come so often now? What's wrong?
There's something up.
No there isn't. And as the evening drew to its close there was only the sound of the announcer saying Good night to which Uncle Amby replied, Good night.
I'm tired, Jenny said and went to bed.
Amby followed to the foot of the stairs,
Shall we go out for the day tomorrow? Where would you like to go?
I don't know. At the head of the stairs the pale face of the Chinese wizard confronted him and at the bottom the bloated and moist face of part of his own flesh and blood.

Where's Mary? he said to Geoff who in reply knocked up Jenny's hand in which he held a cream puff and covered his face with cream. Amby laughed. He got you that time!
I'll kick his bleeding teeth in! Jenny, trembling. They laughed.
I've had enough of this.
Amby was plucking at his knees.
Don't be daft. It was a joke. He didn't mean any harm. Held his knee in a pincer grip and said Submit.
Don't be such a baby. Here. Go to the pictures if you want to. Jenny left them. Amby was washing the tea things. Geoff was sitting in the television room, reading the evening paper.
Amby solicitous for his comfort cooking for him. Good meals. Taking pleasure in his eating. The boy hard, tense, volunteering nothing. Watching him. Abrupt.

Amby developing the habit of grabbing his knees, squeezing the nerve over the knee-cap. Making him laugh then. Ha! Ha! Get off. The dog yapping and jumping up while Jenny and Amby struggle. Its voice high with excitement. Saliva elastic drooling from its soft muzzle. Wrestling the dog on the carpet, rolling over and over with it, clasped to his bosom, while it yapped and nibbled, licked, drooled, nipped, bit. Ouch! That's enough now. But Jenny with his fists clenched punched and kicked at the dog, into a corner, took hold of the collar, Bloody brute, dragged it over the lino, four feet stuck out, holding back, into the kitchen, took down the leash, held him and hit him, hit him, hit him, until he had finished. The dog squealing, yapping. Smack. Smack. Of the wicker basket against the cooker. Stop it. Stop it. Stop that, Jenny. That's enough now. He didn't mean it. I'll kill him. I'll kill him.

That's enough. Punch crouched. His chin flat out on the cushion, his eyes bloodshot. Jenny stroked him. The dog leapt up, stood, trembling, wagging its tail, excited. He tickled the dog's ears. Scratched its belly. Smelt it. Hairs on the sleeves of his jacket. All right, Amby said. All right.

They drove about the town while Ambrose paid calls, business calls on business people. Jenny sat quietly in the car. Comfortable. Too hot. Watching through the windows. The dog scrabbling in the back seat, its long pink tongue out, panting, looking out between them. Jenny sat watching the traffic. Amby smoked, changing gear, with the column lever, with open-gloved palm pushing upward. Alone again Jenny wandered about the house looking into drawers, looking for magazines, under the eyes of the Chinese wizard, the gallopping stallion facing Rebecca whose breast he fondled. A round diminishing mirror on the end wall contained both.

Mary came back. To stay with another girl. She had broken with Geoff. Jenny loved her. He was elated. Springy. But he must sleep with Amby for Mary's friend must have his bedroom. Mary and Amby smiled at each other for Amby was so good to her and she was so grateful. Jenny chattered at tea. He dressed up in costumes afterwards to entertain them. They all laughed. The two girls sat together on the sofa. Amby seemed relaxed and good-humoured. He teased the girls who in turn teased him. Mary's friend was a tall blonde, running to fat with big breasts and big hips which Jenny's eyes fondled. She flitted from bedroom to bedroom wearing only stockings and suspender belt. She smiled at him as she saw him watching her. She walked slowly back, past him, drawing her hand through his hair.

Amby was waiting for him. Jenny put on his pyjamas and climbed up into the luxurious bed. The soft rough blankets were pleasantly warm. Amby's shoulders crossed by the spring vest poked out. His back was turned. Jenny turned away and lay quiet. Breathing regularly. Remained. But felt Amby's hand on his hip and then groping round inside his pyjamas but he grunted pretending sleep as though about to wake and turned to lie on his belly while the hand returned to its master. Thus unconsummated they sleep until morning.

Amby was up early. He cooked a large breakfast for Jenny. Who ate it.

Did you have a good night's sleep?

Yes. It's a comfortable bed, you feel as if you could go down for ever. When will Mary be up?

I don't know, soon.

I'm going home today.

What time's the train?

The girls came down. Laughing. Amby grew jocular with them, fathering them, cooking for them, keeping them with him.

He took his glasses off to shake hands with Jenny at the station. The eyes bloodshot and the nose having wire-worms of red veins straggling accross it, the green trilby which he had taken from its resting place on Rebecca's marble head, on his head and the leather gloves with their three veins held in one hand, Remember me to your father and mother, he said and Jenny watched him diminish, lonely on the platform, holding his dog.

They handed him a triangular sandwich. Mrs Dunmore's red hand, on which clinked charms, signs of the zodiac, snakes, horseshoes, a little naked woman, the Lincoln Imp, Big Ben, and the Houses of Parliament. It came over her black fur shoulder. Jenny took the sandwich and ate it. She opened the flask. The hollow plastic and the glass moving against each other inside the thin case. Like a quiet turkey the coffee slopped into the mug, she handed that to him, then another sandwich. He shifted what remained of the first sandwich into his mouth, to take the other, the plastic cup hot, burning his fingers, resting it against the window through which now the landscape snakes past. They are on the way to Blackpool. Down, round a bend, a stone wall, ivy on it, house, yellow, a yellow beacon, then out, out into flat fields and the hills before them mounting, the road leading to them and the cloud flat and the sky suffused by the elegiac light of the sun. Lancashire. A straight road before them to Blackpool, to the Conference.

The hot coffee slopped over his hand. He sucks the damp from the back of his hand, nibbles at the hairs. Mrs Dunmore's neck is settling into her sleek black fur. Beside Jenny is Timothy and driving, his uncle. Mr Dunmore gone on by train, a chief delegate with a chain of office, to arrange the social functions.
Would you like another one, Jeremy?
No thank you, Mrs Dunmore. Comfortable, in the navy blue mackintosh, something respectable the uncle had bought him.
He does look smart.

So as not to let me down. Down. Underneath there was a brown tweed sports coat his father had given him.
Go on then, have it, bugger it, how much? It'll do. And new flannels, the mother anxious to turn him out well.
He opened the belt of the coat and the jacket button, settled. We'll be there before dark. Through the flat of St Anne's along the coast. The grass a steady green. The grey road. The grey stone of houses. Look out for Blackpool Tower, Jeremy and Timothy beside him, Timothy, wearing the blazer and cap of Worksop College, a public school.
What are you going to be when you grow up, Timothy?
I think I shall take up medicine.
And Jeremy? What will he do?
Mrs Dunmore's head half round, looking at him, through the bulging gristle of a yellowing eye. Smiling at her,
Yes Jeremy, what will you be?
Who? Me?
Yes.
What will you be? He's been dreaming. Thinking of a lass, I'll bet. Their shoulders shake and their necks redden. They laugh. He likes them. Enjoys their laugh.
What will you be?
What will I be? Circumstances don't alter cases.
Uncle Harold. In Australia having sold up at the age of eighty to die with his wife in the loving embrace of a favourite daughter, who had, though, got on. He wrote after arriving:
Why should I give them the trouble of burying me?

I'll see you on the other side of the great divide, lad, he had said to his father and kissed him on the cheek. Kissed him. And his father kissed him back with moist eyes for as he said Harold had been good to him when he was a lad and had taught him a lot. He was a man of character. The foreman of a steel foundry for thirty years. Statuesque. White-haired. Erect. As a young man he had been under the Niagara Falls sealed inside a barrel. But the favourite daughter did not welcome them feeling as she said, ashamed that her father was so vulgar. His wife developed dermatitis out there and was compelled to wear white gloves. So they stayed for the two years necessary to honour their free passage and returned crestfallen to live I think in Bridlington with an unfavourite daughter who took them into her lodging house. They had not visited her when she was in an asylum because they thought she was vulgar. Her husband too, a bus driver, a psychopathic Communist, who beat her and left her without food or clothing for weeks on end. Now, waiting impatiently for death Aunt Queenie in white gloves, nervously fidgeting because she can no longer knit and Uncle Harold reading his manual of Pelmanist psychology to formulate to himself now in the hour of his death a sense as he calls it of perspective, while the savagery of their daughter's husband, abated by his having lost his faith, broods over them and their daughter grateful at last for this opportunity to show them her love, serves them with devotion. Jenny rode out with her, on bicycles, when she came on a visit, in a warm spring, a girl, fluent, laughing with his father, whose rich affection quietened her and steadied her so that made more satisfied by the

love she was able to lavish on Jenny, she was returned to Sheffield where soon afterwards that bus driver broke her spirit.
I thought your Aunty Queenie was my mother till my real mother belted me and told me it was her. She was twenty years older than me. She was a lovely pianist when she was a girl. He leans forward holding his bare elbows, collar and tie on the mantelpiece and thus comfortably the firelight flickers on his own gold marriage ring:
Poor old lass. They've never written since they were back in England. Too ashamed. A man who's been independent all his life.
Mrs Dunmore and the uncle their shoulders shake,
Dreaming of his lost love.
Don't be silly, Amby, he's not old enough.
We're precocious in our family.
What's he going to be?
I don't know. I can't get owt out of him. Ask him again.
She turns to me. That yellow and bulging eye, the wax of her cheek,
What are you going to be, Jeremy?
What shall I be?
He's always smiling. She watches him. Look, he's always smiling, smiler.
He's good-natured, isn't he?
Doesn't he know what he wants to be then?
I know what I want to be. Again they laugh.
Or where. She says Ha. Ha. Ha. Ha.
Give up I can't drive.
Ee, we do have some fun. The red neck came out and in, to and fro from the black fur coat, his uncle, fat,

shaking.
There. Now. Look. The Tower. You can see it in the distance. I crane forward pointing. The quiet sea glimmers as we sweep through the long strip development of the coast town. Oh, outside the window there the air like fine dust settles over the stable world. Open your window. Smell the sea. Timothy. Open yours. Can you smell it? I can hear it. You can hear the pebbles grating. Stop the car, Uncle. Let me look at it. He's woken up now I see.
Look, oh look, there's a ship out there. Look how big the sun is. A red disc visibly falling across the line of the horizon while the light remains steady. Mrs Dunmore remains in the car. The uncle comes with him as does Timothy to look at the sea and to feel that sudden peace. The fresh breeze gentle coming from it, out of the heat and smoke of the car and the flesh creeps in the altered climate. They watch the water, sucking, lapping, and hear the pebbles roll, for a little time, Jenny there, eked out by the quiet ineluctable swell and recess of the sea, his face absent of intention and itself suffused by an inward flow, open it seems, just a little burnished by the dying sun, his wide soft mouth closed and compressed into a smile. The light of the sun runs along the water making a glittering path between it and them The clear complexion of the boy and there is light in his eyes. He and Timothy lean over the rail together, their shoulders pressed together in a moment of perfect love. Or at least that is what it is for Jenny. The uncle's hand is on his nephew's shoulder and there is pleasure in his voice as he says:
Are you enjoying yourself, lad? Jenny turns smiling

up at this fat and amiable friend and his smile like a wide half moon softly returns his thanks:
It's beautiful he says, the sea.
Hark at him, Mrs Dunmore says. Namby Pamby.
But Jenny leans his head into the wind as the car moves on and feels its soft touch on his offered flesh. No. Feels the wind on his skin. No more than that. Through the quiet streets of Blackpool.

Down, into a garage. A uniformed attendant walking before, turning, to the right, come on, beckoning, his hands forward, stop. In the lift, quiet and the boy with two rows of buttons and a pill-box hat, watches him. Smiling. Smiling.
He's still smiling, look, she says.
He is, isn't he. He's all right. His uncle's hand is on the back of his neck and he feels its warmth.
Yes.
Nothing on the face of the lift boy. The fat uncle, around, above, with Flossie Dunmore.

When he'd put his case on the rack in the bedroom he closed the door. He opened all the drawers and the cupboards. Nothing. He lay on the bed, on the ribbed bed cover, feeling it. Alone here. The uncle and Mrs Dunmore had rooms on the floor below next to each other. Dinner they had told him was at half past seven.
Shall you freshen yourself up a bit, Jenny lad.
What are you smiling at? Help me with this, Amby, her arms round the back of her neck, back turned, touching the zip, a slit of white flesh as the zip opened.
The door closed.
Down in half an hour then in the lounge.
All right.

The open sky across which promontories of cloud stretch, that might be land, beyond the red sun, low, touching the edge of the sea. Jenny's face is alight as he stands at the window now and smiling watches the light on the wet sand, the red light like a path of fire burnishing the steel supports of the pier, reddening the red sandstone of the wall and beneath in the placid air the cars of residents. He stands there and his gaze stretches out to the flatness and calmness of the sea, moving, flecking with light, the beach empty of people. Behind him he can hear the internal sounds of the great hotel into which he is reluctant to enter. For here he feels his father's voice about him as the expensive jacket keeps him warm, hears the tone of that rich voice, the reverie he allows deliberately, it might almost be true to say that he seeks it. He generates his own warmth here. He may feel flesh inside the shirt inside the jacket growing warm. He sits on the bed and wraps his arms round his waist and in the gradual warmth which suffuses his body that expression of sweet docility again asserts its dominion. Thus he stays bathing in the sweet light of recollection, home-sick. His father like an emblem of lasting reflection, there, before the embers of the fire considering the quality of his life and that of his children, concerned lest he should seem to them to be poor, his toothbrush moustache, moist from his heavy breathing. The light in the room is palpable to Jenny's eyes. The wood of the wardrobe shines, pine, light, straight-grained, like the belly of a violin which he plays at home, faltering, in the room in which he spends so much of his own time, often the ends of his fingers cut from boning meat so that it is painful to place them on the gut and wire strings. He listens to his father's speaking late when the mother is in bed. Now here his shoulders hunch into the configuration of his father's back and he sinks wilfully into a doze of sweet comfort. The sea laps in his head and the quiet air buoys out his heart. His pale clear skin seems only lightly to feather him.

What are you doing? It is Timothy. Who has changed his shirt, brushed his hair.

I was looking at the sea. It's calm.

Shall we go down? In a blazer and creased trousers.

I think Maggie and Nick'll be there.

Timothy ran down the stairs, quiet on the thick carpet. Jenny follows at his own pace but hurrying a little.

There they are, Maggie, Nick! This is ... where is he? ... Jeremy.

Come on, what are you waiting for?

White, Jenny advances. She Maggie arrested for a moment poised for flight, surprised, to Timothy, looking nicely at Jenny:

I'd didn't know you were bringing anybody with you.

I didn't exactly bring him.

Hello, she says.

Hello. She was wearing a kilt. They went into the thick-carpeted lounge and sat in the deep armchairs, looking at each other.

I was stung by a wasp yesterday, look. Her thigh white and the skin, shining, the muscle moved, the long thigh muscle, narrower on the underside of the leg, her tendons stretched at the back of the knee, the muscle firm shaded, flexing high on the thigh near the bone, an edge of white lace. Her finger is pointing to a red spot. Then she threw down the skirt

again and smoothed it over her knees.
She's always showing her legs off. Her brother speaks to Jenny.
You shut up.
We found a transparent nightdress under Mummy's pillow this morning.
When did you come?
Yesterday. Do you want to see it?
Jenny followed running, when the three of them ran up the stairs, on to the first floor. Nicky drew out the black lace thing from under the pillow.
You can see right through it, look. She stretched her fingers out and drew it across the palm.
They ran downstairs again,
Before Mummy catches us. Jenny followed. Nicky told him, walking with him. She's always showing her legs off. Maggie turned and looked at Jenny as he followed her down the staircase. She smiled at him. And he smiled back at her.

Wind. A strong wind. In the morning and the tide in so that the waves splashed over the sidewalk. They hit the wall. The stone of the pavement trembled, sucked, slopped, screamed, the wind, flicking spray from edges of white water and they pounced back again and up, threw themselves over the wall and the wind whipped the spray along, until the water ran down from the shining pavement, the colours of the rainbow iridescent in it, into the gutter which took it back through the sea wall.

The water caught him as he ran. The wind plucked and thrust at him. The salt water seeped through the navy blue mackintosh. His feet grew sodden in the swirl of the water on the pavement. His hair is wet. He is intent and meets great sheets of water as they crash over the wall. He places himself in their way. And they shock out the breath for him. At Easter. The water chilling and Jenny low in spirit further saddened by the smacking sheets of solid chill water. It is early. His uncle and Timothy and Mrs Dunmore are not yet up. The cloud blusters. One or two cars drive towards the crown of the road as far away from the sea as they can get. The salt water swirls about them. Saddened. Sodden. But he feels cleaner. He goes back to the hotel for breakfast. As the tide has receded the wind has dried his coat and the salt water has left white streaks on it. His belly is chill. The damp shirt clings to him. He returns to his bedroom where he changes. As he descends the stairs for breakfast he sees his uncle and Mrs Dunmore exclaiming over the streaks in his coat which he has hung in the hall.

A new coat. You don't deserve it. Can't you look after anything?

He watches them, his flesh still tingling from the salt spray, his clothes warm on him and hungry.

Later they sat at breakfast and Jenny watched Maggie. There was a glow on her skin. She looked golden. Sitting at a table on the other side of the breakfast room, near a window, looking at her dark-haired mother. There was a tall spare spent solemn genteel man sitting opposite, her father. She did not look towards Jenny. Who was at the same time smiling at Mrs Dunmore, at his uncle. Mr Dunmore had not yet come,

Unaccountably delayed, his uncle said and winked at

Flossie who fresh and pink this morning had wanted Jenny to kiss her but he had evaded her clutch. Now she laughed until his uncle said,
What is it this morning, Tim? Who was taking a little from the pat of butter he had put on the edge of his plate, spreading it easily on the toast which he held in the palm of his hand and then adding a touch of marmalade which he had spooned on to the rim of the plate also.
Aren't you eating anything, Jeremy? Mrs Dunmore.
No, I'm not hungry. I'd like a cup of tea.
Don't you want your bacon and eggs?
No thank you.
Are you ill?
No.
Is he moody? What'll his mother say if he doesn't eat?
He'll eat when he's hungry. He's upset about his coat perhaps.
Oh, you've no need to bother about that, love. Everybody complains some time. Your uncle didn't mean to upset you.
I'm not upset. It's just that I'm not hungry.
We'll go out with Maggie and Nicky, Timothy replied. Will you go, Jeremy?
No. I'd rather look round on my own.
Unsociable.
Isn't he?
His uncle gave five shillings to Timothy who took it with aplomb. He gave five to Jeremy who blushed and fumbled, failing to say thank you.
He likes going off on his own. The uncle apologetic to Timothy.

Who sat indifferent watching them.
Does he?
Poor love he's missing his mother. Flossie's thick ringed hand settled on his own and squeezed it with a moist pressure.
No. He's what you might call a solitary, aren't you, Jenny lad?
Don't make your coat worse by getting it wet again.
No. I won't.
Did you buy it for him, Amby?
Ay. Well, yes I did. His father can't afford much. He's not tearing many trees up at the moment. A marvellous tradesman but a bloody fool. I've always said it. And I don't think he gets much help from his wife. It's not good for business you know to have a woman with no tact. She calls it honesty to speak her mind but is it honest to get into debt, not to pay your way? That's not what I call honest. I've lent them money before and I don't suppose I shall ever see that again. Yes. I bought the coat. I'm not ashamed of it. I don't see why t'lad should suffer. I'll see to that. He had to have something respectable to come in. We can't have him showing you and Timothy up, can we? Besides I want him to feel equal. He's as quick as lightning you know when he wants to be.

Jenny bowed over his tea smiling. The sea laps in his head. I spent twenty minutes tying my tie after I came back. My appearance is impeccable. I am turned out as they want me. At Christmas he lay at the stairhead listening to his mother and father. They had hidden an air gun under the till in the shop. Which they had bought with some effort. His uncle had offered him a more powerful, more expensive

one, which he preferred.
It makes you want to weep. That's as much to us as Amby's was to him - more. Bloody kids.
And he crept back across the landing. A board creaked. Rats ran over his pillow in his dream that night. And in the morning he threw the gun the uncle had bought into the garden.
Show me how it works, Dad. He did, bending over his son. They fixed a target and grew absorbed during a long Sunday morning. The target pinned to a door, half the paint of which was burnt off in preparation a year ago to be painted again. That project like many others abandoned. But the man with his brass collar stud in the open collar of his shirt and his son played. From a pear tree to the door, shooting,
I'm sure that was a good 'un. It must have gone through the same hole as the other bull's eye. Look you can see t'paper chipped a bit.
So. Until Jenny said:
I threw that other gun out. And his father put his arm round his shoulder and pulled him to him with pleasure reproaching him, Nay lad, you mustn't abuse presents. You should be grateful to your uncle. His thick hand softly holding his son to him. Jenny ashamed. Are his parents in business on their own then?
Yes. In a manner of speaking. Flossie and his uncle smile at each other. Mrs Dunmore looks warm and soft this morning. Daintily she buttered her toast and spread her marmalade. Daintily put it into her mouth between her shining red lips. Daintily plucked out a white lace handkerchief from the black cuff and pressed it lightly to her nose.
I'll tell you about it later.

And yet the sea rose and sucked back, boomed, against the wall, and leapt over it to drench the boy in his stained mackintosh. And yet he ran forward and back, forward and back and back as he heard the ebbing, sucking, looked at the still calm, heard the pebbles moving as the water rolled them over, clattering. The water ran down like hail, whipped into his face. The salt on his lips. There. The tang of it. He ran along the sea wall. The spray thrashed across it. Balancing on the wall. The sea like wild hair beneath him, like a mouth open and then chewing. Towards the tower. The wind in his wet hair and the lovely concrete, the film breaking spreading light then dulling as it breaks, the lovely concrete awaiting his return to it, the colours of the rainbow there at his feet and the wild sea, white horses plunging and steadily pressing forward. Towards the Tower. The sun comes out. And he feels its warmth on his cold wet neck. It draws him out.

There were a few people about on the promenade. Maggie and Nicky and Timothy were in the amusement park. The sun and wind dry him. His coat is encrusted with salt. He moves freely. The ground is steady beneath his feet. He saw them and went towards them.

Hello. Maggie smiled at him. She wore a kilt. But stockings today and low leather shoes. Jeremy smiled.

Where've you been?

I've been dodging the spray.

You'll catch it. And she still smiled.

Shall we go on the swing boats? I'll pay. I've got plenty of money. Money. Not to let his father and mother down. Not to have to cadge from your uncle.

To spend on Maggie.

Her white legs showed as the boat swung. He pulled at the rope, high, above him, her kilt billowing to show white pants and white legs as she came, falling, down, on him, and then up and away, from him, until she was below and then hesitating to drop again, at her, for her, while she rose in a closing circle away above towards him. And her skirts flew.
Stop it. Stop it, I feel sick. Feel that. She put his hand on her stomach. They stood together, warm through the green cardigan. They stood together.
He helped her down. The wool slipping over the smooth silk. Under. They had lost Nicky and Tim. Jeremy had taken her hand to help her down. Now he held it. They walked through the people.
Has the sting healed?
Not yet. She blushed.
I wonder where they are.
Do you want to find them? I don't. I want to go on the ghost train. Dark. Warm against him. Holding her waist. An illuminated skeleton screeching while wet hair brushed over his face and chains clinked and a voice I am the spirit of Christmas past. He came out smiling, Did you like it? He smiled at her. She was fresh and clean. Her blonde hair feathering her forehead. Down on her skin. She was supple and lithe and open. She came smiling towards him. Held out her hand to jump from the other side of the narrow rail and jumped, so that she was near him and he could smell her. She looked at him with light in her eyes and warmth so that he could say:
Let's go back to the sea.
What for?

To look at it.
All right. And they went back. The tide was going out. The waves no longer splashed over the wall on to the pavement. The sand was hard and wet. The pebbles banked against the bottom of the wall, shone. The sea thundered on the sand, the white froth coming at them, receding, coming again. The sea higher than them and the breakers rearing as they broke to fall, the sand grated and shifted. Maggie ran towards the wild sea. And screamed. The white water surged towards her and she ran from it, screaming, shouting, laughing. It receded. She threatened it back. Towards her again and this time it caught her. She danced in it,
Get back. Get back. The sea ignored her. Jenny watched.
My feet are wet.
You got caught.
She was leaning towards him, her hand under the kilt which was pulled up, over the knees. She rolled down the stocking. Then the other. He watched. She smiled at him. Ran away with the two stockings trailing from her outstretched arms. Into the wind. So that they flew horizontal. Then back towards him. The kilt pressed behind her. Leaning back. Her white feet and legs in the wet sand. He watched her smiling.

They crouched beside the sea wall, a buttress protecting them against the wind. Which seemed to pluck and tear at them. Snatch. The blue mackintosh covered them both. The tide was out in the distance now. Now they stayed for each other's warmth. I'm tingling. Feel. She held his hand to her cheek. The pebbles were strewn about with brown opaque seaweed, like rubber, and the salt hung in the air. Jenny told her about his father. She said that she had seen her mother in the black nightdress. You could see right through it. He was watching the sea. She looked like a film star. She's got a lovely figure. We'd better go. They'll be wondering where we are.

Hadn't you better put your stockings back on?

Nobody'll see. I'll go straight up to my room.

Do you sleep in the same room as Nicky?

He's my brother.

I know he is.

Well then?

Nothing.

So this is Jeremy, is it?

Maggie was smiling. He said Hello to the man.

This is my mother. He smiled at her. A small dark-haired woman with light in her eyes, wearing a red dress that he could not see through.

The uncle and Flossie Dunmore were of the party. They were drinking round a table in the bar.

Can I go out to the pictures, Mummy, with Jeremy?

Young love sprouting, I can see. The uncle laughed and Flossie smirked kindly at them.

I think so, don't you, love?

The tall man answered. Yes. Come straight home.

Maggie's face was crimson. Jeremy smiled and waited for her.

I'll go and get my coat then. He sat with the four people until she should return. Older now with her hands in the pockets of a flared tan coat that covered her kilt.

Straight home. And no hanky panky!

All right. I shan't run off with him.
Don't be cheeky.
All right.
Straight home.
All right.
Look after her, Jeremy.
Yes.
Silence. Then, after a reasonable period, they went out together. Through the lighted foyer towards the dark cold street. Tim and Nicky were playing table tennis in the games room. Aren't you going to take them with you then?
They don't want to go.
And they didn't.
Jeremy was happy to be with Maggie on his own. They went to see a film and came straight back. He held her hand as they walked back. Then he thought about it, waited, prepared and kissed her, felt her clean soft mouth, her nose with his own, nuzzled her. Once.

Come on. They were in the amusement park. He loved her. The kilt hung on her hips and swayed when she moved. Timothy and Nicky ran from them into a revolving tunnel. They followed. As she rose up the side of the tunnel her legs showed. They crawled through. She ran after Timothy and Nicky. Jeremy followed into a centrifuge. He watched them. Maggie was upside down. Her skirt round her thighs. Spinning. They came out, laughing, pulling at each other. In his well-cut trousers, in the jacket his father had bought him, he followed. Smiling. Maggie ran with Timothy and Nicky. They went into the crowd.

Jeremy watched but they were not there. He went out of the park and began to go back along the promenade towards the hotel. The sun was warm. The breeze blew slightly shifting the sand sprinkled on the concrete walk. He thought they must be ahead of him. There were a few mothers with prams about but the place was not crowded. Out of season. So that Jenny does not hurry after them. If they have gone they have gone. This is my pace I walk at. My father brought me this jacket. He strolls. Strolls. I walk at ease here while they slave. I walk.

When he met them they were playing tig. He joined in. They tried to catch him. He turned about. About. And he enjoyed his movement. Hands stretched for him but they did not touch, did not reach, other hands. It was a warm afternoon. The rubber soles of his shoes bit on the dry concrete so that he could check and turn, at will. They failed to touch him. There was a hawthorn hedge growing beside the path. They broke twigs from it. And reached, reached, out, for him. Maggie, flushed, too. Get him with that. Maggie flicked it at him, touched him, on the arm. He avoided her. She touched him again. The pavement not wide enough. Cars passing quietly along the road. She touched him. Timothy touched him. He ran straight out along the pavement from them. They followed, touching him, touching, touching, laughing. Got him again, again. Then hitting. He felt the sting of the twigs. There were little spots of blood on his hands. He dodged but they hit out at him and with the twigs, caught him, on his hands and arms, on his face and neck, he felt the sting of the pricks and stopped, holding his hands over his face, while they hit him until they had finished.

That'll teach him to touch her.
That'll teach you to touch me. She looked at him.
Look. He's crying. She took hold of the hands which covered his face. He looked at her.
You're crying. Hey, Timothy, look, he's crying.
They came and looked at him. Then they walked away, talking, arguing, laughing, and looking back at him.

White. Plimsolls. Socks. Trousers. Shirt. Blond hair. Dust on the canvas shoes, stains from cycling on the socks, oil on the trousers, the grease of hair on the loose collar of the shirt. He tries to clean it for there is blackness of mind, seething like an angry sea to overwhelm that clarity. For he holds to his whitened plimsolls, holds on, as to a straw, or debris, clutched, on to it, loving it, loving, loving his white plimsolls, to propitiate, to render them faithful, to woo them into confidence. Part of his mind maintains a silence as an airtight compartment which keeps buoyant the rest of his body. Here he is now. Alive to that river along which he runs with his dog, yapping. A pheasant slaps out of the wood, the dog jumps at the bottom of the tree, up, to startle it again, out of the branches. Heavily, its wings clapping on the twigs, on the branches the fat pheasant flies over. The dog yaps. He has dived into the undergrowth where there are rabbits. There is a scurrying, rustling, scampering, scratching, a natural urgency and then a sharp squeal, he's got one, into the wood to get it from him before he has torn it to pieces, but he has, its body is dismembered, he has not killed it cleanly, its fur is ripped away from its side and belly, its intestine hangs out. It is trying to drag itself away. The dog has it by the back of the neck. It is rigid now. It watches the boy. So he thinks. There is white fur on the twigs about. The dog is hysterical. The boy watches. But he pulls away the dog takes up the rabbit by its wet back legs and swings it to smash its head against a tree, the blood spurting out, on his white trousers, warm to his hand and then he holds it down and presses between its back legs to make it pee so that the meat will not taste. It is at last dead. The dog loses interest. Merely sniffs at the rabbit as Jenny holds it. Loosely about there now the rabbit is inert. It merely lies. Jenny drops it and stirs it with his foot. Feels the soft warm belly. The dog pushes it with his nose and the rabbit rolls over, flops, on its back.

Out on the bank again, out of the wood, which is rotten, half-flooded, bog, where trees have fallen and rotted, where there is a thick tangle of brambles, tall nettles, away from that along the green bank. There is light on the water, light and air, the sun shines down on the river, a long river of red glittering light. The water ripples. It smells of the fresh grass beside it. Bits of stick float along it, little flecks of white foam, from the slight fall of the lock, further up, slowly, steady, moving, quietly. Yet Jenny has more energy than that. There is a large ash which he climbs, climbs, stretching for it, up, the lovely stretch of his back, swarms up a branch, his arms and legs wrapped round it, rapt, as the dog wraps his front legs round his leg, trying to make love to him, on the branch to sway out there over the water and smell the fresh and lovely green. He remains there. It rains. The air glows, is luminous, greenfly come thick into the air, they stick in his hair, bite, the sky is white and the rain silver in it. There is a cuckoo. A blackbird. Through the flicking, interlacing, trembling, leaves and branches of the tree the soft light is figured as in wrought iron. The branches rise and gracefully bend over the boy to embrace him, hold him. One after the other, many times, all ways. Like embroidered cotton, like wire mesh, like God knows, anything. Any rate he is up there with the lovely bark, his skin grafted on to it, green mould over his face and arms, on the white trousers, the plimsolls green on the instep, at the toe. Clinging for dear life on to that branch and longing to let himself go, let himself fall, into the water and be carried by the current through the mill race or merely down stream out of the wood in which he trespasses out into the sea where he will be gradually transmuted into other elements than that which he now inhabits for the mood weighs on him, this solitude, his limbs tack moist. Poor Jenny in his hebetude presses his cheek to the bark of the ash and rubs himself against it. He smells its dank smell. The rain patters on the leaves. The tracery of the tree like black wires about him like the veins in an old woman's eye making a dome where all things are taut, where everything snaps, hard, in which the mind moves only in its gristle tethered on all sides as a body buried in sand where no grain weighs but together they make a weight against which no muscle has power. Jenny clinging to his branch while his dog searches through the undergrowth of a dank and rotting wood looking for rabbits where the wood is rotten and crumbles, powders under the foot and where the underside of the pine, the yew in particular is dead under an interlocked canopy of preserved tangle. It was sold at the dissolution of the monasteries to the family which now owns it and is still a game preserve as it was then when the monks held it, the bridle path along which he has come, leased to barges, which are obsolete now. The right of way is fenced in by barbed wire. He picks at the green mantled rough grooved bark of the ash. It is a kind of wood light brown on the inside. The water quietly presses beneath him and reflects the brilliant grey of the sky. And so he remains.

But the cloud passes. The shower has stopped. The sun has come out and the light is alive again, dancing, jigging, tripping, like tinfoil, white, with dots the size of a penny the under sides of the branches are flecked, dappled, moving, changing, swift shadows scattered at random. Bless this child. He needs it. He holds on to this tree. The tree sustains him. Although it is in England in an urban culture, such as it is. I can't help that. The white of his clothes is an eggshell the grit for which he has picked up on roads amongst traffic. Let us take off his shirt, take down his trousers and slip him out of his shoes and plimsolls to send him naked into the water. There was rain.

On another occasion,

We're wet anyway. Let's swim. The water was swift. There is sand on the bottom here. A tree grown out over the place, from which they dive in summer. He stood naked on the soft grass of the bank while the rain fell quietly on him. Charles demurred but seeing him naked, undressed and entered the water. He swam, quickly, out again and dried himself with his shirt, shivering, blue. Jenny stood, glistening with the rainwater, erect. Charles's eyes were on him. He ran down the bank into the stream, into the sweet and tasty water. The rain pattered on the surface. He crouched bouncing gently on the sand, the current feathering him, turned up stream, mouth open, and looking along the flat level, top lip over the water, bottom lip under, blowing out now and then, felt that soft and feathering touch along his loins and Charles, white, goosefleshed, in his shirt tails, dressing on the bank. Chilled, he became soft again so that he rushed from the water, up the bank, where he jumped and danced. High on the bank raised over the level of the flat land with the rain driving, warm, his breath hot on his wet arm, his hands sliding over his slippery body. A coldness, emptiness in his belly. Hardness, nothing surplus. All taut. All useable, all felt, all at once, no interlocking series, all urgent, clamouring, clamouring, this is me, enough, naked, I stand here, under Charles's eye, Jenny, Jenny, indestructible here with the lightness of my final contour, designed, figured, my fingers like shoots out of my hand and my back will bear what weight is placed upon it. Ah, as I touch my body I know that I am perfect and that what I celebrate is perfection. High, naked, on this bank over the level fen, the drizzle drawn with a lead pencil across the sky and the quiet so soft patter of the rain, the smell of beet rising from the field across the river and this lovely chill. No one sees me here. The blood throbs in me. I feel the grass under my feet, jump, to land so quietly, there is no give in the earth, I hear my breath and slap my sides with open palms to turn them red and then back into the water, drink it, the river water, the Slea. Both Charles and Jenny are quiet in face of the mystery. They sit in the rain on the wet grass, together, bathed in a common element, of love, watching the water, their faces suffused by an elated quietness, alert, all alive I think and the rain fills the river. The sound of its flowing more like settling through the ground. In peace.

They continued their walk Charles with his arm round Jenny's shoulders until they came, wet, intimate, loving, home.

But again there is a surge and swell of unsure feeling in poor Jenny's mind, a male and female element, in his androgynous soul, soft and pliant and wet while it is hard and dry. Violence coupled with loving kindness. He loves Charles, giving and expecting nothing, so, just so, neither more nor less than what they've got, neither asking, searching nor straining. Easily. But I'm afraid not one thing or the other, sometimes carelessly, sometimes not, in the middle air, with the rest of us.

What was the matter with you there? What did you get excited for?

I don't know. He didn't. Neither do I. Do you?

I do when I go into woods and when I'm walking by rivers. I always do. Do you think there's something wrong with me?

I don't know. Shouldn't think so.

I like the taste of the water.

You're barmy.

Jenny smiling at him, beaming, his face soft and pale under the redness. Beautifully clean and unspotted, such a fine complexion, as his mother said, he takes as much care of himself as a girl. Have you seen his shoes? Look at them. Look at that. Every day. They're always like that. He likes dressing all in white. He's so fussy that's what gets me. He's more particular than a girl would be. He spends hours cleaning his plimsolls. He's a dreamer. He's all right. His father said. He's a grand lad. He'd do anything for anybody. He won't let you down. Wait till he sets his stall out.

Thin, Jenny picked at his food, chewing with his mouth pinched, delicate, yet strong.

Can you hear his heart pumping?

After a race run, where he had sunk on the ground, too heavy, had tried too hard, the hand of Mrs Doughty, Charles's mother, there, feeling the pulse throbbing. He'll hurt himself. He tries too hard. He doesn't know when to give up. All in. Having been defeated but satisfied to have been absorbed. The circulation of his blood so excited that it strung its own net round him lacing him together into a living wholeness. Collapsed on the grass near the thirty-mile limit, near the cemetery. Wind in the yew. The branches creak. The grass is covered with daisies. Wall-flowers before him. Oh, it is fine here. While his heart gradually slows to a more regular pulse.

Outside the back door of the house there are white marks where the plimsolls have been put to dry. Jenny places them again in the same position. There is light in his face. He plays with the dog on the lawn, rolling, the dog watches him with soft eyes, panting, Ha! Ha! Ha! a pink tongue dangling out from the side of its soft mouth. A Labrador cross, small, black, a retriever, able to hold without damage or blemish. Jenny plays there on the lawn, today he wears grey trousers and does not care about the stains on his plimsolls.

I won't sit here. Look at it. Look at that. It's dirty. It's filthy. Why can't we have a clean tablecloth. It's plastic. Plastic. It smells. Look what it feels like. Querulous. But the mother proud. He's so clean. A gentleman. It comes naturally to him. It's in the blood. The blood. The blood. Like his great grandfather, who rode to hounds, to point to point, his skin white, creamy, like my father's, Dada. Who had healing hands, who was devout, who always used to say, who had green fingers, who never told a lie, nor cheated a man, who was never in debt, who never owed a penny, who lived happily all his life, who was ever so good to my mother, Dada, fostered and fed to grow to establish, that, against the father who drank, fucked, spent, failed, in business, in love. Yet who was loved by his children. She prepared parties, tea, scones, cakes, butterscotch, parkin in November, decorations at Christmas, as it was in the beginning, at home, with Dada, who taught her to walk again when all the doctors had said that she would be paralysed for life. Get up and walk, and she did, follow me, Dada, one of God's own gentlemen, whose mother must have been a lady because when I was just a little girl I can remember hearing the rustle of her skirt. You see it must have been silk, only silk rustles like that, only ladies wore silk. Thus encircled, Dada, by grandmother's silk skirt, by the O'Connors and the Reynolds and the Fitzimmons she made what it was she wanted. But not defeated as that tone implies. Not defeated. Rather with vigour then, having done that, having made that base, with sap and juice in her, to have three sons, of whom Jenny the youngest, now cycles, white, about the village, wheeling, turning, slowly, serenely, this way and that, to hear the free wheels licking, to hear the hum of a spun peddle, near a chestnut tree, where there are other children.

Can you pull up this grass, this tuft?
Yes. Easily. Bent to take it in his hand while the smell came just then into his nostrils and they laughed, girls, too, Ha! Ha! Dog shit. It's covered in dog shit. Ha! Ha! Ha! Ha! He ran away to wash, wash, wash, away the smell.
What's the matter? He scrubbed with a plastic nail brush to clean himself, clean the smell off, clean it out of his mind. Out. Dried he smelled his hands and then catching a faint odour he washed again, again, while he watched gnats, like touches of light, flitting, back and forth, across the sunlight before the open window while the leaves of an apple tree offered shade and light to the surface of the clean water, there, in an aluminium bowl, where his hands were pressed out flat, while he leaned on them and left himself over to the pleasure of the soft water and the quiet light which came through to his unseeing eyes. Jenny invoking the light. Come to me. Come through to me. Come to me. Lounging about with his dog, over the fields, after rabbits or wood pigeon, with a catapult. The sun on the heavy and shining dark grass where the rabbits sat up, feeding, throwing long shadows, the light thick, gnats, greenfly, in the air. Jenny lounging free over the springy ground, into corn, waist high, with red poppies in it, into barley which rustled like his grandmother's silk skirt, ladylike barley. And oats which he must needs sow wild. My poor Jenny, amongst this and invoking that soft and complete touch, here now on the river bank, with sand martins forked and white gliding into this quiet place under the tree, easy, clean, to land, alight, here, beside him, so, as he sits, now, watching, again, the water, the water,

listening, to it, but easy, easy. Today, rid of his fetishes, his plimsolls forgotten, and in comfortable disarray. Here. Amongst the lovely lighted branches of a wild cherry or rather looking at them, while he sits under the great sycamore, the leaves planing, shading the sun, palming it through to dispose it moving about the sloping heavy grass at his feet. Bless him. Such black branches and such a light green, some ivy, which seems to be dying, on it, having failed to climb, brown, rotten, dead. The leaves brush through the noise of the rippling water. The hollow cough of a bullock.

He had swum in it in the morning. Naked. Straight into it, before breakfast. These lovely lilies, out now too, there, at the edge of the bank, where the narcissi have fallen away, as the daffodils, that plane there part of it, as the car, parked say seventy yards away from which two fishermen, father and son, have come to sit, through the day, casting in this heavy current for the fish which it is too light to hope for. Gnats now in an indescribably complicated pattern, knitting the air out over the water, at the edges of the long branches, just where the light is, at the burning edges of the green leaves. It's the noise that's like the shook foil, not the light, which is in fact, much steadier. Bless the tree, wound it, let it bleed, teem over my Jenny. He is after all his mother's child and would turn it into Dada if he could, will it. Sand martins bathe at the edge of the water. He can hear their wings in the water. In balls of light, clashing, spluttering, one flies through the willow over near him. There. A drop of water flicked from its wing on his beaming, dreaming, softening, upturned face, turned up to the light, placid. The air force is exercising the air. Perhaps they are having a mock battle, perhaps they are not, another martin has swooped, turned, belly up, white, past him, under, drop, lunged under the lowest branch and through the gnats, do they eat them? The light comes through the spread and planing wings of a sparrow, against the light, here oh here Jenny between land and water, between earth and air.

He has cleaned his hands. He has gone out again, what to seek? To wheel in that luxurious spring, where the chestnut sheds pink blossom on the tarmac road, where the children have left now and that tuft of grass remains, pointed, which he avoids. For there is in his mind still that clarity. To the river where he swims, dives, from the tree, the sycamore, overhanging, with the son of the woman who had put her hand on his heart. Charles. The banks of the river rise above the flat marsh field, the grass there is clumped, hard, tall, round, spiked, there are willows sprawling, hawthorns, stunted in pools of warm sweet-smelling stagnant water. It is a playground. They must climb a gate, cross a grass field, crawl through a hawthorn hedge and then they are there, sheltered from the wind on this sunny afternoon, quietly they sit in a ring, they have been swimming and have wrestled, the water drying on them attracts flies.

Stop it. You mustn't do that. Charles with his hand on Jenny's sex.

Leave me alone.

And yet persistent.

You mustn't do that.

But that older boy persists and will not leave go. Jenny

softens for he loves Charles and allows him to fondle him sitting quietly there, not much bothered, feeling good, thinking of nothing in particular. Though there is to be a first class journey soon and he has that at least partly in his mind. Charlie masturbates not Jenny but his small black dog. While Jenny runs back to the water and in it erect, naked, with the dog pushing across the water like a cape round his neck, under the sycamore tree, Charlie having found other playmates, he flips, somersaults to stand on his hands legs up out of the water, the water stings in his upturned nostrils, till he falls, over, with open eyes, watches the wealth of whiteness about his eyes, welcomes it, feels the feathering tickling of the trapped air, in the silence, except for the grating of the sand as he stirs it gently with his feet, swimming under the water, to turn, to look up, at its surface, softly the light touching, fleeting, flecked, dappling on to his weightless oh weightless body. The flies out of his foreskin where Charles had taught him to catch them, waiting for them to land, on the top, and then up with it to trap the fly, swift, and to lift it off its wings wet. He's been back to the river. Oh the light, all that light, more here, light at home, though it is stiller today. He is inside now. There is a drizzle. He broods over the empty grate. There is sickness in his mind.

Are you cleaning your plimsolls, love? Thus his mother, sturdy, with flowers in her hand, to arrange in a vase through the quiet stone kitchen, cool, the birds chirping, imitating the sounds of the car, of children, Dada always used to have clean shoes, Dada, Dada. Undeterred he went on preparing himself until

the door opened while he sat reading The Odyssey, and his father lurched in, Oh, reading, what? That'll do you no good, think about your future, regret, you'll regret it, you'll live to regret it.
Where's your mother?
In bed I think.
Ay.
Into the pantry then where he threw about cake tins and other significant objects, opened and slammed shut cupboard doors,
Where's the bloody food? There's not enough to keep a cat alive, May, where's the food?
There is none. You should come in at a reasonable time.
He was growling, snarling, grinding his teeth. Only feeling himself. His mind a black turbulence which only violence would satisfy. That drop through, smack, in the bedroom, at the figure in the bed, the anonymous figure, but she, her eyes wild and growling, gritting her teeth, she hit back at him, while Jenny hung on to his book and rode it, smartly dressed, without a mark on his plimsolls, through the storm of blows that followed, of screams, of shame he felt, of willing silence, of half-hidden smiles, of whispered comment, of significant looking, of concealed gesture that he could feel, feel, himself, his hands, filthy with the sound of that dogfight upstairs, of the filth of his mother's mouth, till the father shattered, trembling, pale, came down the stairs and sat in confused silence, comprehending nothing, having been up and having come down, having been brutal he who was so gentle that the warmth of his hand offered made a strange child smile, who was

now sitting shaking in a chair so carefully so expensively so endlessly recovered by money from Dada, which supported him, solid, while he shook.
She's always been the same, your mother, what a temper, hysterical, false, lying, talking about Dada, always the same, unreliable, can't depend on her, May, vicious, perverse, had never loved him, never known him, always wanted to change him, would not let him be, wanted to stop him drinking, stop him enjoying life, always crying poverty, a conservative, a retractor, a holder-in, a prudent mover, step by step, little by little, but him No   Out   Open it up   Do anything you set your mind to   Set your stall out   I was ambitious but she stopped that cramped me   Crabbed greedy   Snob   I've never been good enough for her   Never come up to her standards   Hubert Bland she should have married   Steady a good steady chap   Take your boots off if you're coming in, Hubert   In the shed, Hubert, if you want to smoke   Don't be late   Don't get into bad company   Don't talk to women   Sing with me in the chapel   Onward Christian soldiers, Hubert   Live in me, through me, Hubert   Be mine   Belong to me   Give up all claim to yourself   I want you   God is in mine eyes, Hubert, and in my heart and in mine understanding, Hubert   Come in here with me, Hubert.
Hubert mended the pipes, put in a new boiler, in a new bathroom,
Will you do this for me, Hubert?
I will and glad to, glad to get out of his own home.
Would you like a cup of tea? A piece of home-made bread, Irish bread from sour milk.
Yes I would.

And another and another stay to supper here here
Here are some flowers from my garden
Oh thank you do you think you could take the dustbin out clean the yard chop the sticks fetch the coal
YOU COME OUT OF THERE
She was at the door. Had thrown it open. Shouting. COME ON OUT COME ON COME HOME LET ME GET YOU HOME WITH THIS TROLLOP WITH THIS PROSTITUTE EVERYBODY HAS HER OFF THEY ALL KNOW ABOUT HER LEAVE OFF MY HUSBAND MY MAN you've got one of your own Ha! Ha! The father laughs. LOOK AFTER HIM COME ON OUT HOME Back to me mine all of you you're a fool she's using you you're a simpleton can't look after yourself no smelling after other women and you should be ashamed to the father, white, astonished, ashamed to let your wife run after other men my Hubert Hubert the good the kind the Christian soldier come home, love, with me away from these people where you belong to me where I can protect you see where you are what you're doing HA! HA! HA! HA! The father roaring. HA! HA! GO HOME HUBERT holding himself up his hand on the door lintel HA! HA! holding his side, his kidney, wiping his eyes, the tears away, HA! HA! Pray for me, Hubert and Mrs now and in the hour of my death HA! HA! oh dear, I never hoped for this Bless you, Hubert. As they went down the street. She holding Hubert's arm who was pale. He called after them so that his voice echoed down the

empty street but brought lights on when he had shouted
You'll rue it Hubert   she'll make you rue it
you'll cop it oh dear   Ha! Ha! look at him
Cavil   old kan   opposite   look at that watch it
note it understand it.

Where she was waiting expecting it, he came back and punched her in the belly   she fell   with a heavy hand he smacked her down down, till Jenny caught the hand and with his own swung   to be shattered

falling

apart

with the blow

His father's eye hard

under the knuckles

Leave her alone

Then later the father having gone quiet, having become silent, having gone out, refusing to speak, the mother, Thank you love, that'll teach him, perhaps he'll stop now, at least I've got you... till he was filled with such a feeling of loathing that his fist the same fist smashed down on her and she lay there spreadeagled her legs loosely open   loosed, the skirt rucked up, in the bathroom doorway, groaning, blood on her, her arms out, trying to get up, slipping, falling, her feet twisted in her high-heeled shoes, scrabbling

Jenny's mind further out

into another country

his stomach jerked   burning   sucking the blood from his knuckles

waves of darkness pressing clamourous behind the white domes of his eyes   collapse mind   hurt she is scrabbling to rise   there   is nothing for

it but to help her her woman's scent and flesh all over him as he helps her to a chair
I'll make you some tea Mother Mother   she is sobbing   as
Jenny   he's gone   my father   he's gone quiet   he won't come back   He's gone away
Forsaken

So that between father and mother let us allow him smartness. Now the father passes him on the other side of the street. He had a black eye. He tried to smile at the boy who wailed inwardly wailed wailed, who wanted wanted to run to him to embrace him   to bend his head down   to be forgiven   to kneel   to be taken in again. But they passed each other while the father cried out to his son silently as he did his son to him   the street empty of other significance than this unheard supplication. No. No.
They heard it. Heard each other's cry but oh why not? did not come together admit it.
But they did though   later   time took care of it   the black eye turned blue   many lovely colours and at last quitted the field,
Are you satisfied now then hey? slapping, gently, not jocular but with love, the boy's shoulder to rub his hand through his hair. Do you want to try the other one? While Jenny blushing, crying, pleading in his eyes, forgive me.

It rained in the night and in the morning by the river the earth was dark. There was no wind. A compatible stillness and the green simply there.

Forget-me-nots, bluebells, out. Where there was a fire of rubbish no grass now grows, nor weeds, the glass in the window of the shed at his back had a small hole through which birds enter the shed and are trapped, beat, against the glass. There is no one there now. Another sand martin. It flutters, mindless, against the glass. Jenny disturbed, opens the door at the side of the shed and the bird flies back out into that sheltered place. Heavy aircraft high up make the noise of thunder. It is sultry. The gnats which have thickened, bite. There are no bees or wasps about, fewer birds, more fishermen, more cars, another plane, another, yet another, a fishermen with a net comes over the hedge beside him,
Have you come to get a fish?
No. My maggot tin.
The wind has started up and there are birds about, diving. Flying low, black smudge over that steely water. The thrush is back. It purls. Listen. Now other birds chatter. Everything is moving about him. The nettle leaves spin, dip, sway, all lean, those palmed branches of sycamore move up and down, sway. That incessant babbling goes on and on and on. It goes on. Gurgle, bubble, slapping, against the soft mud bank, a hollower sound, like a pop. On and On and On. Water. The willow leans with the current. Only the cherry, up the bank, stands erect. The bridge. A lorry crosses it. In the arch, the middle arch, at evening, the sun is perfectly reflected, a red ball, it illuminates Jenny's pale and gentle face, burns in his reddish hair. He looks up into the sycamore but he cannot. The wind in it. On his face. Down. The water is flecked with white, where there are

snags, which stand no chance, but are all swept away, sooner or later. Above that bridge the water is quiet and then under the arches between the two pillars it leans down, slopes, to break, round the bend, as now, then, the sun was out, but is gone, out. He waits for it. Oh there is a lovely swift curving in its diving swooping flight, under the bank, out of sight, and the wind, fitful, the martins do aerobatics over the water eating flies in flight. He waits for the sun. He looks up. In his right eye there is a small v, the forked tail of a sand martin, come to? what?
land   simply   on that branch   there's
another   over his head   say three feet   so
quiet   Surely

The sycamore has green mould on the bark. The trunk is thick. It divides about twelve feet from the ground. The branches are thin, there, that fat trunk, sticks, like the arms of a baby. The sky behind it is a uniform silver and those green leaves which the wind furls, shiver, springing back against it, larger gaps open as the branches bend and the sky comes in to light Jenny's shade. He rubs a hand on the trunk of the tree and then the green mould onto his bare forearm. But nothing is given. He sits brooding over the water, preying on it, until he returns to the house. There he sits in a chair, reading, one hand gripping the arm of the chair. It is resting or gripping? poised? is it? in the other he holds the book. Jenny. Jenny. Thinking. I am inside. I have failed. The sky outside lightens. It is glowing now. I'll go out again. The journey awaits him.

He packed. Into his rucksack he put pyjamas, a toothbrush, a change of clothing, the regulation equip-

ment. Leaving nothing out.
Are you ready? His mother.
Yes.
Have you got everything?
Yes.
Can you manage it?
Yes.
Write to me, love.
All right.
How long will you be?
A few days.
Where are you going?
I don't know till I open the orders. A sealed envelope with the tasks in it. The observations to make.
Have you packed your plimsolls?
Yes.
Have you got everything then?
Yes.
Goodbye then, love. She kissed him. He kissed her back. His father watched him with his eyes twinkling. Relish for him in them. Love. He leaves. He walks away. With Charlie. Shouldering the heavy rucksack. Towards the wolds, where there is limestone, vast air, beneath him the cultivated land, up here, gorse and heather, furze, plovers which show off, fall, to plane, then up, tumble, even stand on the grass verge of the road to be fed by the passers-by, amongst whom now Jenny and Charlie as though alone. They make the camp beside a silent stream, hot after a day's walking, tired, and out of their clothes released from the weight of the packs, falling forward, they lean stagger, laughing, joyously, wrestling, into that soft pool. The sun sets and leaves them panting,

wrestling, rolling naked, abandoned, on that soft moss, so smooth and quiet that it is like velvet, though in Jenny's abandon there is some awareness of Charlie, the smartness of his uniform. The duck's arse of his haircut. The ring on his finger. The transistor radio. The wrist-watch turned inside the wrist, off now though, all that off, and Charlie's taut thin lovely body on him over him, hairless, smooth, lissom, that tall body not like his own, different from his stronger, squarer frame. Free. Nobody there. Ha! Ha! Charlie on him. Is on him and holds his hands back sitting on his chest. Jenny feels his balls on his belly. There before him. Jenny abandons himself to this, to the fight, the free, lovely surface feeling, he lies back. Charlie sits back on his belly, pressing it down with his buttocks so that the skin of his sex is tautened and it rises. But its rising, its reacting makes him want to stop it, so that he twists, squirms, turns but Charlie does not fall, rides him, but, yes, he does, over slowly, topples, and Jenny is away

laughing

Ha! Ha! He runs like a deer, jumping, feeling that soft moss the warmth of the sun still in the stones under his feet when he stops, triumphant, alone, the water, dripping, glistening, from him, on a rock, in the river. A warm rock, which he holds with his thigh to shout,

I'm here, here   come and get me   in that silence
    it's me Jenny.

Charlie crouches beside the cold water, arms crossed to hold the points of each shoulder, with his head down and Jenny loves him,

Charlie   come over here   over here   here
try and get me off this rock   I'll fight you for it
Charlie remains crouched turned in   cramp in his
stomach and some bleak intention in his mind
Jenny stands up on the rock his feet pointing down its curving side feeling the weight pulling at the nails as gravity wishes to displace him into the water.
Eros. I'm Eros in Piccadilly. Shouted out. The muscles of that one leg, trembling, over, splash,
Ow   oo ouch   argh   Ha! Ha! swallowed to cough   Ha! Ha! but Charlie has jumped into the water and has his hands on his neck and is pressing down
I'll duck you   I'll show you   will you let me?
will you?   will you?
though in Jenny's ears there is only the noise of the splashing water as he struggles in some kind of limbo and finally caught gripped, bursting, to come up, into the air, into the atmosphere, into himself, he lashes out, out to punch, scratch, bite, his way clear, his way out, until Charlie leaves him go and the air like cold water after a long hot day sweeps announcing itself into his open lungs.
I am air.
Charlie is crying, gasping, there at the side, his face is scratched, he is holding his balls, his thighs clasped over both hands where he tries to comfort his member, reassure it, that all is not lost. Let him go into the police as he did later and let that bleak intention fasten on his soul where let it foster, thicken, grow, choke his blasted and corrupted his willed forced falsified oiled scented and decorated mind.
For he too loved Jenny whom we may release from that

triumph for it is not his own. It is mechanical. It is false. Jenny is shivering. He is sitting with his knees together and the muscles of his stomach cramped and yet enlightened, up in the air. There is no Charlie here in his mind. He is back, in his tent. Jenny runs over the moor, naked, and falls, rolls in that soft bracken, in the springy heather, rolls and jumps, dives headlong, flat out, into it, scrapes himself over it, drags his loins over it. He is panting. He whoops. He smells the flowers. He has seen the many bees on the moors and has found the Roman road, paved, and walked along it to the Scamridge dykes where there are flint arrow-heads and in a neighbouring field the unearthed stone tomb of a bronze age man. In this sunset red grouse rise from his feet and he chases them, shouting, jumping, after them, away there over that brow, down into that valley, they alight and he comes near, they cluck, quicker, louder, then braced, up again, low over the heather while he lunges after them then, at other times, on other afternoons, when the heat is stronger, when he is with his father and they have spent a quiet afternoon trailing their hands through the water as it glistens over the pebbles and have drunk then walked with it to dry with that odd smooth and soon soaked linen handkerchief.

Jenny is so gay here. He is so free. He is at liberty, lounging. Uncouth. Gayer. Well, the sun is not too warm. He is trembling again. Time has passed. He's had what he needed for this afternoon. For the time being. In this wind though and in that lightly flowing moorland river there is such energy for him, such springs of lightness, such a rage of understanding, such a kindness, that he must oh must go on, continue, such great pleasure. How much he loves these blue forget-me-nots in these green leaves. Now the sun has really come out. So that lake of light like beaten metal illumines his face here leant down over this iridescent river. His hands taut with the cold and the fresh air are clasped. The sounds change with the sun's coming. It is deeper. Now he may see under the water, under the willows which stretch over the stream, the green of the weeds trailing. He can see what a variety of green there is, at his feet, over his head, on his left, around him. There is no loss of light here. No loneliness, nothing but necessary strain. There is time to wait for Jenny. Lounging, praying, takes time. The moors are beyond, a rim, to this narrow level close-cropped grass on which he sits. Through the branches of that willow he sees their shadow, rather their own blue light and it is their own so that he can wait. South are the Howardian hills, north Kirkby Moorside, the North York Moors. West it is the Hambleton Hills. He is in the centre of all that here at this bend of the River Rye where it breaks through that bridge sitting on the level grass of the bank and listening to the water in the silence. The river floods the valley in winter. Forget it. Break the word. As the river. Jenny. Break him open and then follow broken.

But in this thicket Jenny must stop his gambolling. It solves nothing. He does stop. The sun has set and in that lonely place in the moors now above the Vale of Pickering, in that sudden valley, in that sudden quiet, there is only his own breathing, to which he listens, and the space between the stars. He is near Cawethorne, a Roman encampment, where the ninth legion barracked before they went north. And he is not far from Fylingdales early warning radar station. And he is naked. When the Romans left this area the Goths, Saxons, then Danes took over; Goathland, Sinnington, Normanby, Salton, Kirkdale on the other side of the valley have Saxon crosses built into the Norman framework. Pickering Chase was kept by William who perhaps only defeated Harold because he Harold had to come north to this area to settle the revolting Tosti. It remains part of the Duchy of Lancaster. In the records dealing with the infringements on the royal woodland almost every case was solved either by making composition or the poacher, woodcutter, builder, lord exercising his right, was let off, having regard to the state of his health, or the rights exercised by his forefathers, for time out of mind. Before William came up here the manor of Pickering was valued at £88 10s. After he razed it and left Domesday says that it was worth only twenty-four shillings. Not far from Jenny now this is the first Prior of Lastingham, according to Bede:

> Cedd assenting to the king's wishes, chose for himself a place to build a monastery among lofty and remote mountains in which there appeares to have been more lurking places of robbers and dens of wild beasts than habitations of men ... the man of God, studying first by prayers and fastings to purge the place he had received for a monastery, requested of the king that he would give him during the whole ensuing time of Lent leave and license to abide there

> for the sake of prayer; on all which days with the exception of Sunday, protracting his fast to evening according to custom, he did not even then take anything except a very little bread and one hen's egg with a little milk and water...

He was educated at Lindisfarne.

So that Jenny, in this sudden quiet, is on consecrated ground. Does that help? All these moors drain into the Vale of Pickering marshes. A lake still forms given a chance and the Derwent still flows south into the Ouse and Humber and not out of the gap to the sea where it was blocked by ice in the North Sea. Jenny, at this point, broken across the back of these moors, Charlie in his tent, I want it, I desire it, let me, let me, on his own, inside his own mind, with his own false desire, having learned that feeling, picked up that desire, dogmatic, with his hand on his own balls, masturbating, stretched on his back, under the canvas. He has on green pyjamas with a maroon pocket, his luminous wrist-watch moves in the dark as he wanks. Jenny dressed in pyjamas and sweater and socks, sits outside, looking up at heaven. I'm glad. This drains into the sea. This morning, as the sun rises, the heat increases, the light shines in the gossamer covering the close cropped grass of the valley, on the wool of the sheep, the lark hovers, sings while that narrow streak of blue, green, widens, breaking open. Jenny cramped, stiff, moves at last. The water invites him. Naked he stands for a time. Letting the sun warm him. It is still. The radiant light suffuses the green and silver grass, the heater glows, steam rises over the sweet smelling water. Which he enters. Ha! Shocked, by the cold. His head drums. The water plashes and laps against the bank, the stone. When he is dry he opens the tent where Charlie is still sleeping.

Get up, it's a lovely day, I've been for a swim, I'll cook breakfast. A hen's egg. A rasher of bacon. Baked beans and then coffee. The smoke blue, spiralling, following the eddying air.

Did you sleep?

Yes. Right through, all night.

Here's your breakfast. I got the eggs from a farm down there, down the valley.

Where are we?

Here. On the moors above Pickering, Look at the map.

They did so. There is light in Jenny's face, hebetude in poor Charlie's. But he comes through that, little by little as the day goes on. How do you measure the height of a church? What is the method? With an improvised theodolite they do it. They piece together the map, the narrative of the journey, the historical information relevant to the places through which they travel. Lend me your knife. Jenny climbs easy, up, to cut his initials into the top of that ash, amongst the clusters of red berries. He cooks for Charlie. Shall I put the tent up? What do we do for pegs? Do you think they'd give us some milk if we asked. We're in uniform.

I should think so.

He found a walnut the inside of which had been eaten, a nut shell. Bounded in that for a moment, its ridges,

the pointed ends, that smooth wood. There were beach nuts about the ground, reddish brown, the colour of his hair. He cracked them, spat out the shells and ate the white oval nut. They walked towards Rievaulx. Which they drew. A hundred and fifty monks, five hundred lay brothers. Over the Prior's door an Annunciation. That bitter streak in Charlie in abeyance for the time being.
Are you tired?
No. Are you?
No.
So they stopped and rested having come to a hamlet where the bell was tolling.
Jenny?
What?
Nothing. They went on. Later, in the dark, still walking, tired out,
What do you know about girls?
What do you know?
Do you like them?
I don't know. Ha! Ha! I think so.
All right. I'll take you to meet one when we get back.
A nice one?
Yes.
Do I know who she is?
Yes.
Where?
I'll show you.

They talked later in the tent. Jenny had a book of poems from which he read while Charlie leant back, dreaming, looking at the ceiling of the tent, Where like a pillow on a bed a pregnant bank swelled up sat we two one another's best ... If that old bard were weather wise who made the ballad of Sir Patrick Spens . . . Charlie slept now. Jenny watching his face. The light from the flashlamp hung from the pole. The smell of the canvas bivouac, and of the warm blankets, pinned together, as of the sweat of clothes. His plimsolls under his head, wrapped in a towel as a pillow. That freedom and looseness from the pack he had carried, on his back, with his hands behind his head, looking up. Outside now. Another night, without the tent, wrapped in it, together. Vast air over him. Looking at heaven, with his hands behind his head, through the branches of an ash. The cows tearing the grass.

JENNY CROSSES FROM HARWICH TO THE CONTINENT

She is wearing a light brown suit. I await her coming in the carriage while she says goodbye to her father. We go from thence to Harwich. The ship is in port. We board it. It is a clear night, chilly, Easter. We watch them load. A boy is playing a mouth-organ, German, from the sound of the tunes. I show her the Pole Star, Cassiopeia, Venus, one or two others. She leans against me. The light reflected, stretches, shortens as the water laps, black. She has black hair, bad teeth, is thin, boyish. Malicious. Her shoes are red. I love her. Poor Jenny. We leave the harbour. And enter into the sea. The boat forges its path. The motor throbs. We walk about, then down into the area of the cabins. I carry the suitcases. We are shown to our berths by a white-coated attendant. A Dutchman with split lips, like Van Gogh's potato-eaters. I saw that with her in Manchester. I won't be a minute, she says. I await outside the lacquered door. Grained in imitation of wood. I am with a white-skinned middle-aged German who is already in his bunk. He wears a string vest. His hair is black, lank.

I come out quickly, to await her. Here. But she opens the door:

There's nobody else in here.

Somebody's bound to come.

Well, you can come in for a minute while I powder my nose.

I sit on the bunk. It is warm in here. She is arranging her toilet articles on the ledge of the small mirror.

Her suitcase is open on the bunk. There is a bundle of my letters in it.
What have you brought these for?
I like reading them.
Are they good?
Some are.
You've got holes in your nightdress.
She takes it from me, closes the case.
I watch her as she brushes her hair. It must be like this when you're married.

In the darkness, in the wind, on the upper deck I hold her hand. The lights of Harwich are still visible. We lean and look back at them. The lights of the ship travel over the black water. The phosphorescence of the wake recedes into the black night. The boat takes us on towards the Continent. I think of home. The places that I love.
What would you do if it sank? My feet are planted on this trembling steel.
Anything would do. I'd get hold of something and cling on to it.
What about me?
You can swim.
You'd be sucked under. You have to swim away from the ship as far as you can, otherwise it sucks you down with it. You'd leave me, wouldn't you? I knew it. She snuggles against me. I smell her hair. Her hip.
What did your father say?
He was all right.
What did he say?
He told me to behave myself. She brushes her hair in my face.

He told me to preserve my virtue. She looks grinning at me. The wind blows her hair about. The smell of the smoke hangs about the air here. A flag thudders against the pole.
Do you like being on your own with me?
Yes. Mm.
Do you trust me?
I don't have to.
Are you frightened? of the ship sinking?
You're beautiful.
She eyes me, smiling, a woman. Her hand in her pocket. Unencumbered.
What are you looking at?
You're beautiful.
I'm nervous.
I know. It makes you jerky.
Well, aren't you?
Why should I be?
Well, I don't know but I am.
What have I got to lose?
Has anybody else touched you?
Ha! Ha! Poor Jenny. And kisses me. Her breath fills my ear. I dislike it. It enters my mind.
Shall we have a drink? I think there's a bar open.
Can we go in there?
We can go in there?
We can go anywhere.

I buy her shandy. She sips it, holding her gloves in her lap and looking over the rim at me. Eyeing me with large black eyes. I untoggle my duffle coat which I have bought at her instigation. And cling to her, homesick. For my dog, my mother, my father. Despondent. The boat carries me away. I look back.

Ruth.
She looks about her, twirling the stem of her glass.
Why do you like my letters?
I like the things you say.
What do I say?
Beautiful things.
What?
You know.
I've forgotten.
You didn't mean it then, she says smiling.
I did, I say smiling.
Then you know what they are.
I want to hear what they sound like when you say them.
Say something now.
I can't write them.
I know. That's different. If I say it face to face I've got to mean it. I don't know. Nothing you can say face to face seems right. I can only write things.
My father told me to be careful.
If you can't be good.
Yes.
She blushes. She laughs at my discomfiture and takes my arm to say again, laughing,
Oh, you're beautiful
I'm going to marry you.
What on?
I could get a job.
What doing?
They offered me the job of organist at the church.
How much for?
Fifteen shillings a week. Twelve shillings for weddings and a pound for funerals.
We couldn't live on that.

Depends how many married. How many died.
Well, you couldn't count on five deaths a week and that's what we'd need to keep ourselves alive. We wouldn't make enough to keep body and soul together.
I don't like this.
Let's go somewhere else.

The ship's lights travel over the water, the white phosphorus widening behind. Harwich is out of sight. Some students with rucksacks are huddled together near the warm funnel, on the wooden benches.
I wish it could go on for ever. She touches my cheek and in the darkness her hand rests there for a moment.
Are you happy, my love?
I'm glad I came.
Do you really love me then?
I think so. She kisses me. I kiss her back. Clasp her.
Claim her. Again. I lean towards her.
Stop it. Wait. Not yet. Soon. Let's stay here for a bit. The wind's beautiful.
There's somebody in your cabin by now.
There might not be. Anyway it doesn't matter.
It does. Let's go down.
Wait a minute. Stay here a minute.
I see that I must but soon she agrees to go down, saying,
There'll be some fat woman there.
They pass the Dutch steward. He eyes them.
There is nobody there.
Will anybody come?
It's a bit late. They'd already be here if they were coming.
Somebody else like us.

There is nobody like us.
Lock the door.
You mustn't go too far.
I won't. Let me kiss you. I love you. She sinks on to the clean white sheet of the bunk. He lies on her with such ease, such grace.
No. No.
You must.
No. No.
This as well. Everything. You're beautiful.
Do you like me?
You're beautiful. You're warm. I was frightened you wouldn't be able to come. I was frightened that your father would change his mind.
Shh!
What?
I thought I heard something, somebody coming.
Who could now? It's past two.
Perhaps you should go now.
Somebody might come.
Nobody knows us here. What would it matter?
We might get into trouble.
We wouldn't. It's not wrong.
Was there anyone in your cabin?
Yes. But he's asleep.
But he knows you're here.
So what. It's got nothing to do with him. He's German.
What will he think if he wakes up and finds that you're not there?
He won't think.
She folds me in her arms.
I kiss her for the sake of the taste of the juice in her

mouth and for the desire which yearns in me.
You must. You must.
I can't. I can't. I'll have a baby.
You won't.
I will.
Risk it.
No. No.
Yes. You must. She is hard. Coarse. Grates. Gasps. In pain.
Don't hurt me.
I'm not hurting you.
You are, ooh, she cries. She is trying to close. I will break in upon her. I will hurt her. I will tear her. I will. I will.
She is looser. Her eyes are open, watching me, attentive. Seeing me watching her she closes them. Startled. Pensive.
Stop now, Jenny, stop. It hurts.
No! What's the matter, don't you like it? I hurt her, again. I see her mind sink.
Jenny. Oh, Jenny. She is crying.
But she does. She's changed her tone. Her face smiles.
Jenny. Oh, Jenny. I love you. Go on. Please go on.
My mind is startled. Is sucked at. Is surprised.
I wake up asleep on her. She sleeps on. I remain inside her. Growing in consciousness. But anxious. There is nothing in my mind, except a feeling of gladness. We read my letters together in the train going down the valley of the Rhine. We sit together near the window. The Rhine passes outside. Such as it is. Another river. My letters are good. I enjoy them. And the train carries us forward through the valley

into southern Germany, past Cologne, past Bonn, the seat of the government, into Frankfurt, into Bavaria, Guten Tag. He lifts his trilby with a feather in it. Hier ist Jenny. Jenny, these are my sisters, Bina, Gisela, Brigitte, Olga. I play the piano during the day. We sing. Each girl sings, plays an instrument. And the mother sings. Brigitte is ample. We dance. I kiss her soft yielding lips, waltz with her in a café in the town, ah, watch her in Frankfurt at The Marriage of Figaro and where in this is Ruth? Where? Forgotten. During the day the girls go to school. In the late morning Ruth comes to my bed. There I love her, love her. We walk in the forest. There are deer there. The late snow gives way to the sun. The pine drips. The grass freshens, straightens, rises, beyond the tracks into the thicker forest up and then out suddenly into a green bowl where a head of deer, scattered, long neck erect, listen, wait, no, nothing, but there it is I hear something, the neck stands straight, the knock knees bunch. They are away. I break cover to charge them. They bound. Jump. Across the green lush grass covered in daisies, across that clearing. Out of sight. Were they ever there? There is no trace. The place is unmoved. Ruth follows. Tired. I make love to her on the warm grass. We lie there. The sun shines on her gentle face. Poor Ruth. My regard rests on the soft flesh of her belly but penetrates no further into the soul in which I have no interest. The German girls speak with a fine sharpness, their clothes are cut, they are fit, shoes of strong leather. Helga runs the eight hundred metres. Faster than any other woman in Germany. Brigitte puts the shot. They waltz. They

love each other. Health, strength, confidence, well from them. They are like men, mothers. But it is Ruth who bears the brunt of my desire. By what it feeds on in imagination my appetite for Ruth grows so that for a time she thinks it is her I love. But, after all, we go out together to an ancient town in which a travelling puppet theatre is performing Goethe's Faust. In the cellars of a castle. Helen is made into a whore. Only Margaret is fresh. The room is without light, except for the illuminated puppets. Their voices fill the small space. Faust is led inevitably to his damnation and we go up, satisfied, up the dark steps out of the dank cave into the sweet light of day. There is an ancient Catholic church into which, with my first love, I enter:
Shall I seduce you in front of the Virgin?
Somebody might come.
We climb the stairs of the tower. There is a turret at the top from which the landscape unfolds. We drink the wine and lean over the carved wooden parapet. I think this culture higher than it is at home in England. We spent the evening with a tax collector, the father of Helga's fiancé. He taught me to sip hock, to hold it on my palate letting the air come through it. Now he plays Bach on a violin. The flat is small. He is a fat round-headed man. At Christmas he conducts an oratorio in the medieval church. He rules his children with a rod of iron and his face shows fineness as he plays. Quietly controlled and intent on what he is doing. That is what I have not seen in England. Hope opens before me in the vision of this delight and in the tones of the soprano, the clarity and lightness of Susanna. My English soul I think is enlightened.

What is there in England? Everybody plays something or does something here. The girls are fit. The fields have no hedges. Each man owns his own land. Dung is piled in the streets. A man and his wife sit on an ox cart coming back from the fields, alike. I feel that this world is more closely knit to what I desire. The people are fitter. It is sealed over with the joy of a sudden opening. The ploughed land arcs beneath me. Ruth wears a flared skirt and a pale blue jumper. She has on a mackintosh. We look out west, towards Frankfurt. I feel that I may piece together a world here. This is further inland than I have ever been. The air is heavier. It weighs upon me at first. But I grow accustomed to it. I have been reading a book on Kant which I do not understand and have not finished. I play more. Mozart. Ruth too plays, out of her ear, anything, in simple chord structures but deft and right.

They live with each other. They talk to each other. She watches me.

Jenny?

Yes.

Don't flirt with Brigitte.

I'm only playing.

I know. But I wish you wouldn't.

Are you jealous?

Yes.

We won't be here long.

Make love to me.

What? Here?

Nobody will come.

We go down later, chattering. I make love to her again on the way home, in a field near a railway line.

A train passes and we hide our faces in the grass as the light flashes over us. In bed. In the fields, in the woods, in the churches.
But watching me, she said:
I'm pregnant.
Are you sure?
Yes.
Oh hell.
Will you marry me?
Are you really sure?
Yes.

She had fainted coming back from a film. I was talking to Brigitte. I carried Ruth, lightly, up the hill. The family came from East Prussia after the war when the Russians annexed it, had built themselves a house. A family of junkers. He had established himself here as a publisher. He had a pointer and went shooting during the evening. A thin man, laughing at the Americans conducting manoeuvres in the valley below. We stood on the terrace and watched the lights of the tanks. He had an Iron Cross as had his brother, killed in action, of whom there was a photograph in his study, in which I danced with his tall and noble wife, tall, and moving gracefully to a Viennese waltz, sporting a silk brocade waistcoat, clothed in the love and admiration of this house of women.

In the woods I made love to Ruth. An afternoon by a stream in a valley, a long way into the forest, drank hock, played Schubert in the evening and accompanied the tall mother who sang arias from Mozart. Ruth looked at photographs with the two youngest girls while I played with the two elders.
Jenny, don't flirt any more.

I'm not doing. I'm only playing.
What are we going to do?
What about?
Have you forgotten?
Oh, you're pregnant, that, how do you know? are you really sure?
Yes, I am sure. What are we going to do?
We'll have to think seriously about it. There's no hurry is there? I eat the gherkins and black bread. I have enough cigars to last me. I must keep some money with which to return. We go to Fulda. Towards the Russian zone. We are told to be careful. People are abducted. Don't hitch-hike. Especially girls. They disappear.

I hold her soft hand on the train which takes us east until we come into the Catholic pocket. There is a baroque cathedral, gilded, azure. It is the first major Catholic shrine that I have ever visited. Seeing the beggar-boxes and the priests, unctuous, I withdraw to enter a smaller, rounder, bare stone church. There I am more at home. There is no decoration. Light comes from an open circle in the roof.
I like this more.
We are alone here. Have put some distance between ourselves and the family. On a hill with other pilgrims we mount the twelve stations of the cross. An old man and woman mount together, the many steps, which twist up the steep hill, on their knees. We look away and hurry past. They have rosaries and there is a look of despair in conflict with a bitter will in the old man's chaps. I had been reading Huizinga's book on the Middle Ages, the charnel houses in Paris. I remind her of them.

That's morbid, she says.
As is this religion.
But in the vaults of the baroque cathedral which is after all Christian I am reassured by the shrine of Saint Boniface, an Englishman, from Ripon.

But still we return. We go out again, into that forest again. We find a watch-tower which becomes a point of vantage. The meadows are clear, fresh, soft. I love her thus. I hope our love is endless.
Why do you flirt with Brigitte?
Don't be silly. We'll go back soon.
Well leave her alone.
How are you going to get home?
I'll hitch.
You've got no money left.
So what? I'm lucky.

I leave her at Frankfurt station, moved suddenly at her departure alone, in the presence of these five Germans I kiss her. She is drawn out of my sight by the train. It is evening.
Leave me here.
Du musst zurückkommen.

The road sweeps on. At first I am picked up by an American sergeant who buys me a steak. I sing for my supper, more than willing, I tell him about England. I have no money except an English halfcrown. He leaves me in the night. I walk on. Elated. No one stops so that I enter the forest through which the road runs to blunder until I find a clearing in which in the pale light of the moon I see a hut. That I enter. There are empty cement bags in it. Into which I crawl. So to pass the night, lying comfortable. I light a cigar, taste the smoke, doze, relight, listen to the wolves, but the door is closed, I am warm inside the bag, the cigar tastes good. I dream of Ruth, of her surprise when she finds that I have in fact returned unhurt. My heart sings. Here alone in this forest I am in love with her. I am glad that I am. England awaits my return. The earth floor caresses my back. The cigar's aroma fills my head with pleasure. I draw at it and watch, in the darkness, the glowing ash. Ruth. She will be at home by now and I am moving through the Saar towards her. As the light thins I pray for full morning. So that I may continue. Though satisfied. Satisfied with my progress so far and in no hurry. I pass a fine night and at last in the grey dawn I leave my bag, cross the clearing, regain the road, the pine smells strong, heavy in the air, and am picked up by a motor-bike. On. On.

I stop in Paris, to sleep by the Seine, thinking to go to the Louvre, but it is closed. My mind signs as I forage about the city. The traffic is fast. I am caught in a shopping arcade and cannot cross the street. Until the light allows me. I cannot walk out of this city. At the Hotel Royale I change my half-crown for the metro fare. In Saint-Denis, in Calais, in Dover, in London, I call a friend who is working in Foyle's, who introduces me to Anna-Lisa, a German, Jewess, with whom I stay, oblivious of time, of Ruth, until awaiting her return one day, in her flat, I open the door, thinking I hear someone there, but the window is open and the draught slams to the door while I listen outside, in the corridor. The door locks for ever behind me. Having no luggage, homesick, I descend the stairs and continue my journey north until in the early morning I arrive home, and awaiting the bus on which I know Ruth must come. It does and seeing her there I tap on the window. Jenny. Her face springs alight. Jenny. Jenny. She puts her arms round my neck and hugs me. Jenny. How did you get here? Are you tired? You've been so quick. I kiss her again. Ruth. Her hair I touch. My feeling wells from me. Thus in the street I kiss her. My eyes close. I hold her. She is fresh and warm. She meets me. She is pleased by me.

How did you get here so quickly, my love?

I smile.

It was easy.

They sit on the simple bed. The pub downstairs is crowded. In the bar a thin, pale man speaks of going back to work. He has spent almost all the money he had earned in the works during two months' graft. Now the gay excursion into leisure is finished and his constitution is still further weakened. He will take up employment again for another short period, until he has money enough to live it up again for a month. They lie on the bed. Jenny caresses her brown hair in which the light burns.

Do you think they mind?

No. They're all right.

She looks a bit of a tart.

She looks after her children. I like them. I think they're happy.

They're easy-going.

They don't seem to be bothered about anything.

What are you bothered about?

She laughs and smiles and moves her tongue in her open mouth. Her teeth shine with the saliva. She lies on her back and her dress falls between her legs. Stop worrying, my love. Her light hand is on his cheek.

Take your dress off. She smiles. A soft odour comes from her. She curls beside him. Her body in truth offers him ease and yet with modesty I think he sees the soft light in her face.

Are you happy?

Yes.

How?

I don't know. You do.

Is that true?
Yes. He holds her upper arm. Her breasts swell in the lace top of her white petticoat. Pliant. No. She falls into easy attitudes. She curls and covers her face with her hair. Which he kisses.
I'm a liar.
You're not.
How do you know?
I know.
What?
You don't believe what you say you feel.
How did you know that?
I'm clairvoyant.
She puts her hand on his flies and kisses his sex when she has found it. He lies back and she caresses him with such infinite grace, tact, that his mind comes clear and he smiles at the ceiling. The wind blows in his spirit and the sun shines on the water.
I'm pleased with myself. You make me feel that I am graceful.
When you touch me you make me feel elegant. I feel all shaped and formed. I feel distinct. I feel full of power.
Take your clothes off, she says.
The silk of her petticoat on his skin fondles his mind. I don't want to make a false claim but I think she frees his mind. It seems to me that as she sucks and caresses him she draws out some kind of venom, vehemence, and he is the fresher for it. He yearns for her mouth. I don't know whether that is egotism. But that is what happens. And as he kisses her and feels himself on her teeth that seems to him to consecrate and to heighten her.

Literally for her own sex swells until it is indeed almost like a globe. And indeed that small bed-sitting room in Attercliffe in a pub named after a highwayman condemned to be suspended after he had been hanged, between earth and heaven, until his body parted from itself, does with sudden and easy acceptance become the entire world. The smoke and effluent in his blood, as the thick and rounded shoulders, as the bull neck, may have been inherited but the grace is his. In his reading and his feeling. And that distempered wall where hair grease marks the sojourn of previous occupants nevertheless shines in the electric light with its own brilliance. He touches that.

He cannot ask for what he wants because I think the words would not represent the desire. Nor can Ruth. For when she says, Make love to me now, she will go no further than to hide her head on his chest and accept whatever delicacy the intelligence of his hand can find out for her. There is plenty of time.

Still she fondles him and his mind still goes out with spring in it. Still she sucks, lightening the air in his heart. She forges other bonds. The publican downstairs addresses him as Love. He tells him of the chief rent he had to pay to the Duke of Norfolk when he lived in a rented house further down the Common.

Ruth uncovers her lovely white breasts and presses his sex between them, holding them on each side. He watches that lovely intermingling. She rubs her cheek over his belly and kisses, kisses. You're beautiful, she says. I think you're lovely. I like you better with no clothes on.

He touches her light back and delicate flank. There is an assumption. Her flesh breathes the freshness of her person at him. It is clothed with soft down. She is warm. She is altogether naked to him. All her body blushes and the pores of her skin are open and as she loves him their two bodies do indeed make an unbroken arc while their flesh clings together of its own accord. Some sense of harmony and fitness seizes his mind, a sense of the infinite play in that tempered embrace. He wraps his arms about her so that she may come closer into him and their tongues play. She lies between his legs as though he were the woman. She sucks his nipples as he has sucked hers and I think in some way he nourishes her. They fuse. They are welded. Their sweat mingles.

THE OVERMANTLE AND THE SEAL OF THAT ALAS SO LIMITED BUT YET, GLADLY, SO ACTUAL EMPYREAN PART OF TIME

Upward through a pine forest where resin sharpens the air and fallen needless crack under foot. It is early Easter. The winter has remained late. The ground is damp. Cones drop, plummet, and pigeons fly. They walk hand in hand. There is, oh, a lovely silence and their fingers are knit into a design which shores, which defines, which limits, which clarifies the world. They wear overcoats. They are warm. Their breath steams from their mouths.
And life springs in them.
I love the tack of her skin and the white breath which moistens on her glowing cheek. Her bright and laughing eye darts into his heart where its barbs keep it. As:

You are grotesque, without form, without elegance, without faith. Now those scars feel again and move as in this high and unprotected delight he goes through this forest with her. The trees drip the cold and brilliant water of the last shower on them, while the brown needles stick to their shoes. Two hands link them in a common usual effort. They go up. And the smell of the pine breathes in the air. Their feet settle as they place them on the soft soil. But they are not tempted to stop. They go forward. Yes. And they come out of that forest high on the mountain. The sun shines fitfully. Now they are irradiated by the brilliant light. Mist and cloud lie about. There is a fresh breeze. They sit together on a log. And they look down across black and fallen trees, down into the green valley. There is snow on the high ground. Beyond the valley another face of rock rises, towers. About its summit clouds break and swirl. The sun dries and the wind rises, drives at them. A white cloud rolls down the side of the valley. It is dark grey. It swirls. They hear it. It descends into the valley. It grows up the slope. The sun pales and disappears as flakes fall. The cloud is above them. It envelops them. It flocks warmth and the quietness of snow falling. The snow envelops them. It flocks over them. It quietens them. It obscures their sight. Fingers their hair. Touching. The sky is black and has closed in. They sit and let the snow whiten them while they hold each other with soft tranquillity in an embrace which broaches infinite possibility, unlimited space.

They descend through the dark wood. The evening closes in. In the blizzard they cannot find the path by which they came. They seek it but are lost amongst the trees. So they follow the lie of the land and descend until they come to a shallow river from which a white mist rises. The water is black. Rushes. Boulders and pebbles clatter. The water chatters. Ruth fears that cold and strength. Jenny takes her on his back. He holds her under the knees. Her arms are round his neck.

His legs are numbed. His feet slip on the pebbles. The water tugs at him. Her warmth, oh warmth swamps his mind, his back is warm, oh warm. He holds her under the knees. He wades through the water. She shouts and screams:
Aiee! For the wind swallows her noise. The pines roar. Yet there is a strange quietness here in the

water. Jenny stops to listen for it. The branches snap, tap. Ruth clings to him.
Keep steady.
He staggers but he does not fall. The cold makes his legs tremble. He is wet with the snow that has melted on him. The current snatches. He steers through this uneven field of force while she as they near the shore begins to laugh and press, jump, up and down, ride him, shout out,
He's mad. Haha! I've got a madman! He's carried me through the water. No! No! Don't! I didn't mean it. No. You're beautiful. No. Aiee! Please. Don't drop me! I'll give you a kiss.
Am I mad? Am I? Hey?
No. No. You're not. No. Hahahaha!

On the bank he lets her down and she turns to the dark pine trees and to the wind and she shouts,
He's beautiful. He's beautiful.

Jenny views his shoes ruefully, with some concern but with more satisfaction. She kisses him.
Don't stand still, you'll catch cold, and leads him through the wet trees to the inn in which they stay. They eat and drink. With voracity later they make love in a crisp and warm bed from which they emerge in the morning glowing, like the snow itself, to eat again, hot bacon and eggs, while their eye contracts at the brilliance of the white world to which they have awakened. And joy bursts out of their hearts, jumps out and flexes itself, overwhelms them. The chairs on which they sit glow. Light burns in the silver cutlery. The cloth exhibits its texture with ostentatious pleasure in its substance. That world snaps, taut, wrought up through high delight into a mad and

dancing joy.

White light stuns their eyes. They go hand in hand through the snow until the heat of walking through such drifts turns to lust and he strips her naked to make love to her again while the snow seizes her flesh, until she asks him to stop, tired out. He rubs the snow over her breasts and belly, over her legs, in her thighs. She sucks it melting in her mouth. She rises wet through. The snow has melted on her. Her flesh is red. The sunlight glints in a lovely sheen in the moisture of her breasts which glisten while melting snow burns with the brilliance of clarity there in that pure air.

They walk again. She is slow. Her face betrays the soft light of dreaming. She is faint but with hot soup she revives. He smokes a cigar and drinks cold beer. They move on in high satisfaction. He has no map but circles through the forest, feeling his way to stones which cross the river, on these they pause while around her hair radiance sucks and blows out, which is suffused by light which looks as though it comes out of the hair and is not reflected. Her face has the pale comely docility of thrilled, uncloyed, satisfaction. All her body thrives. She feels her flesh to have one substance. She is consistent. Inside and outside are knit and fused. So she smiles. And with modest confidence offers herself with such sweet understanding. Rich, docile, doe-like, vibrant and trembling, with high-strung nerves, just a little loose, ready to snap tense in alarm at a slight jar, some slight unexpected sound or movement, alert, and yet so delicately feeling the present delight, she goes on with him, trustful and quiet, while he too only nervous lest his freshness of spirit should not endure goes with her, ravelled together in an insouciance which passes understanding, which is like grace, a quiet thrilling delight which invests all the visible world with the radiance of sacrament so that as though itself awake to the startled activity which may be seen to clothe it, dead nature rustles its skirts proffering the filigree of branches laden with white snow while mist and cloud and shafted light design the overmantle and the seal of that alas so limited but yet, gladly, so actual empyrean part of time.

THE SOUND OF THEIR PROGRESS AND ADVANCEMENT

Smell that. Isn't it lovely? There are orchids in the sparse grass. See what a beautiful day it is. Stop brooding. Her hips swing in her full skirt and sweat seeps through on to her forehead. The air is cold. The track goes uphill. You even walk as if you come out with me out of good nature but you'd rather be on your own.

A grouse rises and with a scream she lunges after it, springs through the heather. He watches in spite of himself, smiling.

Well, as he unbends he chases sheep. Their feet spatter on the broken stone of the track. Her feet are lightly clad. They run, finely balanced. The sheep start. The heather flowers and the cloud is fixed, high and does not impede the clear sun while a fresh breeze carries behind the sound of their progress and advancement. She wears easy clothes. In the ruined hut at the top of the disused cut he lies with her until that so necessary crack and snap of the world through this tension is wrought up and there again there is that so full and fine empyrean moment when the stone blazes and when the spring of the heather sends such force through its branches that they are torn from the ground. On the return Jenny with wonder in his face, carries such a flower as a token while Ruth walks quietly and softly beside him.

They walk on, as though on air, on a high plateau, and their minds sing, snap. Ruth withdraws, quietly, slowly, from her unfolding.

Did you like it?

She will not answer.
How did you feel?
She will not answer.
What do I look like?
She will not answer.
What am I like? Ay? Why won't you answer?
I don't know what you're like. I don't care.
Am I thin?
I don't know.
I'm not fit.
No.
What are you agreeing to when you agree?
I said no.
But you agreed.
I said no to all your questions and to all the others you want to ask me.
Tell me...
No. No. No. No. She gaily and with no trouble at all defeats his curiosity. He with earnest insistence goes on asking her questions. And he grows used to her not answering, he loses interest in the questions and having lost interest realizes that he lacks nothing he previously had. That he gains from her silencing that insistent and inquisitive interrogative mood.
I don't see why I should tell you everything I think, she says. I wouldn't anyway. And I don't see what use it'd be either. So shut up.
He holds her hands. She shouts gay insults at him. He smiles pale while tenderness like a fox entering a hen-run stalks into his mind. And the uneasy hens cackle and move expecting some descent. He smiles as she goes on and on until at last she places the palm of her hand on his cheek and with a tender smile says,

laughing, light, courteous, with infinite weakness and her voice like water which drips in a fountain in bright sunlight,
My love. All her body moves and all her body goes into the gesture she makes and there is no effort to understand it so that she is all significance. As though painted. All that fine activity of poetry in graceful line. Jenny is left smiling and pitied, clumsy, watching her.

Now he goes with her into a green park. And there in the fresh air they strip and dance, surrounded, overwhelmed, by the grey stone. They bathe in the water running down. Ruth jumps up and down, rubbing herself, to get dry. And Jenny, he plays. They may see high over the valley. Ruth lies on a high ledge and he looks over her breasts and belly and away out into that vast air, oh into that huge valley where a river gleams at the bottom. Her lovely body is as big as the landscape and he watches over it, until with her black hair she turns and smiles in luxury at him, the close grass soft behind her. Wind thuds against a cliff face above them. An ash which bows over them as they lie.

Fresh. Clean. Peace in his heart. Centred on this lovely girl who so freely divests herself and so easily loves him.

On the soft grass, with her, watching her. Her hand comes over her body, moves the flesh of her breasts, moves over her belly, over her shoulders. She slaps an ankle. She lies out and stretches her arms out over her head and her legs full out, arching her back to gaze with delight at the moving cumulus cloud. Her flesh stirs in the sun. Her eyes close to feel it. He lies on his belly eating grass, watches her heart beating under the white skin. Milk white her body. There is no noise here. There are no people. The mountain grows behind them. They lie. One or two insects move in the grass. The light is pure white. Now. The sky is like pearl. He quietly accepts it.

So. Lightly. She flexes her arms and legs in the air and careless of Jenny she hums with her own pleasure. She caresses him gaily, stirring him to the chords and fibres of his being, deeper. Richness and the warm idleness of a cat mingle in his blood. Good-humoured. His mind signs with its own freedom. Pure air. He has no second thoughts. She loves him again and again through the long afternoon. They descend the mountain. They enter a warm wood where desire takes hold of them again and they find a green place between the trunks of the trees. They lie in it. Ants crawl over Ruth's legs. There is juice and sap in her. That warmth. There is no difference between the surface and the depth of her flesh. It is all there. It does not shiver at his touch. Nor contract. She eases herself so that he is in her in a more comfortable manner. And watches him softly. She will move as he wishes her to move. More natural naked than clothed she loves him in that green grass till his body is air and lightness. So that it is purified. He changes state. Ribbed and knotted feelings are planed out. Formed into a fine distinctness. Grown confident. He lies in easy sensuality. She examines him, smiling. It is warm here. There is a fine scent of pine. In his stretched fingers he twirls a forked needle. The needles crack, prickle, as he moves. Ruth's head is on his belly and she fondles him, draws hair across him. She hides her face in that black hair and blows her warm breath over his belly.

Like the warmth of spring itself. Like the scent of orange blossom, she fans him. She hums. Is dreamy. Like a cat she rubs herself against him. They lie and listen to the sound of cones plummeting and to the song of birds. They have time to spare. Sharp. He is lean but his youth is soft and pleasant. And his mind is made active by surprise and easy for he becomes confident.

So, easily, docile, gentle, his flesh like the fresh air and his soul open to the wind from heaven and oh this quiet and modest girl who lies on him with the freshness of a child, abandoned to his caresses as he to hers. In sympathy with himself. All knit up, all himself. Here. Touching. An ineluctable line between his flesh and hers. She smiles at him. Quietly watches him. Under the soft down of his skin a flush shows. His heart moves the skin at his ribs. She smiles down at him. She envelops him in bracing air and now he moves with her till the sky seals over and the world is membrane. Let the air about him offer him fragrance. Let the sky keep its distance. Offer him the richness of the earth he stands on. Offer him the thickness of the wood he is in now. Offer him the kind light.

He thrives. With Ruth his body thickens. His flesh clears. He moves on. Pleasure. Strength of purpose. Grasp. Of himself, and of his family. Of Ruth with whom now he goes to the sea. There they stroll. She is prettily dressed. Her black hair falls over her eyes. She tosses it back. She is gay. The beach is crowded but they change. He watches her grinning as she clutches her towel. Her breasts bound in the soft wool of her swimming costume. They play with a ball. She wears what she thinks fit. Quick. They bask in the sun.

The beach empties. They climb across rocks, further away, there is a calm evening. They swim in the soft swell. The sea rocks her as she floats, washes over her soft belly and lulls her to the rocks over which she clambers. He swathes her in a blue towel and they sit and look at each other. She watches him. She breathes warm air on him. Her hair is wet. She pulls fingers through it. She is panting. Her arms inside the towel pull it round her knees. Thus she stays. There is satisfaction in him. Interest. Glad acceptance in the way he feels. He fastens his shoes. Sand grates on his feet. The salt sticks to his flesh. That hard rock refreshes him. The sea laps at it. He watches her dress. The dress over her head and then flimsy, light, with her underclothes in the bag she carries, they return to a full pub where there is light, noise, heat. Where he looks at her, flesh of his flesh.

In calm meeting. Undeclared confidence in his manner. Humour in his eyes. With conviction. She sits and follows it through, able to meet it in her flesh, able to absorb it, to feed on it. The glance. The yearning. She eyes him as he watches her. She smiles to his smile. Her face clouds. Enough. She feels though satisfaction as she drinks and follows the cool liquid into the intestine of her loose and fragrant stomach.

But this cannot last. Such joy cannot be endured. Ruth grows tired of his demands. She turns:
You think you're God Almighty, don't you. You think you can tell everybody what to do. You think you've no need to bother about me any more now that you've done what you wanted to. I suppose you've told all your friends. You laugh about it with them, don't you. Well, don't get too sure of yourself.
They are in Lincoln, on a Monday afternoon, his half-day. He has come in the van to pick up lambs from Swift's. They have loaded them into the back of the van and now they sit together while she arraigns him. I'm sick and tired of it. You're always pushing and straining and talking about your family. What about my family? Why won't you do what I want to do sometimes? I'm warning you. You'd better be careful. Don't threaten me. He smiles at her and puts his head down to her breast. She fondles his hair, the nape of his neck. I don't want to hurt you, my love, she says. But, pushing him away, I'm not going to be trapped. You won't let me breathe. You're changing me. I never used to be het up like this all the time. I used to be happy. I could talk to anybody. Now I hardly dare say a word. You're making me into something else than what I am. I won't stand for it. It can't go on. You can't expect me to change just because you want me to. Change to what? Sitting boozing in pubs, that's all. We never have any money. If I marry you I shall have to marry your whole family. And you don't love me. You don't even know I'm here. You're like a piece of stone. You'd be unfaithful to me and you wouldn't even give me the

right to be upset. I don't know what sort of a thing you are. I don't like you. I have to apologize for myself all the time. All you want to do is get my knickers off. You're pleased enough when I do. Yes I know. You're very good at repartee. You're not listening, it's not good talking to you. You're all right when you're in a pub.

You're like your father.

Be careful.

It's true. You think you can always frighten me. All you care about is your father and your brother. Look at the way you treat your poor mother.

Leave my family out of it.

You can't frighten me. You're always trying to browbeat me. I'm not like this. I don't like myself any more. You make me into somebody different from who I am. I won't stand for it. You'll have to change or I shan't go out with you any more. I don't care what you threaten. I'm not standing for it. You can go and run up a gum tree. I'm not going to make love to you in ditches and woods for the rest of my life. When could you ever marry me? You've got no money. You're not interested in your work. You're always wanting to do something else. You never make your mind up about anything. All you want to do is talk. I'm fed up of talking.

Steady! Keep steady! Quiet! A quiet man. Knitting. He was sitting on the sofa, knitting. Stitch after stitch, deliberately. I shall be finished in about thirty seconds. Legs crossed, black jeans, sandals on. The same. Everything the same. No changes. One pair of jeans worn out. Buy another. The same. Identical sandals for time out of mind. At his waist a bunch of keys on a faded leather belt. A bottle-opener there too. Joe's bottle-opener. A little red barrel dangling from the key-ring. Dependable. Steady. Knitting. Elbows in and the green thread like a cut across the end of his index finger. Over and in, up and through. The wool trailing over his little finger, held there to keep the tension, under the palm, over the index finger, slipping it on and off, on to the other needle, stitch after stitch along the line. Clicking. Clicking. And the hands moving as in a web. The wool inching through the net of fingers woven into the sweater pattern, gradually coming together on the left needle. Knit one. Purl one. Drop one. Go back. Pick it up. Start again. When I've finished the row. Keep it going. Above the black jeans a black sweater, a beard, closely, evenly, regularly, cropped, hair. Poised. Serene. Steady. Woven and kept together in the green wool his mother's face. Now in a bed-sitter in Birmingham doing exercises out of the Penguin book to keep body and soul together. A bit of knitting after he'd finished work. Steady his nerves.

He finished the row and pierced the ball of wool with the two needles so as to keep them together.

Then he put them into a polythene bag and left them on the arm of the chair. In the kitchen he broke the eggs into the white basin and gave them sixty turns with the whisk. He had put the heavy frying pan on the hot plate. When the fat was melted he poured in the egg into which he had ground black pepper from a wooden mill. His omelette. With it two pieces of sliced bread. Two. Later lettuce with olive oil and two large cups of tea. His diet. He ate, feeling the food on his teeth. The warm tea, drunk quickly, to catch the pepper, burnt in his stomach. He put a hand there. Always the same precise quantity, an identical meal. The same every day. Each evening. The Daily Telegraph was propped against the milk bottle. So he constructed a world.

His mother was pouring tea into the pot. A large, open-hearted, loving, fat woman, bustling, bustling, feeding her children, too much, too much, all fat, all lazy, except Joe now. Tea, omelettes, any time, biscuits, new baked cakes, scones, meat, chops, steaks, fillet, loin of pork, of lamb, crop, silverside, sirloin, sirloin, sirloin, with fat - I like the fat - fat, fat. She too eating. The father, fat, sitting there. His heavy jowls and black bristle, his under lip thrust forward, jutting, talking about church tithes. I won't pay 'em. I wouldn't before. I took the church to court. Not many people have done that. Windbags. The lot of 'em. Why should I pay tithes to keep windbags? Graft. Corruption. Stop it. It must be stopped. Somebody's got to make a stand, take up the fight. The working man has been pushed about long enough in this country. Things have changed or they should have since the war and where they haven't I'm going to make 'em change. And one change I am going to make is that I'll be damned before I pay one penny piece for church tithes. I don't want a parson. I don't send my family to church. Why then should I be imposed on by an archaic law passed when there was only graft and corruption? It's the same now as it was then. Everybody's in it. Well, I'm going to stop it. Nobody'll make a fool out of me. I can tell you that. Let 'em try. I'll take 'em to court again. And if I'm convicted I'll take it to a higher court and a higher court and a higher court. They can lock me up. I'll go to jail. But I'll not pay.

Or with his bees in a black veil hanging from a pointed, broad-brimmed hat, an inquisitor, dripping honey from a suspended cone with linen inside it, through, down, on to the table where one jar after another stood in rows. Yes. With phlegm in his throat when he spoke. Not clear. His teeth jutting, yellow, neglected, and clenched together, lines deep in his cheeks and forehead. He was well over six foot. He kept his belly in with a thick leather belt. His head was sunk in his shoulders and his eyes glittered underneath his black eyebrows. His honey one and six a jar, You don't want one free, do you? Ha! Ha! Tithes. Tithes. Tithes. A penny an acre. Why should I pay it? Why? Why pay it? Tithes. He had one field in Rutland. Fought a court action over the boundaries. A house in Leicester. An orchard, a lovely orchard where the bees were. Yellow leather gauntlets.

Get out of my house you whore, trollop, hussy. His jaw jutting, his teeth out, beetle-browed, to his daughter who had come home late from a dance, too

late, Out of my house! Where've you been? Missed the bus. Missed the bus. You'll have to do better than that. If you're going to lie to me.
The daughter, Helen, fat, heavy, randy. Lying on the floor on one occasion, lying on the floor kicking her legs up, brash. A cook, a professional cook, wanting oh wanting a man. To the dance at the local town, rubbing herself against the man. Missing the bus. Thumbing a lift. Yes. Her skirt over her knees to take the man's hand in his flies, till they stopped and went into a stooked cornfield where on sheaves he had her. Hot wet then back again later to the village, now, You dirty little whore. Get out of my house. Out. Out. Out. The mother stopping him. Don't, Harold. Stop it. Don't hit her. The huge arm raised. The man six foot four, seventeen stone. A war hero.
She's bringing shame on the family. Smack. The hand down on to Helen's face. Smack. Smack. The mother screaming. Helen screaming insulting her father. You mean old bugger. Wouldn't give a penny away. Mean. Mean. Mean. I'll come in when I like. When I like. I'll do what I like. I earn my own living. Not while you're in my house you won't. You'll do as you're told. Get upstairs. He stood over her in the pointed hat with the black veil, cowed her, till she went. Out. Up. Sobbing. Mrs Corby sitting down. I don't know. That'll do now. Harold. That's enough. Get on with your honey. I'll make some tea.

Now the second cup. The editorial finished. There in Birmingham. The arrow shot from the cross-bow into the sheet of glass. Measure it. The area of shock. The effect of impact. The extent of the shattering. Look at the pattern. Triplex glass. Aeroplane windows. Make them stronger. Reduce the loss of light. Reorganise the crystalline structure so that it comes straight through. Whoosh!

When he had finished the meal he put the cup in the centre of the plate and placed them in the sink where he squirted on a little of his chosen detergent and turned on the hot water tap, four turns, to the right, watching the lather gathering. With his plastic brush, from its nail, he cleaned the cutlery and his pots. The black sleeves of his thick sweater pushed up to his elbows. His silver strapped wristwatch off. Thick black hairs glistening softly with the soapsuds.

His mother was pouring tea into the sugar bowl. Harold! Harold! I feel funny. Harold. Here's the tea. Here it is. Then fell. The kettle lid rolling about, clattering, spinning out until it stopped flat. She, crumpled on the floor. Harold in his black veil stooping over her. Her mouth open. Yellow saliva dropping from her dropped jaw and her eyes open and white, her face slipped to one side. Dead. Emmie? Emmie? Grunting to kneel down beside her. Patting, softly, her warm cheek. Emmie? What is it? Shall I get the doctor? Too late. Too long. The gardens of the crematorium a mere formality.

His father down beside his mother. Patting his cheek. The doctor kneeling beside her with his stethoscope to her open breast. Taking it from his ears and standing again, quietly. Joe. You're sensible. Try to calm your father. Here are some sedatives. Try to get him to take one. Sedatives. His father's shoulders and long thin arms all that was left now of the flesh that had generated him. Emmie? Emmie? What's the matter? Why are you like this? Emmie? In her oak coffin, covered in flowers, she was burned a week later in Leicester. They drove there in silence and in silence they returned. The honey was put on sale in the shop. Helen continued to miss the bus. The father cottered but did not threaten to strike her. A younger girl fell from a bus and damaged a thigh. They visited her. She had grown fat. Glandular derangement. She ate. At table she ate the bread. All the bread. She began to steal food from other plates. Without asking spearing with her fork pieces she fancied on other people's plates. She grew. She put on a stone, in a year, and would the doctor said until she too died. Silly, young, with a girl called Thorpe she covered the walls of her room with pop singers. He's lovely. Oh, he's lovely. Better looking than you, you silly old bugger. To Harold, her father, who sat at the table, in his shirt-sleeves and braces, no collar on. Unshaven. Going through his papers. Box after box of papers. Reading his tithes correspondence and growling and muttering. A few men of integrity. If more people complained. Graft. Corruption. It'll never change. But they'll not do it to me. I'll see to that. I'll not give in to them. Reading the correspondence about the action brought by the local council for the compulsory purchase of three yards off the lawn at the front end of his bungalow. His counter action. The court case. The press cuttings. Harold Corby defends Liberty of Individual. His loss. His anger. His irritation. Snarling and grinding his teeth. There at the table. Graft. Graft. Corruption. Don't you tell me about your local councils. This country stinks. It's a matter of principle. Principle. Cantankerous. Don't tell me why they built that housing estate at Helpringham. Out in the street a girl unmarried, pregnant, walking past. To the bus queue. He saw her. Out after her. His seventeen stone and his jaw jutting. You should be ashamed. Standing here with decent people. Walking down this street where the children can see you. You're a whore. A whore. You should be horse-whipped. Now you get on a public bus. I shall write to the council. To the council. Complain. Choking with indignation. Phlegm up there in his throat. Cough. Swallow. To the council. The girl away, running, crying, holding her belly. Leave her alone! You're no angel!

Nobody's perfect. Poor lass. Leave her alone.

Standing there above the bus queue like a falling mountain.

Beetling over them. Six foot four and seventeen stone. Have you no principles. No shame?

Back again, shambling back from the street, back to his boxes. To his proof of graft. A sergeant pilot when he came out in 1945 after thirty years' service, a pension enough to live on. With inflation not enough so that now he is a meat grader.

Graft there too. Butchers slipping a pound to the grader to let a carcass through. Not me. Not me. Never. I cut it down. Straight out. If there's disease there. Thc liver's on the floor. No truckling with them. Black marketeers. While we were fighting the war. Price fixers. Tricksters. Like scrap men. Thieves. Gypsies.

He was trying to get on the council to expose it. Not

elected. Writing now, at the table, Mary-Anne eating salad opposite. Buns, just baked, had left school now and since her mother's death, cared for her father. Growing. Writing an analysis of tithes. To his M.P. A letter about the corruption of driving instructors' examiners. About the eleven plus. About religious instruction in schools. About this, that, this, this, this. Here! Me! Now!

His mother falling as she poured the tea into the white sugar basin. The sugar brown and set. Keep her out of mind. Switch on the television, and take out the knitting. Later prepare tomorrow's work. Finish the calculations from today's results. Plot the graph. Hold to the fine hairline of the slide rule and follow it across until you come to the right answer. Make your cocoa at a quarter past twelve, one sugar. Do five of the exercises out of the Penguin book after you've tidied up and placed your instruments neatly together again and breathed deep over a window looking out on to the wilderness. In carefully folded striped pyjamas. Your sandals together beside the chair. Jeans neatly folded over the back of it. Belt and keys over the jeans. Read your twenty-five pages now.

Soon after his mother's death his father crashed his van and broke his collarbone. He sat subsequently in the chair with his arm in a sling, waiting, bad-temperedly, for death to come. Scowling. He would not eat. Nor drink tea. His face was black with stubble. His eyes were half closed. The corners of his mouth were turned down. His jowl fell. His chin was sunk down on his chest. He looked out of the top of his eyes. At bay. In him black stubbornness. Like a cornered bull. His head down. His feet out. Waiting. Like a bull. Watching his daughter eat and grow and Helen ignoring him. Dirty. His flies undone. His shirt front unbuttoned, food on his flannel shirt, his black chest and the yellow coarse wool vest. Joe made omelettes there late at night. In the big low kitchen where the mother had died. Two eggs. Sixty turns. Two minutes. The keys at his waist. His father sat in the chair wearing a frayed pair of carpet slippers. Sloppy. Glowering. The sling for his arm was dirty. He would not have it changed. Occasionally he shambled into the orchard to look at the bees, wearing his tall hat and black veil and stayed there for periods of time. A tall figure, aimless, in his orchard, watching his bees. Under the veil his face set like a gargoyle, fixed, stubborn, that lower lip jutting out, out, the forehead brooding contracted, concentrated, willing himself to death. Bent on it. In the chair. In the same attitude.

Come on, father. Rouse yourself. Rouse up. Rouse up.

Let me be. Slumped. Lingering. The collarbone not healing. The bone not knitting. Joe with soft voice, modestly about the house, quietly, softly. Softly trying to keep down his sister's weight. Bribing her a pound money for a stone flesh. Each stone you lose I'll pay you a pound. And then precisely to work in sweater and jeans and sandals his keys at his belt on a green well-oiled bicycle to the school he temporarily taught in while his father sat, and muttered, sometimes, tithes, he was forced to pay them, you must make an inventory of the stock, Mr Corby. So that I can assess the profit. You must pay some income tax. I'm not paying tax for public waste. Public money squandered. Unmarried girls about the street. Filth and corruption, graft. No principles. Welfare state. I want no part of it. I want to see justice done. Why should I pay for fat priests and city councillors, begging, for schools, playing fields, whist drives, for the Mothers' Union, for the restoration fund, for the Easter offering. Emmie. Emmie. I think she squeezed my hand before she died. I think she did. As she was going. Nothing. Now she's nothing. As dust into dust. As ashes into ashes. Emmie.

Slumped. Concentrated. The room about him in disorder, cardboard boxes filled with litigation. A derelict piano with brass swinging candlesticks. The chair collapsed, the springs gone, lining, flock, the rugs threadbare, souvenirs of his air force career, from India, Burma, Australia, a silver dish presented by his mess mates wishing every success for the future. The children, Mary-Anne, Joe, Helen, in the kitchen. Ignoring them. Like sand in his eye, goading him. Irritating him. Distracting him. Let me be. Trying to prise him away from his purpose. She was fat, she was warm, she treated him like a naughty boy, she knew how kind he was, how gentle, how loving, how generous, misunderstood now since she had gone. But how to make it clear that this was only a rough outside, that he loved them all in his own way, for himself. That he had their interests at heart, that everything he did was for them, everything. That it was their patrimony that he wished to protect. He would leave them a house each. Unentailed. Unmortgaged. Free. Independent. That they could keep out of the hands of the usurers. The Jews. To keep clear, clean. Now to unbend, to show them. He felt silly. He loved them there, in the other room. How much his son's softness pleased him. His quietness. His good sense. His head screwed on the right way. How to be kind, to be loved, to be pleased, pleasing, to be pandered to. Why Helen ignored him? When he shouted at her he hardly meant it, more the pleasure in shouting. Why Mary-Anne swore at him. She got her own way in everything now that her mother was gone. Emmie. Why Joe was so quiet. Emmie understood. Emmie. She knew that he meant no harm to Helen, they didn't know that, Emmie understood that his cruelty was not cruelty, that his bullying was not bullying, that his meanness was not meanness, that his litigation was not litigious. Emmie understood. After all he'd done. To leave him alone there, willing him dead. Out of the way. So that Helen could bring disgrace on the family.

Mother wouldn't have wanted you to give up Dad. Joe beside him, with food, an omelette, come on, rouse up, it's not the end of the world, you ought to try to take hold of yourself, take hold of your responsibilities.

I'll be best out of the way.

You won't. Don't talk daft. Eat this.

I can't. Clenched. No, opened out so, accepting it I betray her, forget her, leave her, if my teeth champ on that food each bite takes me from her, if I open my mouth she will fly out through my teeth. Keep it shut. Die. I won't. I can't. I mustn't. I must sit here. I must stay here. I must not change. I must not compromise. I must not bend. I must not try to make them understand. I must not bid for their love. Emmie loved me. I could do what I like. Whatever I did. She loved me. I knew that. I proved it. Corby she called me. Corby.

Black. Out. Running out. He sat in the chair, slumped, or he stood in the orchard in the spring and watched his bees in the blossom. Waiting. Short of breath. Dirty. A pain in his chest. Here! At last.

They found him lying in the orchard with the black veil over his face. His features had slipped. Breathing. Paralysed. His face innocent of grief or of anger. Softer, cleaner, rounder. Calm and vacant in the hospital bed, fed with a feeding bottle. In nappies. Dad? Do you know who I am? Dad?
So for months, for years perhaps, a coronary thrombosis, too much good living, too fat, too old to change. Good living.

He'd got such a strong personality, such a fine physique. It's awful to see a strong man fall. So Aunty Mary, the mother's sister. She came to help them, to help manage the house. That's enough, Mary-Anne.

Joe at this time loved Solveig, a Swedish girl. She came to stay. Helen and Mary-Anne were nice to her. She stayed only a short time for she was needed back in Sweden. She would return in the summer. She did not return. First her grandmother fell backwards down the cellar steps and so died. Then her mother committed suicide. Then she married, had a miscarriage, divorced her husband and by the summer was in a mental institution. Joe, calm and steady, on his well oiled bicycle, continued to teach. At the end of the summer his father died, intestate. It was necessary to sell all the property. Mary-Anne was under age. Helen wished to evict Aunty Mary from the bungalow where she lived, part of the estate, Joe would not allow it. They quarrelled. Helen left, disenchanted, to marry.

In the factory in Birmingham he parked his Hillman. In the laboratory he donned his brown smock, felt for the slide-rule in his pocket, the breast pocket, patted them, there in a row, red, green, black, and the silver measuring tee-squares, slide-rules, celluloid protractors, keep it going, the further the wider, and between ends there were logarithm books. He sat at his chair. Sandalled feet together. Open your brief-case. Place the graph you drew last night square to the end of the table. With your arms flat out and your head bowed, watching your line stay there. Keep yourself there. Steady yourself there. For you must keep down the next girl, Josephine, whom you met in Paris. Yes. At a lecture. Next to you. Ginger hair. Oh, ginger hair in a green costume with green eyes and long thin legs. Silent there beside her, quiet, until you said,
What did you think of that? Freckled and then pale, smiling back, straight, Come and have some coffee. You come back to my flat. Let me tell you about Julian. In Oxford. Champagne. And then he left her but wrote saying that he loved her, could he return. Did. Then he left her again when, after some time, he re-wrote the letter. Her mother came,

This is Joe, Mother.
Joe? There as someone to be introduced. As proof. Being steady and sensible. They went to Versailles. On the train Mrs Trickett pulled down the hem of Josephine's skirt, nipped it between thumb and finger, adjusted it, smoothing it down with the other hand, sitting opposite.
Oh mother, blushing, smiling, glancing, at Joe, from her good eye. Her grandfather had had syphilis. Her eyes would not work together. On her right side she knocked things over. After a long visit.
Oh, the gardens were lovely. What I'd really like is a nice cup of tea. Joe. They were in bed for a time while she talked about Julian. He had been reading law. He was going into his father's solicitors' firm. Joe understood. Yes. He realised that she could never feel for him what she had felt for Julian. But if he could help, be of any help, it would be enough for him. He demanded nothing for himself. He wanted nothing for himself. It was for her. If he could see her happy. If he could help to steady her and give her confidence that would be his reward. She was grateful. She left him for Julian who had re-written his letter again and who again left her. Satisfied. He finished his course there in Paris and returned to England with nothing to reproach himself for.

Mary-Anne grew. His bribe failed. She sat in that low kitchen and ate her own baking while it was still hot. At sixteen she weighed sixteen stone and at seventeen, seventeen stone, at eighteen she weighed eighteen stone. Surreptitiously she popped this and that in her mouth. Chocolates, biscuits, slices of bread and butter, the new bread's crust, broken off.

Gnawed the edges of the loaf when she brought it from the baker. Like his mother she began to move, bustle, bake, feed him, who remained. Making the inventory. Taking the stock, realising the value, with equity, sobriety, quietly, steadily. She kept him, his cheeks rounded. His jeans grew tighter. He and Mary-Anne ate with savagery. When he got in the table was laid, loaves of new bread, celery, cold meat, pickles, onions, beetroot, red cabbage, piccalilli, anything, cakes, buns, biscuits, tea, endless tea, smack, chop, grease dribbling off her chin, off his chin. We must stop this, Mary-Anne. It's bad for you to eat like this.
Listen who's talking.
You must get a job.
What can I do?
A nurse. Too fat for a nurse. Slim. Eat. More. Some more. Another piece. Another slice. Just a little bit. Just one. Then I'll slim. Tomorrow. I'll start tomorrow. Oh please, Joe. PLEASE.
All right, since you can't slim you'll have to be a child nurse.
Oh, that'll be lovely.
Omelettes later then. At night. More. More. She ate and grew.
Joe too was growing fat.
Now look, Mary-Anne, stop it. You must stop it. Mary-Anne stop it. Now. You must stop now or you'll make yourself ill.
Who are you to tell me what to do, you silly bugger. I cook your meals and do your washing, don't I? Don't I? Shut up then, you're not my father. Do you think you're my father? Do you think? Do you? Her eyes in his mind. Do I think I'm her father? Perhaps she's right.

What's the use of trying to interfere. I wouldn't let anyone dictate to me. She'll get over it. She's only a young girl. Withdraw. Keep out of it. Keep away from her.

Aunty Mary was forty-five. She no longer helped. Mary-Anne had called her a silly old bag. She had retired into her tent, the bungalow. Joe called on her. Like an armchair she sat before the fire surrounded by her little comforts. Her crochet work, her knitting Her slippers. Her photographs, of her husband, dead of her sons, away, of her childhood, with Emmie, Emmie, in Leicester, there, in prosperity, at the piano. She standing, an arm on Emmie's shoulder, the singer, upright and proud while Emmie sat beside her, bright, alert, vivacious. Joe sat with her while she made him tea. He listened to her complaining about Mary-Anne. I don't know where she gets it from. I don't think it can come from outside of the family. His tea in the cup which was in the saucer. Proud now of his delicacy of touch, his precision. His hair clean and sweet-smelling. His sweater fitting tautly. His body disposed about him as he had ordered it. Joe, sat, and drank tea with Aunty Mary. Mary-Anne was at the village dance.

Quieter still then. And even steadier. My lovely Joe, eking out his life, letting it play through his fingers, not much, inching it out, piece by piece, little by little, withdraw, Joe my darling, keep steady. Mary-Anne ate too much. At twenty-one she weighed twenty-one stone. She died in the low kitchen, pouring out the tea. Joe quietly finished the inventory and divided equally with Helen who, disenchanted, was married. He withdrew then to Birmingham where he is sitting in his brown overall making calculations.

When he had finished work, in the Hillman he stopped at the first garage as always, to check the oil and water. While the attendant did that Joe checked the tyres. Every thousand miles he sent it in for service. It was undersealed. Simonized, comprehensively insured. Nothing was too much trouble. This evening he is going to visit the next, last, girl. Divorced with two children. He buys sweets for the kids at a small shop where they know him. You can tell the time by him. A box of chocolates for Margery and arriving there he parks his car where he always parks it and in the evening when the kids are in bed, having welcomed Joe who had brought a new element of security into their lives, he sits, rather relaxed, on the sofa, with Margery, watching the television, eating chocolates with her, soft, quiet and steady.

Married. Easter. My daughter's second birthday. Ruth, whom I shall now call Nicole, my French wife, is going to Leeds to buy clothes. She went to mass in Malton on Good Friday and again last Sunday. Last night I caught her praying. She has been gayer since than for several years. I can say that already, I don't want to say it. I would like to stop this. I shall be thirty this year. Never too late to break or mend. We have come through a storm in the last month or two which might have destroyed these safe arrangements.

Her hair is piled loose on her head and hangs down. She is wearing the blue jeans in which she painted the house, parti-coloured, and a black sweater, black boots. Her movement is loose. She is teasing me. We eat lunch away from the children who won't eat if we're there. Green salads with the olive oil her mother sent, spring onions. In a room painted red and white with a polished wooden floor which burns in the sun, the lettuce crisp and my mouth alive, my papilles gustatives, as my father-in-law calls them, doing overtime, now, at the thought of it.

Arthur and his wife came to visit us at the weekend with their child. For Easter. Making money now. I was reading a lecture by Hammond called The Growth of Common Enjoyment when they stopped at the gate in my father's new Triumph, which gives him prestige. My first handshake was reluctant.
How do.
Nicole came out. Hello Anne. Her head on one side, half proffering her hand, never sure here whether to

shake hands or not, when she does her supple fingers stretched out bend back, her thumb curls back over, her whole hand grasps. She clutches and shakes, her elbow out, like a French child, peremptory, once up, once down. But not with Anne who hardly sees her. Her jeans attract no attention, nor does the loose black wool of her sweater from which all the vitality has been worn.

The boot of the car is filled with folded blankets. There's a box of food in the back. I take it out and into the pantry. Meat. Bacon. Farm butter. So they are welcome. It is time for the baby's feed. She has several tins.

Have you got a clean spoon, Nicole? Arthur takes him. Hold him. Never leave him except at my bidding. Obey me. Watch me. My feelings are of the utmost importance. My sensations constitute a value which you must recognise. I am a mother. Other people seem to take no trouble over their children. I however fulfill my duties. I will have satisfaction. I must have more, money, clothes. We'll never have any money, not enough for me to dress properly. Properly. He spent a fortune on her for a fur coat at Christmas. Then, wearing it, on Christmas Eve, she was good-tempered. It's a new kind of fur:

It's very nice, Anne.

That must have set you back a bob or two.

His father smoking his pipe. The light shining in his hair. His eyes twinkling. The glass of whisky in his hand. Here Anne. Have a glass of brandy. He gives her a glass. She takes it from him smiling. Her white fur coat wrapped about her. Dyed, I think. Or dead. Now Arthur must hold the child which is fat,

heavy, good-tempered, dressed in blue, smiling, while she prepares his bottle.
Do you need anything, Anne?
No. I've brought everything with me. I have everything I need. Hold him then! Look he's crying.
Come on then. Was he crying? Did his nasty daddy make him cry? She didn't feed him herself, frightened that he would pull her dugs out of shape. Though she is flat-chested now almost because she won't eat as an exhibition of her narrow sensibility.
She is thin. Her mouth is pursed. Her teeth bad.
Will you come out for a drink?
I can't. The baby. His feed. Somebody's got to do it. You go.
What time shall I cook the lunch, Nicole says.
Half-past two, that'll be about right, not before, they don't close till two. Not that I want to go. I'd rather stay here. But I'd better...
Yes. It's a sacrifice, isn't it... Poor Jenny... never mind, my little darling, you'll survive. Doesn't want to go... you should be ashamed.
We went to several pubs in the villages about here where the people stop talking when you enter the bar in order to listen to what you say in order to find out who you are what your income is and how much capital you have.
We found a pub with a few people in it in Kirkby Moorside where we could talk.
How's business?
We had a record week last week.
We sit near the empty fireplace.
I can hardly believe it. It must make it a much more pleasant thing. Working there. Oh, it is. There's a

different atmosphere. They're better tempered. We don't get on each other's nerves so much. This car's made a new man of him. He takes Mother out on a Sunday afternoon. There aren't rows now as there used to be. They get on better. He takes her out to the sea. They take the dog out for a run. That's the best thing you ever did for them. They love it.
I know. And your pipe. That stops him coughing. He smokes it before he goes to bed.
When I saw him the other day he was breathing easily. They'd come back from Mablethorpe. The dog was tired. It's a beautiful animal. You should see it jump. I throw a ball against the wall and it jumps for it on the rebound. It turns itself round in the air. It's a beautiful thing. They love it.
We'd better get back. Perhaps we could come out tonight.
Anne'd like to come out.
I'll see if we can get a baby-sitter. Nicole'd like to come out too, I should think. That'd be all right, wouldn't it, if we could all go out to a pub, together. Nicole would enjoy it, I think. I hardly ever take her out.
Anne'll want to go out.
Yes. I'll see if we can get a baby-sitter. I think Nicole might enjoy it. I think we'd probably better get back. I said we'd be back by half past two.

She had fed the baby which was sitting cooing in Gilles' pram. The lunch, Yorkshire pudding, beef, spring cabbage, roast potatoes, was ready and Nicole pretending to be angry. Arthur and I in high good humour brought on by the Guinness perhaps.
What shall we do this afternoon? It's a good idea to

eat lunch late on Sunday. My eye on the clock. Nearly four already. How about a twenty-mile walk over the moors, Anne? Pick baby up. Look. He wants you.
Let me finish my bloody dinner then.
Go on. Pick him up. Ah, look!
Nicole took him, smiling, looking at him, thinking about him.
Oh, what a heavy baby. My word. How much does he weigh?
Over two stone.
My word. Yes. Are you a heavy baby?
He watches proudly. I think he spends a long time playing with his son when he is alone with him.
He also plays with my father's dog.
What do you want to do? Shall we go out somewhere? There's a Roman road, still paved, as it was, we could go to see it.
All right.
Aren't you coming? She was sitting on the sofa, watching television. You'll ruin your eyes. That won't do you any good. You want to come out and get some fresh air. It's cold.
Nonsense. It'll do you good. Come on.
Aren't you coming?
Oh, all right. What about baby? He'll get cold.
Wrap him up. He'll like it. He'll be all right.
I don't want to see a daft Roman road. What is there to see? Another one of his ideas.

We drove out to Goathland. Up through Pickering. Across the moor. I showed him the monks' tracks paved during pilgrimages from Rievaulx to Whitby. The area criss-crossed by tracks used by monks going from one monastery to another. I watched her in the mirror as I drove, with her lips touching the baby's head, her eyes closed. There was a high wind. The wool of the sheep standing by the road, blown in, pools opening in it, the white soft down underneath exposed and on the other flank the wool streaming out and the wind roaring. It was cold. The light was clear, brilliant, the wind seemed to blow it clean. Out of the car.

I'm not coming. It's too cold. He'll get cold. It'll be me who has to get up to him. It's all right for you. I'll sit in the car. Nonsense. Give him to me. He'll enjoy it. He's a boy. Come on out. I took him. She got out. The skin stretched over the bone of her face and her teeth bare, like a sheep, white, her eyelids blue, already cold.

Under the shade of a random built wall. An oak tree growing in it. The track rising beside it. To it. The boulders here near the oak vast, black, the oak surmounting them and looking up through the bare branches into the blustering sky where white cloud hurls across through a blue which burns with its clarity. Gravelled by the blown cloud and in the shade the air like palpable dust, its delicate texture creating peace while the fresh smell of the moss now under foot, the grass cropped so close that it is like moss, enters us into a cleaner world. The sun is low down in the sky. We are walking west. The grass at out feet is velvet. Dense. Firm. Yet with a freshness, an innocence, is it? No. Not in this process. But there are plovers which gambol, play, in the air. The wind, oh, the wind blusters. Blusters while I run with the child, which is laughing, watching the cloud, watching the sheep. We chase them. Over the

heather. Lunging over the springing turf. Laughing. Come on. Ha! Ha! The sheep too nimble. I hold his head as I run. Smoothly. So that I do not jolt him My nephew. Swaddled too much. Heavy. Strong. Ours. Happy. His mother away behind, walking. He hands thrust into her coat sleeves, her features chisel led into acerbity by the wind.
How much further is it?
I cannot help but bound in this clean wind.
Twenty miles. You see that high point there, there, in the distance, beyond that, beyond that plantation of fir where the ground is ridged so that it is difficult to walk on it, see it? There. Here take him, Arthur. I'll take Cathy. Nicole has been rolling in the cropped grass with her. She can walk now, well. There is after all nothing wrong with her leg, which I have imagined buckled, knock-kneed, hen-toed, anything. Iron is all she needed. Nicole's cheeks are red. She is glowing. Proud of herself to like this fresh cold. I'm resilient, aren't I? After all I was used to heat. I like this now. I'm glad that I like it. I think I'm a fine woman.
You are.
She runs after me, knees in, feet out, elbows in, hands out, working sideways. Shouting. She can't catch me until I let her, panting. I smoke too much. The children. Gilles is climbing the wall. He is on top of it. The wind blows his long hair.
Come down!
Papa! Papa! Regarde-moi. Cathy ambles beside me. I pick her up. We run. I will enjoy this if she doesn't. After too much beer, too much food.
Is it much further?

Yes.
I'll go back to the car. I don't see why I should just walk about.
Come on. It's not far.
He walks with her at her pace, my brother. Nicole is behind us now, with Gilles. She is holding his hand as he picks his way along the top of the wall. There is a gate before us. I open it and she passes through. Arthur carries his son. The folds of his coat she adjusts and closes the gate so that Nicole must open it again.

There is a river. Over which stepping-stones. I take Cathy and hold her face close to the brilliant water which ripples, chuckles, plashes, over pebbles, over the rounded granite. Here a vast bank shades us from the wind. The water looks deeper further up. Perhaps it is possible to swim in it. Shall we swim? The sea at Whitby will be rough.
I'm not going any further.
She sits on the broken bracken. The clear water is at her feet. It's stupid. Just walking about. Arthur holding his son sits beside her for a moment. I leave them. To keep her sweet. Running with Cathy up the steep slope. The narrow track toward a great granite boulder where I will stop if I reach it with one effort. I don't. I stop. Turn. Below Nicole is through the gate, crossing the stepping-stones. I can hear her shouting with Gilles who dances. Arthur gets up and turns uphill, towards me, with his son. She follows him. He runs to catch me. He will. Does. I stop again. Nicole is with Anne. Talking to her. They come up together.

The Roman road goes north-east, to Whitby. It

is paved. The stone broken a little and stretches out, straight, over the top of the moors. Built by slave labour. For the further enrichment of a non-productive empire, in the economic sense. England for its tin and copper and iron. Villas at Malton. The settlement thick in this area which is now more or less depopulated except for farmers and retired businessmen. Though the real estate is still high. This being a green belt and Goathland a fashionable place to retire to from Middlesbrough or Darlington or Tyneside. A National Park. The second major development the building of the monasteries in this area, Lastingham, Ripon, then later Rievaulx, Fountains, Bolton, Kirkham on the Derwent where it flows away from the sea, south. Cistercian settlements mostly, French. Like my wife. Some of them. Others from Lindisfarne, Cuthbert. Whom Bede wrote of. Who is buried in Durham, a great Norman cathedral finished, at least the choir, by Gilbert Scott in pre-Raphaelite style. Though the pillars of bare stone remain. As they do at Rievaulx, at Whitby. Whither the road goes. My feet ring on it. The sun sets. The wind still blusters, dies, again. The sun suffuses the sky with pearl, mother-of-pearl. That I remember to have found in a tip in Sheffield, fragments, flakes, which glinted, which I collected. Now I find that that tip was the remains of the handle-making industry, handles for knives. That the dust of that pearl may well have killed with phthisis some relative or other. Her white skin stretches tight over her bone.

Look at it, I command her, it's nearly two thousand years old.

Where does it go?
Whitby. That's a spectacular coastline. Let's go.
The sea'll be rough. Let's go to see the waves.
Another one of his daft ideas.
What's the matter with you now?
I'm cold. I don't want to go to Whitby. Why should I go to Whitby? Just dragging about. It's time for baby's feed anyway. We can't go. He accepts that. His face shows it. All right. I agree for the time being. He'll take it for so long for his son's sake. She will have her own way for some years. But as he knows she will not be able to go on blackmailing him. The baby will grow up. He won't need her too much later on. He can afford to let her bridle him, curb him.

We go back down the bank. The baby's mild broad face smiles out of the wilderness of his clothes. She is perkier as we return to the car. Gilles and I are late for he wishes to climb the gates. He runs on the mossy ground. He looks into the brilliant water. He rolls down the heather, springs up from it. Is tired so that I must carry him as I do.
Look how tall I am. He shouts out. High. I stand on a boulder, tilt, tilt, fall, holding him.
Look, mummy. Look. Look.
I'm hungry. At least the walk has accomplished that.
The car is filled with smoke. I offer her a mint.
Which she takes.
What about that, hey? Did you like it? But I talk too loud. He cries. He is in fact hungry. It is time for his feed. So that we return at once. I smoke. Nicole's cheeks glow red. Her grey trench coat she wraps about her shivering now in the sudden heat and stillness of the car.

She snuggles against Cathy. She is quiet. Looking out of the window.
Showing the world to her daughter.
Yes, she is all right. To my question. I would have her chiefly as she is. Her tact. Her modesty. That she lies, conceals. That she fears men. Craves ecstasy. She is more pliant than is fitting for my peace of mind. Her grace. She is proud of her daughter. Confessed her jealousy the other day for a dressing-gown her mother sent to Cathy. She'd have liked one like it. Gayer now since she's started going to church again. The pores of her flesh open. I would bless her if I didn't know what the world meant. Like a bird at the window over which my hand closes to free it, which scrabbles, pecks. Wiry. She has a hold over me more than the legal tie. Of knowledge. Feeling the adultery in my heart. Touching it. Watching it. Watching me with it. Mastering it. Her success complete in her gentle tactics. We shall soon have been married five years. Five summers and the length of five long winters. The sound of the river is in my ear as I write this. Nicole is in Leeds buying spring dresses. I do not expect her back yet. Though I have been to watch for the car. My wife. What does it mean? Wife.

We ate salad. Spring onions, boiled ham. Tea. Anne could not eat yet. She had to put the baby to bed. Somebody had to do it. We had almost finished when she said that she was ready. We'll go to Whitby tomorrow. Did you enjoy that, I say?

At Whitby she said that we must get back for it was time for baby's feed. We could hire a boat. We could go out to sea. Nicole had got her feet wet, the

high spring tide coming over the pavement. We ate whelks. She refused to come here too until Arthur persuaded her, looking at me, saying, pleading: Aren't you coming?
She refused to go out to the pub the night before. I don't feel very well. I gave her a glass of brandy. She did not drink it. Sunday night. She started washing nappies. Somebody's got to do it.
Is she all right? I said in the pub. What's she started washing nappies for?
Do you take notice of anything they say? I don't. She says one thing one minute and another the next. I bought her a dress not long ago. It'll make Elsie jealous, she said. That's all she thinks about. I laugh about it.
She had left the brandy. It stood as a reproach on the mantelpiece. She came downstairs soon after we had returned and said,
Pillow!
Nicole ignored her.
Pillow!
Have you got a pillow? Arthur pleads with me. His look anxious.
Give her a pillow, Nicole.
She did.
I resent her. She's selfish. She's cut off. I gave her these - clothes - for the baby - she forgot them.
But she is smiling. He's a lovely baby.
The abbey dominates. Whitby. Standing on the point of the cliff 'unprotected from every wind', as Bede said.

MY IMAGINATION IS NOT ALLOWED TO WASTE ITS SWEETNESS

Nicole and I had been estranged. I had been watching a black-haired girl, like a boy, easy in movement, thin, sharp, talking to her, working late at night, not going to bed till three or four, sleeping late, so that I never saw my wife or exchanged more than a peremptory word with her. She looked drab. Five years. The house empty. Retreated into herself. Watching me. Feverish to my touch.

She caught gastric flu. After a fine spring the weather had suddenly turned cold. There was very little fuel in the house. She vomited all night. Could not eat. Lost weight rapidly and said,

I'm sorry. Sorry. It can't be much fun married to a wife like me.

The characteristic turn. Accusing herself of my meanest feeling. So. If he wishes to be unfaithful to me that is because I am drab, mediocre, uninteresting Uneasy. It is because I am frightened of men. It is because I am boring. I have no claim to happiness. I should suffer. I have had too easy a childhood. I should expiate my sense of well-being as a child. What right had I to so much privilege? It is good for me that I should feel pain. That I should meet trouble. I will face it. I won't give in to it. Poor Jenny. It must be boring for him to be married to me. I've got nothing to offer. Who can give nothing. I can't help myself. I always withdraw. I can't help it. I lie. I take. I don't give much. I crave my feelings, my pleasure, not his, English, and his pubs, friends, jollity, laughter, clowning.

She sees herself differently from the way she sees other people. She can think that at twenty a girl may still be childish and so thoughtfully treat her in a chosen manner. I cannot do that. Thus I have no sense of dignity. No sense of what I owe myself. She lay in bed visibly growing even thinner. The sour smell of vomit in the room. Which was cold. The sky, lead, and the rain seeping through the palms of the yew outside the window. Silence except for the drizzle. Lost in the North Riding of Yorkshire. She whose element is the sun. She has no friends in England. No one she loves. Bleak. Against her nature. She stopped going to church when she came to this country. Yet goes when she is at home. She is still there. She is getting up later and later now. She wastes away. I am losing her. Should she die I would take the children to her mother who must in conscience accept them and thus I would be free.
I thought that I might stay in the flat in York. Leave her to her plaintiveness, her gloom. Her despair. For I said,
You depress my spirit. You sigh. When I hear you sigh my heart sinks. Into my boots. Why should I lose my life to your constraining? I am not yet thirty. Should I defeat all my appetite? All my energy to hear that? Oh dear. Her wax face pale and moist with tears. You cry. You say nothing. You lie. You make me feel guilty, anxious, you worry. I used not to worry. I was unconcerned about money. You do no work. You have no warmth or generosity of heart. You should never have married. You should have been a nun. Contact distresses you. You shrink at my touch, or you crave a holy consummation. Not a

little easy feeling. Not a little squalor, blood, sweat. Clean slimy self-reproach to me in your wasting frame. While I fatten, put on flesh, feed off you, do I? You reproach yourself for it, rightly. Should I then enter with you into your anxious world where there is that purling sense of righteous feeling and official duty? As: one should be conscientious, doing what one is paid for. I think that is not so. Though I agree that it is difficult to avoid it yet I think one must Should I be more like her father? Would she rather I represented some principle of authority for her?
But she says,
If you are going to be unfaithful for goodness sake don't talk about it.
You coward. You are not interested in the scruples of my conscience. Soon you are bored by the realism of my confessions. If I want to fuck some other woman I will. I don't see why I shouldn't. Marriage dies when it only constrains.
Oh shut up.
You should listen to this. It concerns you.
It concerns you. Why should I listen to it. It bores me to death. Go out and have some adventures if you like. Only don't spend all the housekeeping.
What reason then does she give me? The contempt for my peccadillo destroys it even as an aspiration. That's what I have against her. My imagination is not allowed to waste its sweetness. She lies in bed like sweating stone.
I'll bring you some tea. I forget. She eats nothing for three days, asking for nothing. Lying, sweating, looking with hollow and gleaming eyes until finally she says:

Could I have a little soup, my love, and a piece of dry bread.

I'll bring it.

I do. With duty. Irritated that she should do nothing. That she has no resistance. That the tone of her voice should collapse into such a Latin sing-song. Up here in the north of England where the wind blows like a wild animal. Without the energy of my country. With delicacy, grace and tact, it is true, but she cowers before these storms.

So at the end of a long winter. Until last Sunday. She had recovered from flu. I had resisted temptation. A fine day. There was balm in the air. Spring had at last begun. The daffodils were out, wallflowers round the house. Primroses, celandine, violets. I'd been dancing the night before. Drunk. Had slept alone in the flat in York. Locked myself out of it later by accident and had telephoned. She wanted to go to a sale in the afternoon. She did. I came back. And she returned with a lovely stone pot she had picked up for a shilling. On the Sunday I felt free. Easy. I walked about the house, and garden, looking at it. Went to buy beer at a pub with Gilles. She had roasted a piece of pork for lunch with apple sauce from the apples we'd stored last autumn. I ate it. I had given her money to buy a spring coat the day before. She took it reluctantly but with a soft look accepting it gently fearing, I think, her own pleasure attaching her to me, her money anyway. But on the Sunday after lunch I mended the electricity. So that lights worked in two rooms in which they had never worked before. I mended broken pots we had bought in Apt two years ago, with one of those new glues. I cleaned the car. Put Vim on the rust and rubbed meticulously, on the chrome, on the bodywork. The clean light of the sun. Gilles and Cathy began to play in the water in the silver bucket. He splashed her. She like it. Laughed. The wetter the better. I cleaned away the mud with a handbrush, went to the kitchen which was suffused in a high glow, the sun warming the tiles, quiet in there. The water gushing into the silver bucket, cold, clean. Gilles on a chair beside me, watching the water. He jumped down to me, before me as I turned, swinging with the bucket to go out, Cathy, checking, Cathy under my feet. It takes her time to get up the step, to get down it, to get over the piece of wood in the door-frame and then shouting with delight as the silver sheet of water smashed against the blue car. Some more. Turning to go in. Leaning over her as she struggled through the doorway. Out again. She is standing too near. Mind Cathy! You'll get wet! She stands still. I throw the water. She is encircled in tongues of light, Here, here in this rich afternoon. Nicole weeding the garden, singing. Gilles skips and jumps, splashes throws earth at the car, rubs it, cleaning it he says. Cathy chortles. I go back. For more water. No. Easily. But throwing more than is necessary for my children to play in the flash of the light in the coldness. For Cathy to skip. It is a Sunday like many others except that here I have a fresh expansion in my belly. Here. Nicole is pale from her effort. She is intent on what she is doing. The children dance. I have mended during the course of the afternoon, two chairs, a broken pot, stuck a knob on a chest of drawers, stuck rubber in the door frame of my car and have wrestled with Gilles. My daughter. Looking at me as she splashes with the water in the bucket. Her face alight. Vivid. Born here. I have no desire to be in York or London or in the south of France. As I grow to know this place it seems to me to grow larger. I clean the interior of my car. I dismantle the cages inside the hut near the river. I will make it into a study. I wash the walls. I set a chair in it.

The kitchen in which my wife and children sit at tea seems a world of lightness and peace. Nicole pours the tea. She is eating heartily. I'm hungry. I love her as she eats. She munches the lettuce. She is thirsty. She drinks. I eat, smoke. Cathy is singing, eating an egg. Gilles holds a pork pie in one hand while he adjusts a car he has made with the other. I go back to my hut. Nicole comes to see what I am doing.

What a good idea. I'll buy you some furniture. Will you do me a favour, my love? I came to ask you.

Yes.

Will you look after the children while I go to church? I've got Cathy ready for bed.

Yes. She goes.

Cathy wears a long quilted dressing-gown on which are white and pink flowers. She runs on the rich grass. Gilles plays with her. She chortles, steps on the hem, falls, laughs. I go on with my hut. Should I take her in? It is growing cold. She is at the gate playing with a farm worker who lives opposite. Who pokes his fingers through the bars. She chortles, laughs, staggers about the lawn, perfect in grace. Born here. The light is dying and it is growing chill so that I take her and swing her about. She laughs. To warm her. Myself. I put her to bed and kiss her soft face. Gilles too. Nervier. Whose English is a whine. Whose French accent is better. And I feel some modesty. Alone. My head reels with pleasure. I listen. There are two pigeons cooing in the garden which I am reluctant to shoot. The water plays. Nicole I think is praying, for me. I sit on the bench by the river. It is growing cold. It is dusk. I am smoking a pipe. I watch the water coming through the bridge. I feel that I would believe in the efficacy of prayer given half a chance. Stooping in a door so straight. Marvell wrote that not far away. I have read nothing today. Well. That doesn't matter. But I stay here. In the enjoyment of this sense. Which I wanted to enlarge.

I wait for her.

She comes to sit beside me.

She puts her arm through mine and leans against me, wearing the grey coat which melts so well into the quiet, shaded place.

I feel her breathing.

There is nothing uncommon about this. We watch the grey water together. That is all. It may be with irresponsible abandon. Untouched by the balance of payments. Which has not been brought home to us. Though the war in Vietnam threatens. I can offer no concern for newsreel experience. I will. I will. But my well-being tempers the pain in my thought. But this must soon stop. But I can leave it here, I think.

COUPLING

She sat opposite in a clean well lighted waiting-room in Venice. Twenty yards away from me. There were one or two other people taking the boat, at midnight. Across the Adriatic into Yugoslavia. A priest, a hard-looking Norwegian, two Dutch doctors. Black-haired, keen-featured, smallish, petite, yes. My wife was, where? anywhere, in France. Somewhere. So that what I might do she wouldn't know about. American. Flat-arsed. In a khaki gaberdine skirt and clean legs flush into low-heeled leather shoes. Good quality.
Hi, she said, to the priest as he passed her on the boat. She was sitting where everyone must pass her.
He did not reply.
You English? she said to me.
Yes.
Have a drink?
Thank you.

A Norwegian in the bar was drinking slivovitz.

Hi, Nancy said to him.
What would you like?
What's that you're drinking?
Slivovitz.
Slivovitz.
No. Listen Sli vo vitz.
Sli vo vitz.
They laughed.
That's better.
Now. Drink it like this. He threw it down his throat. Smacked his lips. Licked them round with his forked tongue. Blond. Pink-fleshed. Bony. Spare. Hard.
She did. And gasped. As I did. The perfume in the

top of the nose.
The second is easier, he said and brought them.
Three. I took mine. Skol, I said, And threw my head back. I tried to keep my tongue at the back of my throat to stop it burning. Nancy too drank hers straight.
He grew confident.
You have much courage travelling in Europe alone, Nancy.
I can take care of myself.
In Norway...
Norway, isn't that a little place north somewhere?
The land of the midnight sun? The winters are six months long.
What do you do then? Don't tell me.
Drink, make babies.
Yeah. O.K.
All the babies are born six months later. It's like the English bank holiday.
What are you?
I am a Captain.
What of?
A passenger steamer which goes from Bergen to Stavanger.
I could beat him I think. Break him. He's taller than me. He looks fit. But he's thin. He's light.
Have another?
Yes.
Nancy?
Thank you. She has soft breasts girded up for gentle touching. I will attain her. Adultery. She won't kno
Her skin is matt brown.
Whereabouts in America do you live?

Detroit.
Where they make the cars?
Yes.
You're a long way from home.
I teach school. This is my summer vacation.
Her hips spring in her clean-cut gaberdine skirt.
Aren't you afraid, Nancy, with all these men?
The black-haired, white-coated Yugoslav barmen watch her. There are the two doctors. A sunburned sandy-haired man from Bradford with his freckled wife. Freckled on her fleshy arms. They call each other Mother and Father. My friend the Dutch doctor whispers in my ear,
They're nudists. I look closer.
How can you tell? Father wears a loose parti-coloured summer shirt outside his trousers. Have that slack flesh and those dangling balls been exposed at length to the southern sun? I wonder. Would Mother now have a big belly and ribbed and mottled thighs? Do they call each other Mother and Father when they are . . .
Can they?
He has his arm round Nancy.
Kurt. His name is.
No. Koo ert.
Koo ert.
Better. You English. Everybody speaks English.
The English don't talk at all. I'm Irish. Don't talk to me about the English. They have killed all my invented uncles in the 'Throubles'. Oh, the thrush of a diphthong and a more gracious lilt. Did you catch that slight cadence, ladies and gentlemen, giving me away, against my will, Irish. It isn't so. But I would have him believe it. In fact. Aunt Poll ran away with

a Black and Tan from Wicklow and they were later married clandestinely in Barnsley where they lived, I believe, a reasonably happy life, until quite early, she was stricken down with a brain haemorrhage. Will he tell me what he thinks of us?
It's dangerous for a good-looking girl like you Nancy to travel about at night with strange men. You ought to have somebody to look after you.
O.K. She takes his arm from her shoulder. And turns to me,
Let me buy a drink.
What? You? Do American women buy drinks?
Yeah.
Well, I'd heard that it was a matriarchy...
A what?
Matriarchy.
Come on, Jenny.
Mother-dominated.
That's a long word, Englishman.
The Captain laughs. Mother and Father getting up stagger out. He turns,
Good night all. Waving his hand. The two Yugoslav communists regard in silence, stolid, imperturbable. Nancy turns to me with a lip curled, an eye cocked. I bend to her ear and catch the warmth of her flesh, her scent. Which is moist. She is sweating. I almost touch her ear as I whisper,
They're nudists. She neither flinches nor moves away. I breathe into her ear. Good so far. She puts her hand on my neck to pull down my head and breathe moist juice of sweet life into my thirsting ear:
So am I.
Argh Nancy, lovely lady from Detroit, So am I, so

am I. Soami. Summae.
Do you know what they are?
What?
The Summae? Summae of St Thomas Aquinas? In which he discusses the nature of being. Where questions are entertained as to the quality and quidditas of the unmoved mover. The Primum Mobile. Wheels within wheels. Ay Nancy? The five proofs of the existence of God? Thrown out as food for uninformed doubters. So that they need not be compellingly true. Just have the appearance of logic.
Have some more slivovitz.
Sli vo vitz.
He's still here. His pale northern flesh pinkens. Again his hand is on her shoulder. O.K. O.K. she says again, again, and takes it off. He holds on to her hand. Grasps it.
O.K. O.K. And laughs though. The two Dutch doctors who have been doing a double-talk act in English, leave.
Good night.
Good night.
Pause.
At twelve the bar closes.
You're not going to close? not now? we're at sea.
Regulations.
Have a drink first.
No. We must close.
Who'll know. There aren't any secret police on this boat are there?
That priest. He lacked charity, didn't he, that's it, in not replying to Nancy.
Where is he?
Out into the night.

Where? Probably tucked up in bed sleeping the sleep of the just.
No. There he is. Sitting on the wooden bench, looking out into the starlit night and listening to the quiet waters of the Adriatic as the boat thrums quietly through them. The sea is calm. The boat ploughs through. Venice is out of sight. The Palace of the Doges, dropped, over the horizon. The warm air. The taste of the slivovitz. But the priest? A priest. Going to Yugoslavia? The opium of the people. He can't be a priest. They burned all the churches. He'll be imprisoned. Poor priest. No. He can't be. What does it matter? There is laughter inside. The Norwegian captain is dancing with Nancy. Jiving. She is having a great time. I watch through the porthole. The bar remains closed. Some slivovitz remains. Norwegian captain picks up Nancy and throws her over his shoulder, somersault, her skirt flies. Her white cotton pants. Her suspenders. Flesh. Thigh. Stocking. Milk white flesh. Argh. What am I doing at this window?

The shutter rattles as I tap it.
No use, the Norwegian says. We won't get more.
Koo ert, I say, Coerce them.
She holds her hand out to me.
I must have another drink. I need one. I tap. The light within this small square drinking parlour is now dim. Another. Tap. The wood is dark. Nothing. Nothing but the bitter disappointment of ineluctable brown stained wood and an unconsummated beginning. The long night.

But the bar opens. The two attendants, solemn before, are laughing, smiling. One hands me my slivovitz without my asking. The same for me, says Nancy. She pants, swigs it, and dances again. Sweat stands on her. They clap hands. Alone. She is alone with us. Her lovely hips flex beneath that American cloth. The Captain and I eye each other. Shall we? We can't. Not with these two beaming faces. The possibility of concord gone for ever through too much company.

Have a drink?

Bitte?

They speak German. Of course. Conquered during the war.

Wurden Sie ein Glas Sli vo vitz trinken?

Bitte sehr.

Gesundheit!

He snaps his heels. Heil Hitler. They laugh. He embarks upon a show conversation with them in German in order to impress my Nancy with his knowledge of languages. Haha. But that is his mistake. She turns, turns to me:

I'm not sure about him. I'm glad you're here, English. I can trust you. Specially with a name like that. Jenny. Ha! Ha! How about Eros?

All right.

You're O.K., Jenny.

I'll see you have no trouble with him.

You could too. Yes. You sure could. She feels my bicep. You're well muscled.

What are you, hundred fifty pounds, five-eleven? Huh? Let me feel you. Boy. That's some muscle. I unbunch it. Proud.

Captain returns to claim Nancy. He staggers, wavers. The Yugoslavs raise their glasses and wink at me.

I resent them. Am ashamed of this exhibition of decadent bourgeois capitalism but entrained in it willy-nilly. They do though. Wink. He grabs her. Tries to waltz. She won't. Stiffens. Shows me she doesn't want him, turning to me with an appealing look. I tap him on the shoulder.

I think you're annoying the lady.

Uh?

I think the lady would prefer not to dance with you.

Prefer not?

She is holding my arm.

I could see you were a gentleman. I can trust you. I thought so when I saw you. You're molesting this lady.

Uh? Molesting? He peers into my face, breathing the fire of spirit.

I regard him with frosty indifference verging on contempt.

I brace. I think he is lighter. I will protect the Detroit lady from the advances of an ungentlemanly Norwegian steamer captain who nobody ever heard of, going nowhere, a row-boat, commercial traveller in ladies' underwear. Captain! They don't know how to behave. Wouldn't trust him as far as I could throw him. All bone. No spiritual life, the Norwegians. None at all. Like the Swedes. All commit suicide. No wonder. Trolls and mountain kings. Peer Gynt and the Banshee. Bergen a city with seven mountains and a small room in which I locked myself for a week, on holiday, a lunatic escaped. Very much afraid of Norwegian lunatics. Here now captain to be dealt with protect American lady from Detroit.

Come to my cabin, he says. Who to? Me? I'll kill him. No. Her.
I will not, she says.
I'll take you. He grabs hold of her.
Let go of her. I thrust him in the chest. He staggers back. I brace. Wait for it. But he draws himself up to attention and salutes:
This was their finest hour.
I'll take you down to your cabin.
Thank you, Jenny. I appreciate that.
What number is it?
Ninty-nine.
Really? We're neighbours. Mine's a hundred.
Well, that's nice.
Here it is.
Well, thank you sir. She curtseys. I'm grateful to you. That Norwegian was scarey. He might have gotten rough if you hadn't helped out.
Don't mention it.
She remains in the door as I before it.
He'd drunk too much slivovitz.
Yes.
It's good stuff, isn't it?
I like it.
Pause.
Well, good night then.
Pause.
Good night.

But I hear her moving about. She climbs into the top bunk. I do. The thin steel partition alone separates us. Her mattress squeaks as she turns, thrashes, about. Restless. As I am. I can hear her breathe. Nearly.

Shall I tap? Ask her in? I can hear her. I lie naked under the sheet. My hands behind my head. I look at the white-painted ceiling. I turn on the ventilating system, a ball with a hole in it. To direct the flow. I allow balmy air of the Adriatic to play over my northern flesh. The sheet thrown off I cool my burning body with the stream of air. Ah, Nancy. Nancy. Who would know? She even thinks I'm Irish. She doesn't even know my second name. I think. The world turns, rocks, slightly. But I feel good. I yearn for her. Y-earn. Yearn. Come in here of your own accord. Seduce me. Make love to me. Then all I must do is suffer it. Thus it is not I who betray wife, self. You want me, Nancy come and get me.

She won't. She doesn't. I burn. Nancy. Nancy. I lie here naked. I await you. But you do not come. Is she asleep? No. I hear her turn. I move noisily to show her that I too am awake.

Hell. I say aloud. Will she notice? I hear her turning. But she makes no advance. My covenant with myself still holds. I am not unfaithful. But there's nothing wrong with interest in people. I don't see why I should restrain myself altogether from talking to women merely because I am afraid that I might fall. That's tantamount to admitting the guilt. I know my own will. Come to me, Nancy. I know that I can control myself. It's a poor virtue that fears to be tested. All right. It's cowardice. It's dishonesty to lie here. All I want to do is talk to her. All right. I tap.

Yes?

Are you sleepy?

Not a bit.

Would you like to come in here . . . for a cigarette.
O. K. I'll be there in a minute. Just let me put something on, I'm not decent. I imagine that I hear the rustle of silk as she sheathes her naked body in the clinging diaphanous texture of a transparent negligée. Will she come in with only that on so that I will be able to see the tips of her breasts beneath it?
She taps.
I hold the sheet about my waist, half sitting in my bunk, leaning on one elbow. Come in. It isn't transparent. But it is a blue dressing-gown. She is carrying a packet of Peter Stuyvesant, mentholated. Her eyes caress my naked torso. Yes. The tendons of her throat dip down towards her breasts. She lies on the bottom bunk.
I couldn't sleep.
Neither could I.
She eyes the part of my thigh which comes over the edge of the bunk as I lean to take a cigarette from her.
I felt like talking.
I couldn't sleep.
You've said that, Jenny.
It's fate.
What?
Our cabins being next to each other. We've been thrown together.
I'm thankful to you for getting me away from that sea captain. Boy, he really was a rooster.
That's all right. Don't mention it. I'm glad I was able to help.
Shall I try to touch her now. Or wait.
You can trust some people. I feel that I can trust you, Jenny. I don't feel that you'd do anything ungentlemanly

It sure is crazy though me coming in here in the middle of the night with hardly anything on, talking to a guy I hardly know. I feel confident about you somehow though, Jenny. I feel safe here. Some people you can feel easy with right away.

She stretched and lay out on the bed. One hand behind her head. The other holding the cigarette in her mouth. Her hair dark. Ah, that. Hair. The blue woollen gown wrapped closely about her. The form of her breasts.

Are you married, Jenny?

Well. Yes.

What's your wife like?

She's beautiful. Elegant.

I wish I knew her.

You'd like her.

I bet I would. I bet she's just lovely.

Yes. She is. Lovely. Yes. Are you married?

No. Well no, I'm not.

Why not?

Waiting for the right guy to come along, I guess. Tell me about your wife. Is she blonde?

Dark.

Is she clever?

Yes. Too clever.

Has she got a good figure?

Yes. I suppose so. Yes.

Like mine?

I can't really tell. Show me. Let me see.

Jenny. How can I? I've got nothing on underneath.

Show me. Show me.

Jenny.

All right. How can I tell whether she's like you?

You saw me dressed upstairs in the bar.
You can't tell when they're dressed.
I wouldn't be talking to you like this if I didn't trust you.
I know. I trust myself. Show me that you trust me. It's only flesh.
What are you so anxious for then? Tell me some more about your wife. Is she younger than you?
Well. Yes. A bit. Yes. Yes. She's a marvellous woman. Everybody I ask tells me so. She is clever. She controls me. I don't know how she does it. She's deft. That's the word for it. She knows me. It's uncanny. I bet she knows what I'm doing now. She can see through me. She's clairvoyant or something. Yes. I love her. Yes. Dark. Clever. Everybody tells me I'm lucky.
It's nice to be able to talk to a man you can trust.
Does she trust you?
Yes. She says so. I've told you. I trust myself.
I know. You can say true things. You don't have to be on your guard.
I mean I know you wouldn't do anything ungentlemanly either to me or your wife.
No. That's true. I suppose it's the way I've been brought up.
How's that?
To respect women.
Yes. I could see that when you came into the bar. As soon as you walked in. I knew I could trust you.
Do you think it's wrong for a man to be unfaithful to his wife?
Depends on the circumstances I should say.
On what? Whether she's likely to find out? Oh my

God her dressing gown has opened and she's raised such a soft white leg, bent it at the knee. The blue gown falls on either side. It is a clean shaven leg. I knew she was a man. The flesh is white and smooth. Steady. She moves it out, sideways.

What?

I said that you couldn't make general rules.

What about?

About what you said.

What? Oh! Adultery? You can't make general rules about it? I want to show her my body. Does she? Will she?

Let's play a game. Asking questions. Truth or dare. If you don't answer you pay a forfeit.

O.K.

Pause.

She stretches that bare leg. Her toes feel the woollen blanket. Her eyes are closed. I look down upon her leaning over the bunk. The rise of her thigh, the soft inward flesh of her upper leg and the smooth paleness of the skin stretched over the knee.

Ah Nancy, you tickle my fancy.

Pause.

Ask a question then.

Ask me one first.

All right. How long have you been married?

Long enough. Two years. Is that all? That's not much of a question.

It's your turn.

What am I like?

That's no question. You're supposed to ask about me. Do you think I'm Irish?

Come on.

Well, it's difficult. Let me see. Do you like making love to men?
It depends. Yes. Yes. I do. Do you like making love to your wife?
My wife?
Yes. Your wife.
Well yes. I suppose I do.
Suppose?
Well I do. What kind of man do you like?
How do you mean, Jenny?
Did you like that sea captain?
No. I think he'd be brutal with a woman. He'd got hard hands. I wouldn't like him touching me. Brrr. He was creepy.
What would I be like? See if you can tell.
You'd be gentle. Yes. I think you'd be kind. Gentle. You look kind. You'd be kind to children. Yes. You'd be a good father. I'd like you to touch me. Let me see your hands.
I show them. She takes one and paddles in my palm with her strong fingers. Yes. I'd like you touching me. You've got gentle hands. I could talk to you if I were your wife. You'd be confident. Strong. Some men are nervous. I'd need a strong man who could dominate me. I need to be dominated, most women do. Somebody I could depend on if things went wrong. Somebody like you.
She smokes with her eyes closed, a soft inward look on her face.
My hand goes down towards her.
I feel almost as though I'm talking to myself. She opens her eyes.
Have you got another cigarette?

She opens them. Her eyes and smiles oh smiles with such a smile as would bring tears into many a good man's eyes. Such beauty. Her flesh clear fresh pure as the driven snow delicately scented soaped caressed laid out here below me awaiting me come and get me take me (it says that) put aside scruple who'll know she thinks you're Irish she couldn't trace you I'd like to? what? where are we? wait a minute. Argh but my hard flesh burns. Livid with apprehension.

Who's turn is it? she says.

Mine.

O.K. Fire away.

Would you like to look at my body?

Pause.

Should I answer that?

Pause.

If you don't you'll have to pay a forfeit.

What will it be?

That depends.

Will I like it?

Depends.

What would your wife say?

That's no answer.

She blows smoke through her pursed lips, through her nostrils. And she watches me. All right I would. Her eyes have retreated and shine with an inward relish. I throw off the sheet and climb down from the bunk and I stand naked before her. I stretch, suck in my belly, I open my legs and stretch out my arms in the two positions of Leonardo's man in the circle. I am erect. She smokes. Her tongue licking the cigarette, watching me. I like this. I turn. I flex the muscles in my back. I feel her eyes on my

buttocks.
My head is down and my eyes are closed. Her gaze is all I need. ALL. ALL.
You're well made, Jenny. Her voice breaks into my reverie. I stand.
Give me a cigarette. She proffers the packet. I take one. I bend to her match.
Shall I?
No. Stay like that. She lies, stretched, ah stretched. The boat balances in the Adriatic Sea. That is where it should be. The floor space is narrow. The Great Bear has slipped into a different position almost without my noticing it.
Let me see you.
All right.
She puts out her cigarette.
She unbuttons the robe and draws it open, holds it open, lies, stretched, out, there, her nipples mounted, erect, her belly light, she stretches out, arms above her head, once, out, her breasts rise as she stretches she breathes her ribs show her back arches so that I see the shape of the buttocks.
Take it off. Off.
Put the light out.
In the pilot light. She worms out of her gown. Turns. Ah her long dipping back to the rise of her arse.
I can't see. I put on the light again.
Her face is buried in her hair. She lies on her soft belly and bends her legs up, crosses her ankles, the flank shows, uncrosses the ankles, opens them, opens her arms, and stretches, for the four corners of the bed ah Nancy Nancy none of this is true. She turns.
I cannot restrain myself. I assault her. She turns

and offers her cunt to me, offers   open   my body is only muscle and drives at her till I break in upon her I damage her I cause her pain I knock bone on bone. She gasps and grunts and clutches me. Her nails score my back my arse she bites spits struggles I drive at her at her she follows sucks clings I have her like a flower in light   easy   she swallows me I am in her intestine in her belly she pulls at me, pulls to disembowel me argh argh Nancy Nancy tickle my fancy. The end of life. My apotheosis in a boat in the Adriatic. Detroit Nancy. De trop. Too much. More.

No.

It fades.

It recedes.

I withdraw from her.

She surfaces.

This never happened.

I never showed her my body. Nor did she offer me the spectacle of her so lovely naked flesh and hair but that one veritable unclothed leg in that quilted buttoned blue gown. But her hair was black, her name was Nancy. I did take her from a Norwegian sea captain. We were in the Adriatic. We were in the same cabin. I touched her. I fondled her. I fucked her. Again. Again. She wanted more. She touched me.

Till I rise again. And I love her more than ever.

THIS IS AN IDEAL SEXUAL ACT. IT IS ENDLESS. ONE CONTINUAL HIGH MOMENT.

Yes. Yes. Up. More. Further. Again. Do it again. Nancy. She wore a transparent black negligée through which in the red half light of the pilot light alone left burning in this first class cabin her strong

jutting nipples jut, no, blue, her blue gown, her leg, her black hair fondling my face I bite eat suck scratch.
That's enough of that.
No it isn't.
You can't go on.
I can. I don't want to stop. I like this. We'll go round again. In her black 'n blue transparent dressing-gown ah Nancy fetched and carried as yes she went, returned, at my bidding, as she was told, hither and thither Nancy de Trop lovely lady from Detroit to and fro my fancy tickled Nancy.
Wait a minute.
Let's get this straight.
Is this happening or is it not?
That's not your question.
Who are you talking to?
Proffered American grace in the Adriatic Ocean on my father-in-law's money, who would not miss it or me. Which is true? Is that a question, Which is true. Contemporary Nancy hopped forty faces down the public street. No she drank slivovitz. Plenty. With Koo Ert and me. She was a nudist. She said so. I've taken her at her word.

There's not much she wouldn't do for me. I've had her a long time. Yes. Yes. I'll fuck her again. Open Sesame. Ali Baba's back on his bandwagon. The barge she sat in like a burnished throne glowed on the water. Her nipples jut. Rub up the lamp. Now my little genie perform again or I'll garrot you, put you in a Chinese lady, strap rats over your belly, you won't get out of this one. Into my pen. Get in. In. Now. Tapered. Behind the balls of a blue biro she still tickles my fancy.

Which I will lay down. I will lay me down. Soon. Soon.
I'll play with you a little longer.
That's enough Jenny. Stop it. You're killing me.
Who are you talking to?
Jenny?
Yes. Nancy.
Take it easy. You're hurting me. I'm not like this.
You think I do this with every man I meet?
Neither am I.
You started it. I came in here because I trusted you.
You don't even know who I am.
I know enough.
You don't know where I am.
I do.
Where?

Over here

I'm not

I'm here

Keep still

It's you who've changed position

Put the light on

All right

I illuminate the room. She lies in her black negligée smoking a black Russian Sobranie in an ivory holder she dangles a golden slipper and opening with a tired rather bored gesture, languid, yes, the folds of her nylon negligée she languidly draws between her pursed lips a chiffon scarf yellow I think yes yellow so light one might say that it breathed all the paleness of a Gaelic moonlight. I come at her with a knife, a ship, she flicks her ash tapping the holder with the index finger

Oh not again darling.
Yes. Yes. Yes.
You are naughty, you know.
Just once.
Well, if you must. She lets the negligée slip from her ivory shoulders and stretches herself on my rack. I fasten her in.
Where will you do it?
Here.
Mm. Yes. That will be nice. Oh yes. Again. Again.
I could kill you here.
You couldn't. What would you do. You'd have to talk to yourself.
Love. Love. Again. Fuck me. Ah fuck me. I can't get free, she says.
All right. All right. Wait a minute. I haven't finished.
What more do you want?
I want to marry you.
You're already married.
Yes.
You can't.
No. I can't. Please.
How?
Please. Please.
Go on.
I will.
In her blue quilted dressing-gown with her leg naked to the groin smoking her Peter Stuyvesant mentholated cigarette she says,
It's nice to talk when you can't sleep. It's nice to have to protect yourself from guys all the time. I like talking. A girl doesn't get the opportunity. It's nice meeting people. An English gentleman. Boy.

Wait till I tell the girls about this. Tell me some more about your wife? I bet she is really lovely.
The trouble is that I'd like to make love to you.
Is she nice?
Are we still playing the game?
O. K.
I'd like to see you naked but I daren't ask. I shouldn't. I owe it to myself not to. You make a covenant with yourself. I'd be the one to suffer. She'd never know though. Never know. Now. I'd like to ask that but I won't.
That's a different kind of question. You shouldn't anyway.
I know. I won't. Would you do it if I did ask?
Probably. If you really wanted to.
It's a pity.
I know.

She had a strong square face and short black hair. Straight. In her manner. She moved about. Moved her leg about.
You've got such beautiful legs though.
Do you like them?
She uncovered the other, pointed the toes. Opened them lifted them, holding the gown. They're beautiful. There was nothing wrong in that.
Do you really think they're nice?
Yes. I do. They're strong and clean. You've got nice ankles.
What are you doing? Are you teasing me, Nancy? I must not fall. I love my wife. I don't want to lie to her. I won't touch her. If it starts now after such a short time. I must keep it intact. I can't afford to trust myself. But I don't like being tethered. My

feelings are my own. That is their trouble. But she'd never know. She'd find out. It would damage her. This damages me. I wish I could make love to you. Do you mind talking about it? No. I like it. You're honest. I like that. At least you admit it. That's all I do. I blow mentholated smoke at the ceiling, turn, feel the roughish sheet on my naked body. She is lying out below me a lamb to the sacrifice. What prodigality to pass such an offer by. The neck of her dressing-gown has opened I can see the soft swelling upward of her her her breasts. It seems unnecessary to restrain myself. I might as well be hung for a sheep as for a lamb. If I've come this far. Shall I? What do I risk? She'd never know. But I am afraid of my posthumous feelings. What if I destroy my soul? What? How? Nancy is a lady. Her black hair is straight. She smokes and watches me. I am excited. If I am why must I restrain myself? Hold says my conscience. Why? My soul keens. It is your duty to yourself. Duty? Nancy?

What are you thinking about?

About your wife, what it must be like to be your wife. Talk some more about her.

Does she wear good clothes. Do you buy them?

I bought her a transparent black negligée once. She couldn't stop laughing when she put it on. There was some transparent pink thing inside it. The girls in the shop enjoyed my buying it. One of them said:

Is it for you, Sir?

I didn't like her wearing it. She embarrassed me.

You wouldn't though.

She kept saying it was cold and giggling.

Do you buy her other clothes?

No. I'd quite like to though.
But a man shouldn't, Jenny.
Do American men?
What?
Buy their wives clothes. I don't know. Tell me about American men.
What are they like in bed. Have you had many?
I won't answer that.
Pay a forfeit then.
All right I will. What?
Wait a minute. Will you do anything?
I have to don't I?
Let me think. She is watching me. Her eyes rich. Waiting for it.
Put the light out. She gets out of the bunk and does. The dim pilot light quietly keeps her in view. I cover that with my hand so that the edges of my fingers glow blood red.
What shall I do?
Wait a minute. Yes. Take your gown off.
All right.
I hear it fall. No. She puts it in the narrow bunk. I see the tip of her cigarette glow blood red, as she inhales.
Now what?
I want to know something about you. Close your eyes. Which part of your body do you like most?
My legs.
Touch them. Are you touching them?
Yes.
All right. I hear her. I have thrown off the sheet and lie there naked. The boat rises and falls gently gently. It is warm here in the Adriatic Sea. I search for you

in my mind. She is lying, on the bunk beneath me again. I say,

It's your turn now.

Are you afraid of women, Jenny?

Not that I know of.

Have you ever had a homosexual experience?

Yes. Well. Nothing much. Not really.

Would you like one?

I'm not sure. I think so sometimes. I think it might be a cleaner thing with a man.

You might be more separate, it might be.

It might leave you more on your own.

Do you think about it?

Now and then. What about you?

When I was a girl there was a beach at home. On holiday. I had a friend called Celie. There was a woman used to go down to the beach and sunbathe nude. We used to hide behind the rocks and watch her. I got a kick out of it.

My wife told me something like that.

I don't like this.

Put your dressing-gown on. Put the light on. I cover. There she is.

Have another cigarette.

I'm smoking too much.

I give her a black Sobranie. The gold of the tip dusts her lips.

What time is it?

I don't know. Are you sleepy?

A bit. Sleep here.

I can't.

Not with me. In that bunk.

No. I'd better get back.

Why?
I'd better. She sounds dejected.
What's the matter?
I'm tired I guess.
Are you disappointed?
In what?
I haven't touched you.
I told you I didn't want you to. What are you playing at? She is angry.
Don't get your heckle up.
What is this? You don't like women do you? You typical? You a faggot? Is it true?
What's the matter? What's brought this on?
You and your games.
Oh hell. Let's start again.
I'll go.
Why?
I don't like this.
All right we'll stop it. You don't want to go, do you? I'll never see you again. We don't want to end it like this.
O.K.
We'll start again.
No. We'll just talk. Sit down again. Where are you going?
Split. I want to get across to Belgrade.
You?
I'm going to Dubrovnik to meet some friends who're coming through by car.
Are you going on?
Yeah. Greece. I've got a meeting with a guy I met in Paris in front of the Post Office in Athens, midday, a week Tuesday.

Will you find him?
He'll be there.
How do you know?
I know. She smiles and says. Ah Jenny. I shouldn't touch you. You're just a baby.
Come on now honey? Let's stop playing games.
Is that you?
This is me.
I wonder if it is.
You're afraid of women, aren't you?
I'm married.
So what? So was you know who.
Well, it must prove something.
Got any kids?
Yes. One. He's all right. He's quick on his feet.
Thus passes the night. I try to arrest it. I don't want to talk about this. I want to find some centre to probe. I want there to be a more dramatic exchange. I am not in danger here. I want to be threatened. Mortified. Otherwise I feel nothing. I don't know what to do.
She's pulled her blue quilted gown about her and is sitting on the steps of the ladder, smoking, legs crossed, rocking slightly, her arms wrapped round her middle, the cigarette dangling from her lips, her eyes slightly screwed against the smoke.
I'm surprised there's nobody in the bottom bunk.
There aren't many people on the ship.
There's another girl in mine.
Really?
She's a nice girl. German. She's going on to Greece. She's going to a Club Méditerranée.
This is too much. Another one. A German. Blonde. Matriarchal. Strong. Tanned. On her own. Asleep.

Through the steel partition.
Shall we ask her in for a drink? I've got some whisky in my case.
Now Jenny. You should be ashamed.
Would you like a drink? I've only just remembered it.
Sure.
Hand the bottle, will you? It's in my grip. We'll have to drink out of the bottle. Her so soft red lips caress that neck. She tips up the flat bottle, once, twice and hands it to me. That slakes my thirst. It goes well with the Sli vo vitz.
I am grinning.
Is she as good-looking as you are?
I won't talk about her. You talk to me. I'm the one you asked here, remember?
Ha! Ha! I turn and blow smoke at the ceiling. Another. Two at once. One on each side. Don't know them. One on top, one underneath. Boy oh boy. In her naked bed, blonde, gold, light, they glow when they're sunburned in the salt and wind. They come at you straight. They're clean-limbed. They're disciplined. They speak English better than we do. Anna-Lise, say. Golden in the sun, drunk.
Hey! Where are you?
Hm? Oh nothing, dreaming.
Jenny. She smiles at me. I at her.
I'll never see you again.
You never know. We might run across each other.
Would you introduce me to your wife if we did? Huh?
Yes. I'd like to she'd like you.
She smiles, smiles.
Why are you so pleased?
I like you. I think you're a nice guy. You're a gentle-

man. I was right. There was nothing to be afraid of with you. I could trust you. That's the trouble. I wish you hadn't trusted me. I wish you'd asked me to make love to you.

Make love to me, Jenny.

What? Now?

Ha! Ha! You see. Come on. I want to be seduced by a British gentleman.

Well, wait a minute. Hold on a bit. I laugh. Just like that?

Yeah.

Are you as it were equipped?

Are you really?

You never know what might happen in Europe.

Well, that's true I suppose. Well.

She is lying on the bed again. Her legs are uncovered. She is moving them. Open.

Shut. Open. Shut: Open her mouth. Her tongue licks, fondles her teeth, her lips, plays. Oh. Take it off. Take it off.

Stretch. Claim. Take me in. I plunge in.

This is American flesh. Style. I'm

where?

Nancy.

She didn't do it. She did not do it. She went away untouched unmoved no it was me, my fault, she wanted me to but I didn't, I didn't know that she did, gone, out, where? America? Hell. I didn't. She did none of this. I lost her. Some of it must be true. What have I gained? I might as well have had her. Nothing. As the French say. She was asking me to fuck her and I didn't even know it. She must have been. I didn't even know her. She was naked underneath that dressing-gown. She was showing me her legs. I could see the rise of her breast where she'd undone the top button. Why else should she have been in my cabin at four o'clock in the morning? I must have known it. Of course I knew it. I'm lying again. I knew it just as well then as now. Was I frightened of her? Am I? Is that true? Would I rather have it in writing? She showed me the white line at the top of her thigh where her swimming costume had been. Ran a finger along it, round the thigh, thigh. Sigh for that. I sigh. Come back.

You want to have it both ways. Playing at it.

So?

She got away. Others didn't. I'll tell you about them soon.

Her hair black, her belly flat, as she opened and closed her legs I climbed down and lay beside her. Kiss her. Strange. She tastes strange. That's American perfume. Her flesh is rougher. It's warmer.

Is it?

No. It's not warmer. But it's different. Tighter. She opens and shuts her legs. I have it. She bucks, bites. She's more aggressive. Physically stronger I suppose. Her hair smells strange. Her hair is coarser. So is the texture of her flesh. Good. I can go on. Nothing happens yet. I am not yet coming to a climax. I can continue. Easily. She is a Jew. I had a Jewess once who was like this.

Are you a Jew?

Yes. Oh yes.

So is my wife.

Your wife? Oh. Don't talk.

I like this. This is good. Yes. It's good. Go on. I've struck it rich here. Here comes the gold rush. Burgeoning. Coming out. More of it. More of it in. In. Out. In. Out. The sun shines. It illuminates the manuscript. I love it. Oh Nancy. Jenny. Nancy. Jenny. Mingle. Fuck it.
She smiles.
I gasp.
Come. Come. Here. For me. I invoke you. Wait on me. Draw me out. Blow me. As an egg. The mountain shall melt into the sea and the sea become a mountain. Que tout craque. This is an idyll I say. So what? You don't think we should be doing this? Where are we going?
What significance has it?
Coupling. That's all. That's plenty.

Like this

I wouldn't miss it. I live on it. Thrive on it. Oh Nancy. Nancy my spikey little Jewess in the Adriatic Ocean.

There was another one in Cambridge. Who climbed through the window with a bottle of whisky after I'd locked the door to keep her out. No. No. I mustn't. While I thought of the self-sacrifice you have to make to conduct life as it should be. They all come in. The German. The Negress. The Yank, the Jew, the Norwegian, the Swede. She comes in a car and will commit suicide any minute. They come through the window, the door. Lovely women with their hands open, panting, their diaphragms expand and contract,

breathing, ah, they are already there in bed.
I'm in the wrong bed. Who is this? Oh? He! He!
Who are you?
In the wrong room. In Paris. In a hotel. Place de la Sorbonne. St Thomas Aquinas University. Josephine. Well, now you're here you'd better stay.
Don't know who I am. Don't want to know. Want to stay with Josephine. Lovely Josephine. Start again. Start it all over again.
You're drunk.
Yep. Sure am.
Where have you come from?
The English Sunday.
Get away.
No. Stay. Nice. Trust me. Nancy trusts me.
Nancy we'd better stop. I'll hurt you. Can't go on for ever.
Why not?
Wear it out.
Go on a little bit.
All my women. All mine. Take it off. O.K. Lift it up. Put it on. Pull it through. All prepositions at once compiled with. Away. To. Even. Nearer. Never. Do it. Yes. Yes. I will. You see you like it. She smiles. Smiles. I think it has come. I've had enough. Satisfaction. The breathing lengthens into an exhalation which goes on until since nature abhors a vacuum there is an indrawing celebrating in the teeth chilling and in the burning pleasure of the lungs and eye of the filling stomach of the satisfying appetite an endless sentence of pleasure in breathing with no beginning or end and still in sight of the actual I shall be able to do this again.

She lies back. Collapsed. Out. Slack. Gutted.
Satisfied. I've made it up.
All right. You weren't frightened. I take it back.
Are you typical?
Was it good?
That's the reallest thing has happened to me on this trip.
Good.
Good.
We slept. The sleep of the just. I awoke in the morning. The steward tapping on the door,
We shall be landing in fifteen minutes, sir.
Thank you.
Loosely she sleeps. Innocently. Unsullied. And.
She said.
I'm tired. It's been nice talking to you. I'll see you in the morning.
Good night.
She can't get away as easily as that.
She's gone. What? It's true. Gone out. Just gone out through the door.
Come back.
Shall I? Mm?
Yes. Do. We're not there yet.
O.K.
Put the light out. Let's do it again. In the darkness. Let me touch you, Jenny. Her cool hands fondle my willing burning present participles. She abets my fancy. I will not touch her. She can touch me though. I break no rules. I am not unfaithful. By no means. Would you like me to make love to you? Oh. What are you doing?
What do you like?

I once went on a trip with a guy across the States.
You seem to be able to go anywhere.
I can take care of myself. I went on a trip with this guy. I was seventeen. We camped in the red woods in California. I was just a girl. I wore a long flared skirt I remember that spun out in a cartwheel when you turned around. We camped by a river. He was my first lover. He was just lovely. So clean. And sweet-natured. We walked about those woods. Those trees. We slept together in the tent. I wanted it to last.
He read a lot.
Did you love him?
Yes I did. But he was drafted. To Korea. While he read I sometimes walked by myself. There was a river. I used to strip and bathe in it, then run in the woods to feel the air on my body. He was drafted to Korea. I used to sit and watch the water. He was killed.
I'm sorry.
You're a nice guy, Jenny.
Do you think so?
I like you.
Do you know the favourite thing in England now?
No. Tell me.
Drag shows. Transvestite men. We're all faggots. As you said.
Were you in love?
Yes.
Were you seventeen?
Yes.
We all were.
Yes. We all were. I'm in love with my wife.

I know you are.
How?
You would have made a pass at me before now if you weren't. God knows I've been asking you to.
Oh? Do you think so? I'd like that to be true. I do believe it. Yes.
You'll stay faithful. You're a good guy. She's a lucky woman.
Would you like me to have made love to you?
Shall I answer that?
Yes. I mean it.
All right. Yes I would.
You're giving it to me both ways.
I can afford to. She smiles at me.
I'll tell you something. If there's anybody I would like to have made love to it would have been you.
That's nice. Thank you. I'm glad you told me that. I'm glad you told me that.
There is a tap at the door.
Nancy? Are you there?
It's that blonde German dried in the salt wind, cured in the sea.
We're in sight of land.
All right. I'd better go, Jenny. Let me kiss you.
She does.
On the cheek.
And goes.

I watch the sun rise. The barren islands flank the Dalmatian coast. The boat threads through them. Grey turns to pale blue. The water is smooth. There is more swell. The boat tips a little but is so comfortable. The chill lifts and flesh contracts as the sun slips up and shines palely at first on the side of the

ship as I look down the grey painted steel into the greyish swishing water. Quiet. Oh, quiet of soul. Joy. It is a clean day. I am innocent. Untouched. I have committed adultery only in my heart. My well-being suffuses the sea. I am elated. The sun warms my face. I look out over the level sea, over the level grey deserted islands. There is neither vegetation nor human life upon them. Hungry. I have kept my marriage vows though not all of the ten commandments. But I will make my understanding literal. It is enough that my body remains unsullied, does it? Is it? Yes it is for I feel curious now. I am excited by Yugoslavia. I look forward to it. I still am what I thought I was. I'm glad that I am as I am. I shall be able to look at my wife, unmasked. My heart swells with the sea. I know that. I am thankful. Argh but I am hungry.
The two Dutch doctors in grey flannels and blue blazers come along the deck, talking, laughing. One later translates Latin inscriptions for me in Split. Disiacta to my astonishment means pieces of money.
Good morning.
Good morning.
In the dining room the Norwegian captain is drinking black coffee.
You look rough, I say. He opens two fingers of the hand covering his bloodshot eyes and looks palely at me.
Too much Sli vo vitz, Koo ert, I say.
I'll send my wife a postcard when we dock.
Nancy enters.
Is that Nancy? My Nancy? She is short, dark, squat, her skin is matt, she has black moles, thick ankles. I am unfaithful even to my dreams? Nancy? She is

with a fat, squat and ugly Bavarian German with matted black hair and two chins.
Hi, Nancy says.
The Norwegian captain covers his eyes. I have further cause for rejoicing.

My head is full of music, mine, and the birds', teaching each other. They're learning anyway. I have in it the sounds of things, the sounds move and change, surprising us. Yesterday Jim and his family came; Anne, Susan, David. They played in the water. Back from Cambridge where I had had one or two conversation with people worried about their weight. Me too. Never mind. Back here things are quiet today. Except for the water, which is quietening. On the other hand there are bullocks playing, pushing each other with their heads. There are narcissi and daffodils about my feet. Over me there is a sycamore tree, around me. I've been here all morning, listening. There's not much going on. But it's quiet. There's an aeroplane. Training. There's a dog. Now there's sun at last, the hedge is growing again and even under those trees, but there's still a hole in it where a bullock got through. Never mind. The Croziers have gone, with their children, so that no one looks out of that house now. Gilles, my son, is without company, Cathy, my daughter, doesn't mind.

Yesterday and the day before were fine too. I see from the papers this morning that there were crowds out on the Serpentine and in the coast towns. Blackpool was crowded out. Red Square was filled with cheering crowds, as they say. Never mind. Keep it quiet. Steady? What I want is the light and chatter of Susan, David and Gilles playing in that water. I brought a white plastic bath out on to the lawn and they put their swimming costumes on, except Gilles who had a cold and was nervous anyway, and played in, with, it.

What did they do? Jumped. In. David in it, sat down, but, agh, cold, oh, ah, oooh, gingerly with his bottom, lowered down to meet the water. Ha! He! Oh!

Argh. Ooh it's cold, Daddy, it's cold. I want to get in, tell him to let me in, Daddy.

David, let Susan have a go. David.

All right. In. Splashing him. Splashing her. Gilles, delicate, little, dipped his hands in the water and ran after David on the green lawn, laughing, laughing, sprinkled him, so that the sun caught the drops flying and made them alight. Shine. Sparkle. Laughing.

Ha! Ha! Ha! Ha!

Look at me, Mummy! Mummy!

David running, jumping, down into the tub again, sprinkling Susan. Gilles, my lovely Gilles, with a French accent, born in Marseilles, Ger off, Bloody hell, two and a half. Like a green and pliant stick. Like a brand of willow. Like the leaves of grass by this river where there is a soft breeze, a gentle and sweet suspiration. Until the water was emptied, all scattered, utterly, had all been thrown out into the light. Out! What remained. On to the grass. Gilles at last while they were fighting over who should get in, tipped up the bath to make a puddle there. They fought to stand in it. Warm on the warm damp soft green grass. Stamped to splash. Gilles now confident came to have his red sandals taken off, and his light brown socks, to dance, to paddle, to splash. There with them. The light in and on the grass like crystals of ice or like sparks with the three children dancing. Dancing. Joined hands to run round in a ring. Gilles's feet off the ground half the time. Susan seven, David five, but strong, built like a man already with a deep chest, strong neck, set, square on his shoulders, with a flat face, and a snub nose, pretending to cry when Gilles hit him, pretended to hit him.

Oh my God perhaps it is possible after all to live in England. There's a thrush. It purls. It's the right word. Purls. Listen to it. You don't have that in France. When they pass you're there with your gun and your bottle of Pastis, elaborately clothed. No shade there, or quiet. Here, there's a black mark on the lawn where they danced yesterday. We lay on the lawn and watched them. Nicole with astonished white legs after a long winter playing with Cathy. How will she come out? Sharp. Yes. As always, but quieter, today, yesterday, much quieter.

Wouldn't it be nice to be a housewife, this morning. She was wearing that thin black and white skirt and a black jumper, her hair was loose, my wife, lying there, on a tartan rug, looking at Cathy, watching Gilles, watching me and chatting, talking, to Anne, to Jim, white though, thinking, I think about her lecture on Ficino, and no wonder, like the moon she came and like the moon she will remain, herself to herself only an imperfect copy. But through that, yes, now and then, as last night, after the long and quiet day. There's a kind of step at the edge of the bank just over the willow which grows out, flat, stretched, over the water. We sat on that in the evening and watched the water. One of the children sitting there with me earlier had flattened a cluster of lovely narcissi and she tried to straighten them up again with her hands like lamb's wool, just feeling them, holding them straight, offering them the opportunity, as she does me, without insistence. Just room between a clump of daffodils and the fallen narcissi to sit together. Yes. Alive to it. What happened. She lay on the lawn. She had Anne jumping about, at her rhythm, but she didn't mind, it's part of her class, her discipline, her sharp edges, wait a minute, her hands on the stem of that flower, that's more like it. She lay and played with Cathy whom she calls Cartouche, cartridge, whom she will direct at the world. The sun was too hot for the baby so they moved to the shade. Sitting with her legs showing, to her knees, her thighs, my eye able to rest there, just look, no trouble. In her blue and white bikini the day before at Scarborough. She undressed on the beach. Watching me while she ferreted about inside her jumper and then her black pants oddly public, ignored, more or less, except for a certain amount of proper attention. Gilles played with the sand, followed a baby on a donkey whom he thought was Cathy, ran with me into the water until he found that it was cold. So ran back to his mother who was gay, open-hearted, yesterday, who welcomed him, me, who chased us zig-zag, anywhere about with her arms open, growling, then on all fours, biting him, Je vais manger. His laughter, like pearls, the sea fresh cold, rolling in, Si quelqu'un m'avait dit que je nagerais dans la mer du Nord, she ran into it, Whoops, in it. Smacked against her and took her breath. Out from the top of her swimming costume popped her lovely breasts, so she said, I was watching the children. She ran down there. I saw her push herself out breast-stroke, head up, like a dog, until a wave came over her, rolled her, turned her. I saw a foot come out, one foot, and then she, gasping, rising, all alight, the sun alive in the water streaming from her, Oh! Oh! I can't breathe. It's cold! I can't breathe. She ran back with her elbows in and her forearms out. Her breasts bouncing, lovely, streaming wet, to grab a thick blue towel, head on one side to let out the water from her ear, drying the other, her long hair wet, hanging down and the drops of water covering her like drops of fire, like lace. Flicking him, me, with her hair, swinging it round, so that the sun caught it, while Gilles on his own, with bucket and spade had made crumbling sand pies which he at once destroyed. Then they watched her with improper attention, as I did. No trouble. All this yesterday and the day before.

We went to Scarborough, twenty miles away. I played with my children. While I've been writing this, blossom has actually come out on the tree. Nicole. Pretending surprise to see Gilles's belly-button, pointing, Oh! regarde moi ca, le belly de Gilles, we're bringing him up bilingual, and he falling, laughing, his hands over it, laughing, laughing, his legs in the air, rolling with his hands over it, laughing, laughing, holding it, hiding it, on his feet again, quiet for a moment, diabolic, his hands on the hem of his shirt, watching, his eyes alight, waiting, for it, watching his mother, then up, suddenly, quick, exposing his belly while Nicole pretended great surprise, faisait de grands yeux. Oh! argh! pointing, he giggled, laughed, his voice like a melody announced. Her own laughter changed from amusement to love and laughing she embraced him, kissing his soft cheek, while he looked surprised by so much nakedness, holding him, looking at it, looking at her shoulders and back, drawing back a little. I too ran down to the sea, when I too had struggled to undress. Let's see how you do it then, while I was on one leg, trousers stuck, at my feet, tottering. Trying to get them off, holding the blue towel with my other hand, while Nicole lay sprawled out, cleaning sand which Gilles had thrown out from Cathy's eye, who had sand also round her lips, had been eating it, and is watching ME with proper attention.

She's gone away to give her lecture on Ficino. I remain, and congratulate myself on it I see. The wind is rising. It is colder. The water makes more noise. There are weeds growing now tinting it green, trailing out. The current fast. Cold. Down from the moors. The river board has left the bends, the meanders, in its course, to halt it, slow it down, otherwise when the snow melts it would flood York and all that valley. The willows are planted to keep the banks steady. In places where it is crumbling they have tied together bundles of willow branches and rammed them into the mud, to keep the bank. This bench I am sitting on is sloping down, as are the flagstones under my feet. There was a kind of patio here when the house was owned by a gentleman. Now it is broken. The shed behind me too is sloping, tilting, down the slope.

She came out of the sea like milk. There is milk in her. When the sun comes out she opens up. Here. Come here. Will you? Her wedding ring is loose on her hand. Her hand is hard where it has had a pen in it.

I've come inside. It was too cold. I was freezing to death. So was she. Here I switch the fire on and settle again into her warmth. Her anxiety. Her wish to be left alone. I won't disturb you. I'm a creature of habit. I like to have my things disposed about me, so that I can come back to them,. when I want to, and they will still be there. We can't work in the same room. Get out. Out, of my mind. I want to be left alone. Je suis decue decue, like a wail, the cry of a cat, disappointed, in the night, je ne voulais pas que ca soit comme ca. Je voulais plus que ca. Il n'y a pas assez! Just there, over there, there's something better, richer, fuller. Out of reach. Just. She strains for it, push it along, hurry it along. Speak in a foreign tongue. If there is sun why then dance, dance, tread it down. If there is quietness mime it loudly. If there is joy be more joyful. If there is love to be loving. Moi aussi je suis decu. Watching your sharp movement. Eating your French cooking. Good. Yorkshire pudding and what's this? a bay leaf, a bay leaf, a mixed marriage. Thyme in the mutton. Fenouil in the mushroom soup. Verveine in the teapot. Rosemary in sauce piquante which smothers the beef. One way and another moi aussi je suis decu. That warmth, that fat and quiet sloth, that condoned eating, that comfort, no demanding, that lack of interest in appearance so that I could be much fatter with a clearer conscience. Sharpened up. Clarified. Made more rigid. Up. Out. Come on. Get up. It's half past eight. Half past eight? Is it light yet? Light? It's been light for hours. You know it's light. You've only just come home. Listen to the birds. Trill. Purl. Warble. Twitter. Chatter. The bloody birds. Let's get up. Go for a swim. Be quiet. Quiet. Easy. Let go. Give yourself a chance. Tu blagues, non?

paresseux, elephant, tonneau de lard, Anglais!

I'd been in bed two hours. I'd sung all night with a lovely girl. I read bits of Shakespeare with her. I came home in the dawn with the light in the mist lying on the fields and the sun swollen, red, the window open. Pigeons, yellow-hammers, on the road, picking up the grit before the traffic started. The May Day traffic. She woke me up at nine. Get up. The cooker's out. How can I cook the lunch?
Don't cook it. Cold. That's it. Cold food. Jim and Anne are coming.
I've only just come to bed.
Get up. Come on. I'll pinch you. Ow! Like goads into my fat carcass her bony fingers, nipping, tickling, pinching. Gilles on me.
Gilles! Mors-le. Ha! Ha! Gilles, vas-y, mors-le.
Ow! I'm tired.
Should come to bed earlier why didn't you see to the cooker? I expected you home Je t'attendais, the cooker, cooker, cooker.
Half an hour, only half an hour
All right half an hour
Out then later ooh steady argh did I drink? can't remember come on all right not all that much was I unfaithful? no did I want to be? yes. Did I really want to be? Thank God I wasn't. No trouble. No hurt caused. No debris to get rid of. Clean. A fresh start. If I can get the cooker started. Luckily the sticks are dry. Take a branch from a dying apple-tree. Here they are! Jim. Anne, Susan. David. Gilles is delighted. He is dancing. Already they have gone out into the garden. Nicole is apologising, for the cooker being out. I make a game of my slowness.

I'm afraid the lunch will be late. She is saying. He let the cooker go out. He did. Me. Pointing at me, that note strident in her voice. She is straining to come into the present.
I've only just gone to bed. Get up.
I don't know how you do it. I've bought a nice piece of pork.
Oh dear. I can't put it in yet the cooker's out.
Never mind. There's no hurry. Relax. Let go. Go and sit in the garden.

I sat there with Jim. He was listening to the birds. The chair was propped up where a leg was missing with a pile of books. He took them. You can have them if you like. I will. My mother does a lot of reading. There are books all over the shop, here. Take them. Take any you want. Take anything. We spent the day there in the open air. We ate at last in the orchard. Susan and David were hungry. Gilles imitated them.

When the water had been emptied from the bath they teased me. I was dozing. On my back, flat out, trying to get some sleep, my mind singing because of the light and colour I had seen coming home that morning. I'd got Nicole up, out of bed, to look at it. They jumped, wrestled me, Gilles, fragile in the melee, diving in, Susan, sentimental, snatching kisses, touching, snuggling, solid, well-fed and then to escape down to the river where we sat, four, in the space between the narcissi and the daffodils.
Do you want to go in?
Yes. Oh yes.
Wait a minute then. Gilles falling down the bank. Into the swift water. Till I caught him. My bare foot

on a thorn. While Susan and David whooped. He pushed her. She fell on the clump of narcissi. Jim held Gilles. I slithered down the bank to stand in the cold water. David came down. I held him. He held the willow with the other hand. I let him down, the water swept him, clinging to the pliant willow, the sun like gold, flecking, flickering, dancing. Like, what? like a gay fire. David in it, the water, solid coils of water over his white strong chest, sweeping him, his legs trailing, up again. The willow pliant, springing, the thin sharp leaves flicking in the water and then up feathering sprinkling it at me. Like silicon or crystal, deep. Then Susan in and whooping jumped at David, Steady! You'll have me in. You'll be swept away. Ow! My foot. You stood on my foot. He was trying to duck her. She responded. They splashed. Splashed, splashed each other. And me. My trousers rolled up to my knees. The lovely fresh smell. The sycamore over us, higher up the bank. Here, holding on, amid the woven weaving branches of the pliant willow tree. Gilles laughing, shouting, in Jim's arms, watching,
Papa! Papa! While the water sparkled in my eye and its fresh smell swept into my nostril and my feet clove to the pebbles while the force of the current plucked at them. Downstream. A few yards. There was a deep pool. Quiet. Froth gliding slowly over it. Shadowed by a hawthorn. There were trout there. Rainbow trout. Grayling. Some carp. Above that there were daffodils. Further out in the stream the long trailing weed streamed out. Susan and David holding on to the branch, sprang and jumped in and out of the water, thrashing the surface. I was amongst

this lovely cluster of light and noise. Water drops flying, the fresh wind, the coldness. Jim on the bank, watching, looking on, holding Gilles who knew him, liked him.

Jim dried them. I took Gilles and sat him on the branch which stretched over the water and did not bend under his weight. He held on with both hands and looked down at the solid stream. His feet almost touched it. He dangled and swung them. I watched with him. We stayed thus, quiet, together, for a long moment.

I brought Nicole there in the evening. We sat together. She straightened the narcissi. She was quiet and calm. I wanted her to stay. She did, for a time, but she wanted to put the finishing touches to her lecture on Ficino. Never mind. While she was there she stayed. Gilles had gone to bed, singing to himself, his face clear and open. Jim and Anne had left mumuring something about the next time. We had not wanted them to come. Too much work to do. We did not want to fix another time. What I did want to do was to play in the water again with Susan, David and Gilles. Nicole and I sat quietly together for long enough, between the narcissi and the daffodils watching the solid stream of dark water. Holding each other. Holding on. Perhaps. Trying to keep out of it. She at any rate. Me too. I think. To keep aloof. To be able to watch. To be the spectator, to observe, watch it, watch it, so that you're not surprised, so that you can tell what is happening. Later, so that you can see yourself watching it. And so on.

No.

Back.

Into that light and that water and with those children. Let it come. Let it through. Listen for it. Watch for it. Follow it. Attend. One member of the polit-buro was missing from the photograph. Mr Khrushchev lit a bonfire in his back garden to celebrate his seventieth birthday. The woods around his house are filled with the sound of firing as he hunts. It is perhaps as well that he is out of the way, Kosygin, a little more sober. I hope he is. Here I watch, look, at the water. Distressed nonetheless, not reassured by the seeming amity between Johnson and Kosygin. Impressed with a sense of the irrelevance of my body in that conflict. Seeing no sense in joining it one way or another but uneasy uneasy what can I do? other than this? what? what?

I finished the evening looking at Nicole's back as she sat at her desk reading her Ficino. The curtains were open and the moon, full, was above her as I looked, shining on to her hair, seeming to correspond to something within her which it clothed with visible circumstance. I did in fact soon persuade her to go to bed where we soon put the moon in its place. Then we lay and listened to the softer sound, the rushing of the water outside. I thought to recreate it. Do it again. Invite them again. Go to Scarborough again. Play in the water again. Again. Again. But you can't. Let it go.